IMAGES
of America

AROUND PERRY

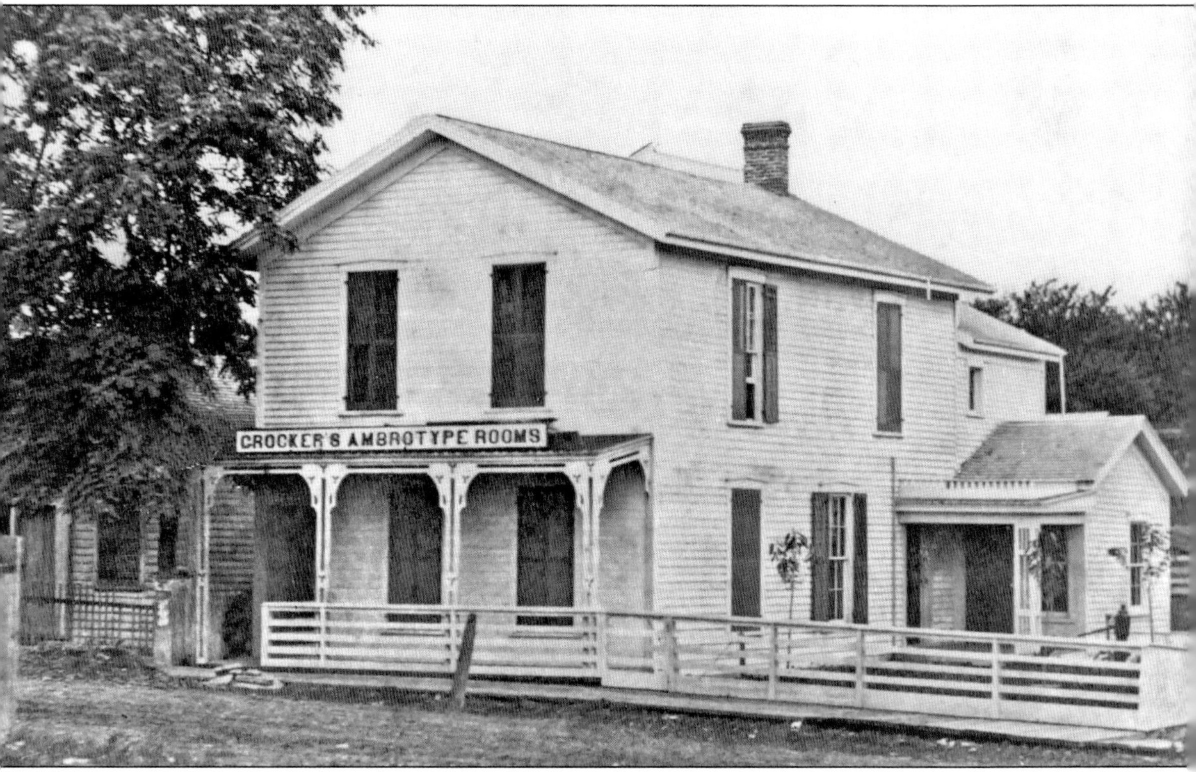

Merriam N. Crocker arrived in Perry with his photographic car in 1853. While parked on Main Street it burned along with several buildings in September 1856. He constructed this photography studio on Covington Street, which later became the Little Studio of Clark and Betty Rice. Ambrotype is a form of photography using glass plates that was cheaper to produce than the earlier daguerreotype. M. N. Crocker (1827–1927) is the source of many images preserved by Clark Rice. (Clark Rice Collection.)

On the Cover: The Perry Academy opened for students October 1854, having been funded by the community. In 1856, the Methodist Episcopal Church Conference took control, until 1872, when the District Union School bought the building. It became Perry Free Academy, later renamed Perry Free Academy and Union School, and in 1897, it was designated by the state as Perry High School. The cannon came from the Civil War and was donated as scrap during World War II. (Clark Rice Collection.)

IMAGES
of America

AROUND PERRY

Christina B. Nolan

ARCADIA
PUBLISHING

ISBN 978-0-7385-7291-8
Published by Arcadia Publishing
Charleston SC, Chicago IL, Portsmouth NH, San Francisco CA

Printed in the United States of America

Library of Congress Control Number: 2009939868

For all general information contact Arcadia Publishing at:
Telephone 843-853-2070
Fax 843-853-0044
E-mail sales@arcadiapublishing.com
For customer service and orders:
Toll-Free 1-888-313-2665

Visit us on the Internet at www.arcadiapublishing.com

This book is dedicated to the people of Perry—the wonderful, the unique, the thoughtful, the patriotic, the curmudgeonly, the inventive, and the cultural—all adding to the fabric of the community.

Contents

ACKNOWLEDGMENTS

Thanks to the past collectors of Perry's history, for Frank Roberts's book, Henry Page's history files, and Clark Rice's pictures.

To Peggy, Janice, Janet, and Amy at the Perry Public Library, thank you for your help, your encouragement, and your patience, as I invaded spaces at the library.

Thank you to Betty Rice whose dedication to history gave us the Clark Rice Collection. Thanks also for the stories you and Ruth Parker regaled me with as we traveled the countryside.

To Rebekah Collinsworth at Arcadia Publishing, thank you for your knowledge and guidance in this project.

Thanks to all who answered my questions as I tried to fill in the blanks.

Thank you to my daughter Jennie for her photographs and to all my family for their patience and support.

Unless otherwise noted, all images appear courtesy of the Clark Rice Collection.

INTRODUCTION

After the signing of the Treaty of Big Tree with the Seneca on September 15, 1797, land west of the Genesee River became available for settlement. Mary Jemison, "the White Woman of the Genesee," received 17,927 acres of land near what would become Perry.

The town of Perry was first settled in 1807 by Joseph Woodward, who built a cabin east of Perry Center, but stayed only two years. The first permanent settler was Samuel Gates who built his cabin at the northwest end of Silver Lake later in 1807. He and his family raised the first wheat crop, and set out the first orchard. In 1808, Josiah Williams built the first log tavern at the corner of Simmons Road and North Main Street.

The town of Perry was set off from Leicester and incorporated March 11, 1814. A portion for Covington was taken from Perry in 1817, and the southern part of Perry became Castile in 1821. This area was in Genesee County until Wyoming County was formed in 1841. The town took its name from Commodore Oliver Hazard Perry, the hero of the War of 1812.

The village of Perry developed along Silver Creek, the Silver Lake Outlet, which runs from Silver Lake to the Genesee River in today's Letchworth State Park. The first sawmill was built in 1811 by Seth Canfield and Julius Curtiss. That same year, the first dam on the outlet was built by John Hammersley at Federal Street. At that site two years later, he built a sawmill and a small flour mill. The village had been called Columbia, then Ninevah, and when incorporated on May 17, 1830, it was known as Perry.

In 1812, a schoolhouse was built in the village of Perry and another in West Perry. A log school building was erected in Perry Center in 1813. The LaGrange School was started in 1815 and operated until it closed in 1958. This school building is now on the grounds of the Wyoming Historical Pioneer Association at Silver Lake.

On July 13, 1855, the sighting of a sea serpent in Silver Lake put Perry and the lake into the headlines. Business had been slow at the Walker House on Main Street, so a clever plan was made to create a sea serpent to put in Silver Lake and cause some excitement. The mystery went unsolved until remains of the hoax were found in the ashes of the Walker House in 1857.

An old folks picnic at Silver Lake resulted in the formation of the Wyoming Historical Pioneer Association in 1877 and the building of the Pioneer Cabin in 1878. The Walker House at the lake was built across from the Pioneer grounds after the passenger trains had come to Silver Lake and Perry in 1872. Icehouses also used the railroad to ship blocks of ice, cut from the lake in winter, to the cities in the summer.

There are many beautiful churches in Perry. The different structures help to date the pictures, since the spires and towers rise above the community.

Main Street changed over the years as businesses changed with the needs of the residents. Stores moved to different buildings, the structures were sometimes moved, or they were destroyed by fire. In 1877, oil lamps were installed, and electric wires and arc lights appeared in 1892. The telephone came to Perry in 1894, and the water system and water troughs in 1896.

Some of the early industries in Perry included the Perry Knitting Mill organized in 1881, the Robeson Cutlery Company that moved to Perry in 1898, and the Tempest Knitting Company founded in 1907. The textile industry attracted the first Polish immigrants in 1903, and the Polish community grew to include a Catholic church organized in 1910.

Civic and cultural buildings were added to the community. The Leicester Street school was finished in 1908, and the village hall was opened in 1913. The Perry Public Library opened in 1914. The Masonic Temple opened in 1915.

Agriculture was and still is one of the biggest industries in the area, and businesses developed to serve this. In the olden days, the Perry Fair, now the village park, gave farmers a time to socialize and learn about new products.

Two collections from the Perry Public Library have been used for images and information for this publication. Henry Page was an unofficial historian of Perry who collected materials and thoroughly researched much of Perry's history. His lecture notes, correspondence, newspaper clippings, and photographs are filed by subject in cabinets at the library. The bicentennial publication *Perry, New York, As It Was and Is,* which he did the research for, was dedicated to him.

Clark Rice returned to Perry after serving as a combat photographer in World War II. He and his wife bought M. N. Crocker's former photography studio, and he took pictures of the Perry area until his death in 1999. He also preserved and reprinted the older images inherited from Mr. Crocker, many of which he shared with Henry Page and others. The Clark Rice Collection contains over 7,500 photographs and other materials that have been annotated by his wife, Elizabeth Rice.

Also used for research were Frank Roberts's *History of the Town of Perry, New York,* the Bicentennial book, Beers's *History of Wyoming County, N.Y.*, *Wyoming County, New York: an Architectural Tour* by James Yarrington, *Wyoming County, New York: Images of Our Past* by Mark Herman, and *Historical Wyoming* publications.

One

EARLY HISTORY

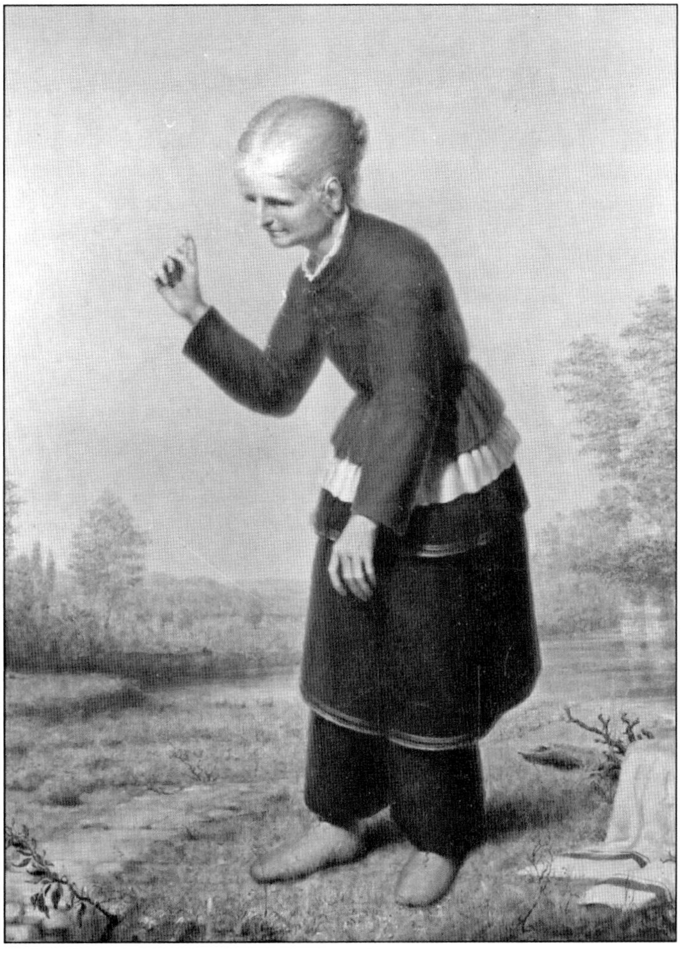

Mary Jemison, "the White Woman," was painted by Carlos L. Stebbins in 1880. Mary was kidnapped as a girl from her home in Pennsylvania, adopted by the Seneca Indians, traveled to western New York, and raised her family in the Genesee Valley. Mr. Stebbins depicted her, bent in old age as she is about to leave her Genesee River home. In 1831, she moved to the Buffalo Creek Reservation, where she died two years later at age 90.

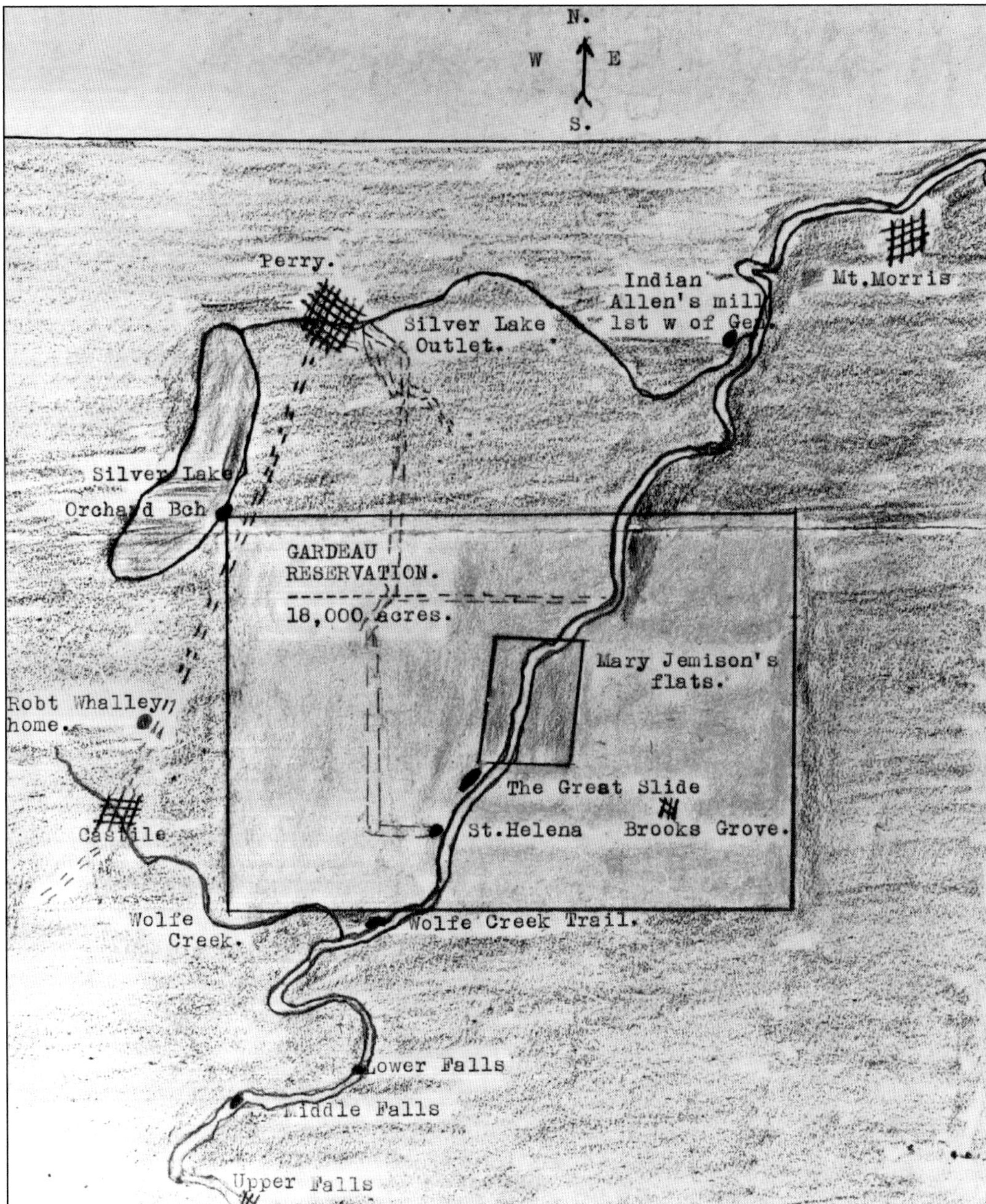

This map by Dr. Frank Crocker shows the Gardeau Reservation, the land Mary Jemison received at the signing of the Treaty of Big Tree in 1797. The broken lines from the village of Perry to the village of Castile represent the Allegany Road, or Route 39. Middle Reservation Road goes from Perry to St. Helena. The smaller road from Perry is St. Helena Street. Dr. Crocker, M. N. Crocker's son, wrote a series of newspaper articles on local history starting in 1922. This map was done between 1922 and his death in 1946.

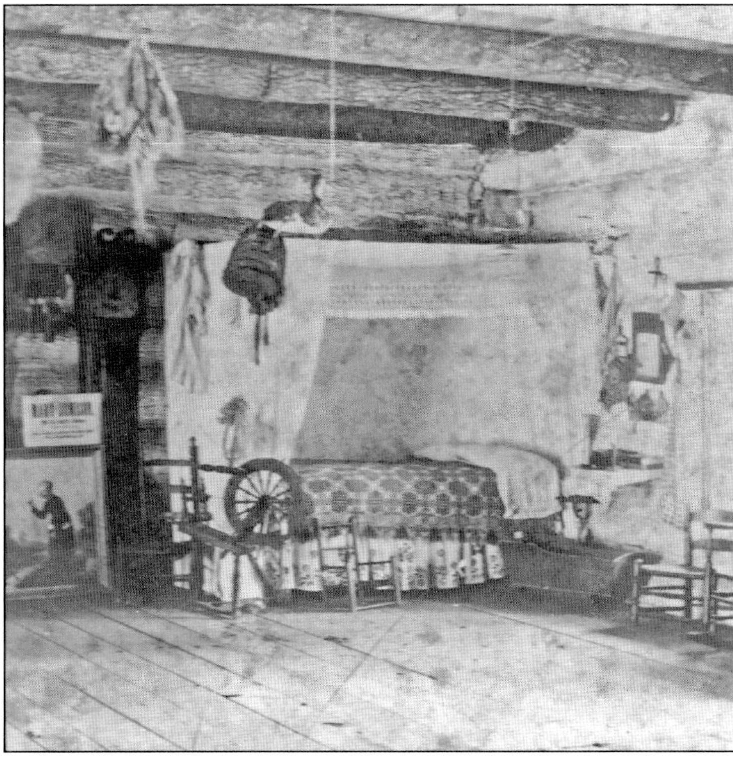

Carlos L. Stebbins gave the painting of Mary Jemison, here labeled, *the Old White Woman*, to the Wyoming Historical Pioneer Association in 1880. It was displayed in the Pioneer Cabin at Silver Lake, along with a chair she owned. Mr. Stebbins interviewed people who had known Mary Jemison and painted a fairly accurate likeness, which met with their approval.

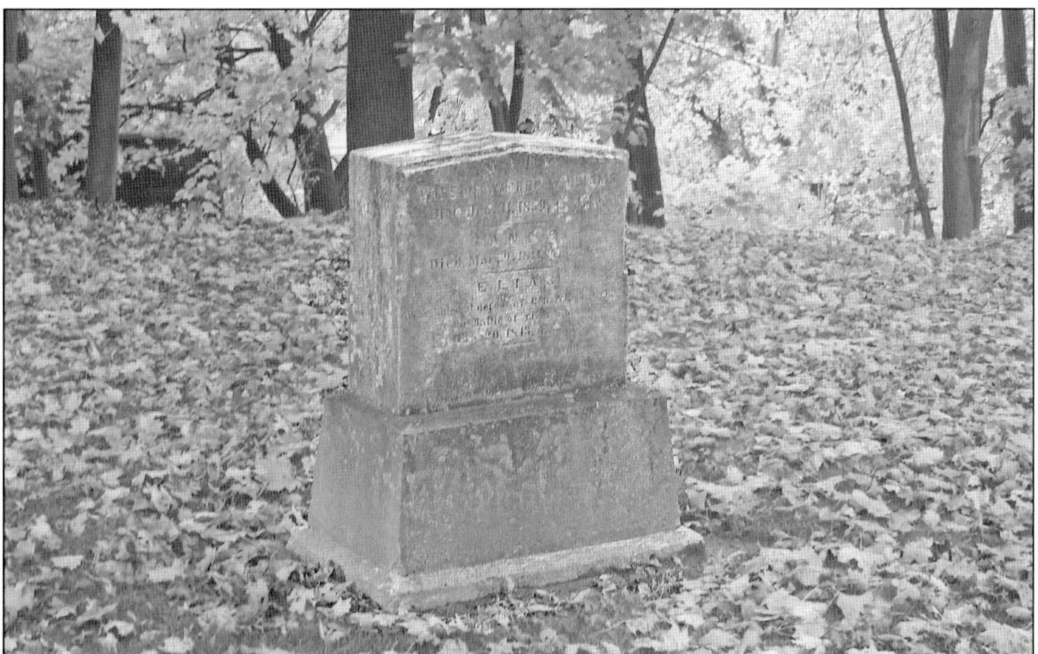

Josiah Williams settled in Perry in 1808. He died in 1832 and was buried with his wife, Elizabeth, in the cemetery where the public library is located today. This gravestone also lists their son Elias, who "was killed at defeat of Gen. Winchester, at the Battle of river Raisen" on January 20, 1813, at age 28. This battle took place in Michigan during the War of 1812. (Photograph by Jennifer Nolan.)

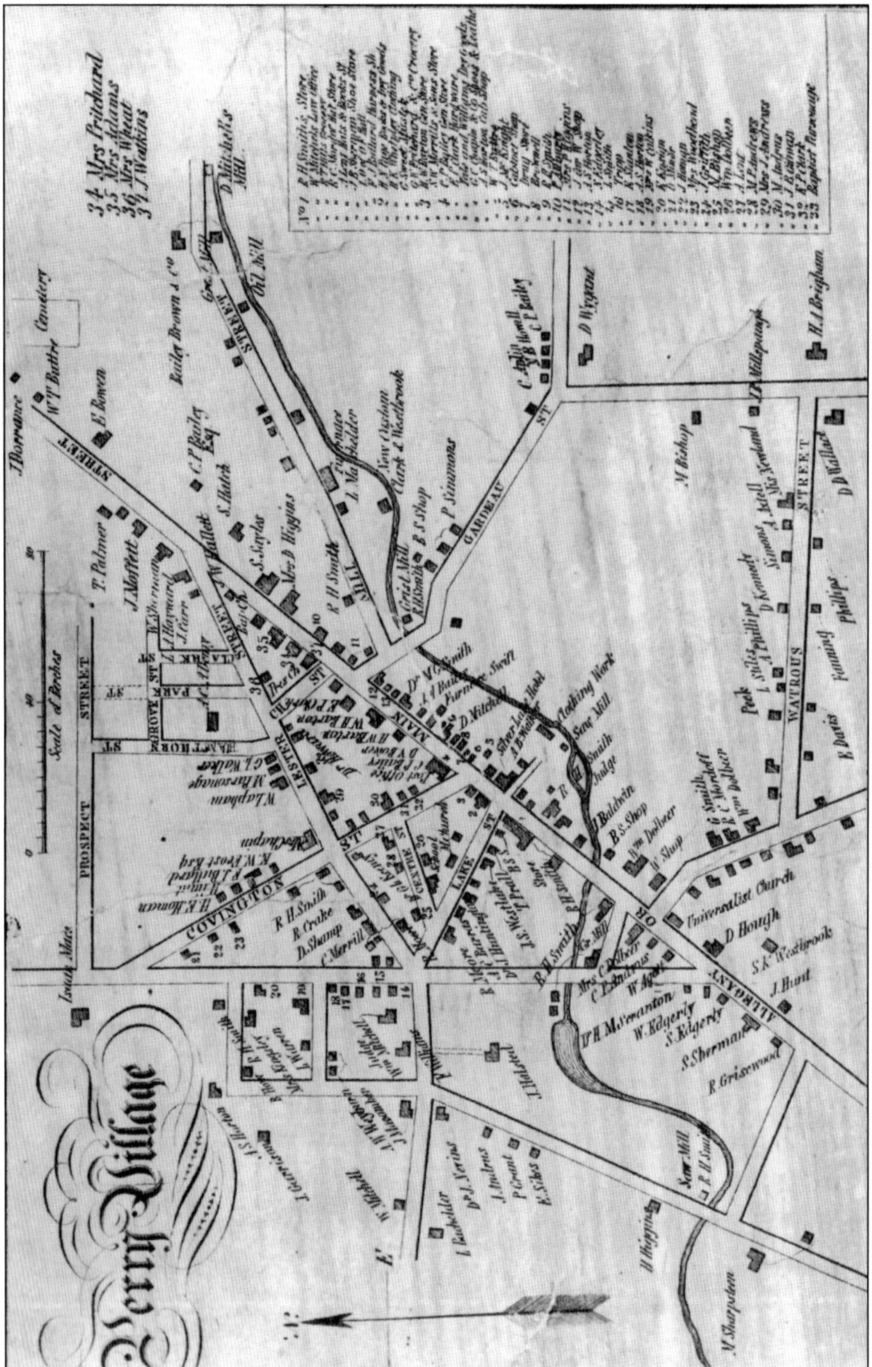

This 1853 map of the village of Perry shows Main Street businesses and development along Silver Lake Outlet. Nine mills are along the outlet, and Water Street was known as Mill Street. Borden Avenue and Dolbeer Street intersections with Main Street did not exist, and Centre Street was changed to Short Street. The academy building is shown on Lester (Leicester) Street and would open in 1854.

The Richmond Flour Mill shown at right was located between the outlet and Water Street near Gardeau Street. This was built as a cloth factory in 1827 and later became a gristmill eventually run by John Richmond. The sluiceway in the foreground runs to Hamlin's Flax mill, out of view downstream and to the right. The flour mill was demolished in 1898. (Henry Page Collection.)

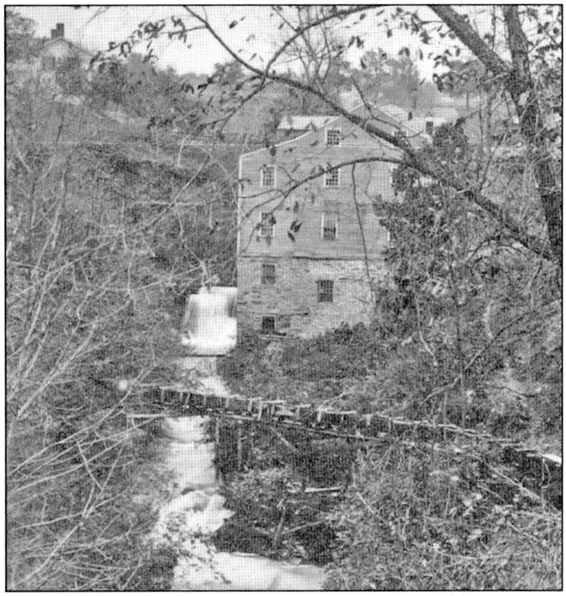

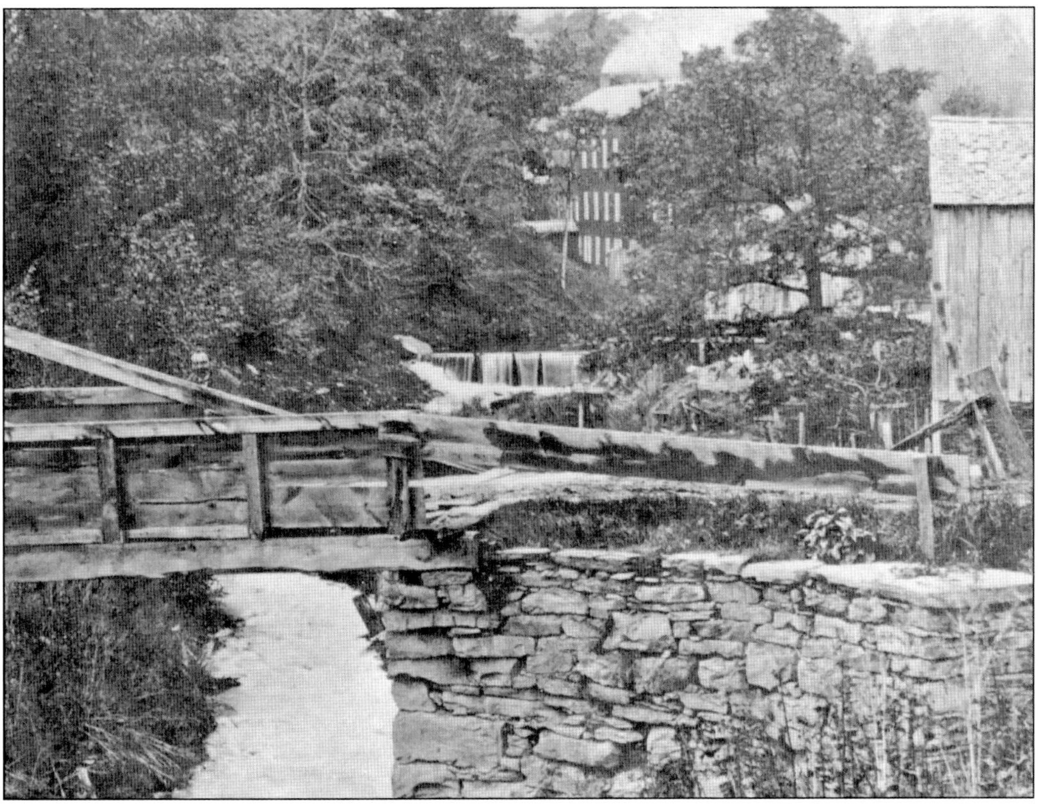

The mill in the background was built along the outlet about 1822 as a cloth factory. It was located behind the Walker House, now the M&T bank drive-through, not far from the Andrus sawmill. It was later converted to a woolen mill, owned at one time by James Wylie and was destroyed by fire in 1880. In the foreground is the Gardeau Street wooden bridge that was replaced by a culvert in 1883.

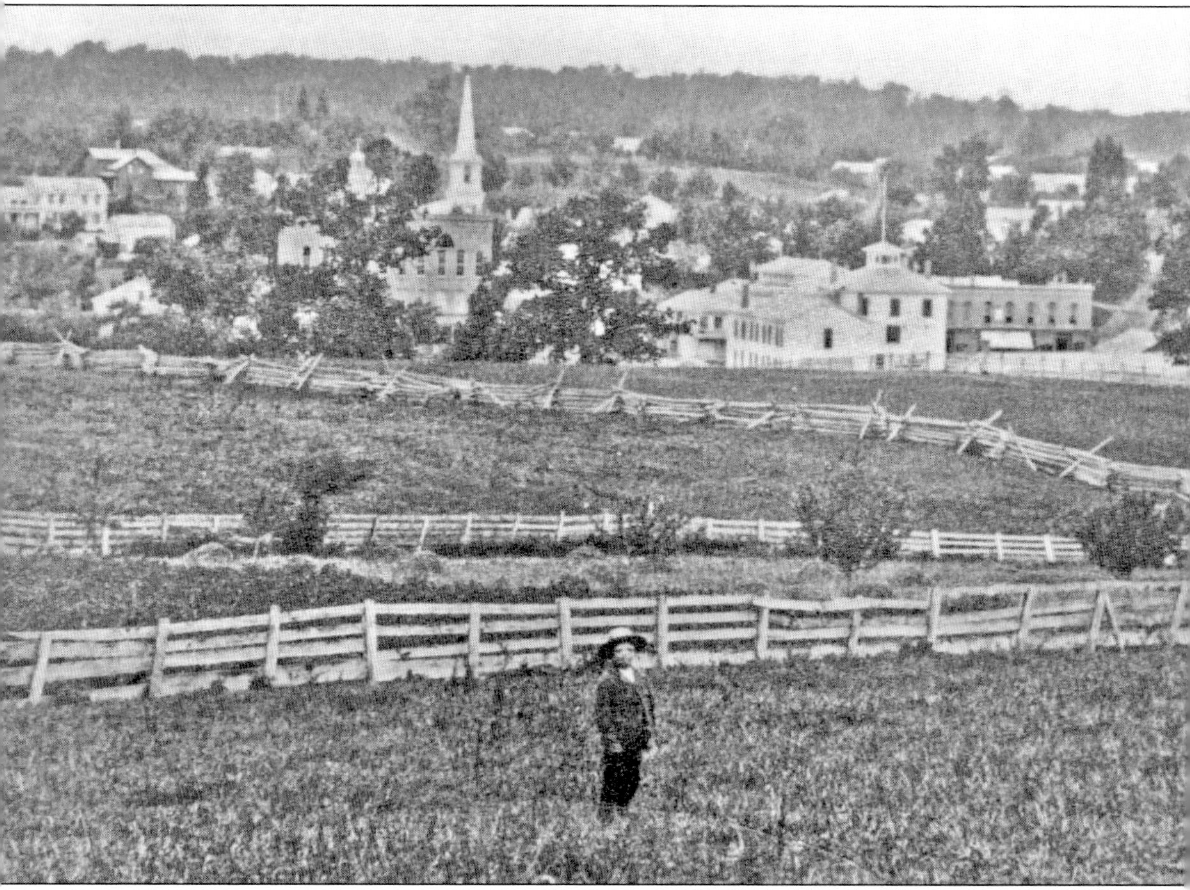

Main Street was photographed from a spot above Spring Street between 1868–1880. The steeple of the Methodist Episcopal church on the north side of Lake Street rises behind the brick Smith building at the south corner of Lake Street and Main Street. The top of the second school at Lake and Short Streets appears beyond the church to the left. The closest white building is the Wylie Woolen Mill on the outlet, and the Walker House with its cupola is in front and to the right. The roof of the National Hotel across the street shows above with the two-storied, brick Wygant and Cole buildings on the south corner of Covington Street.

Two

Schools

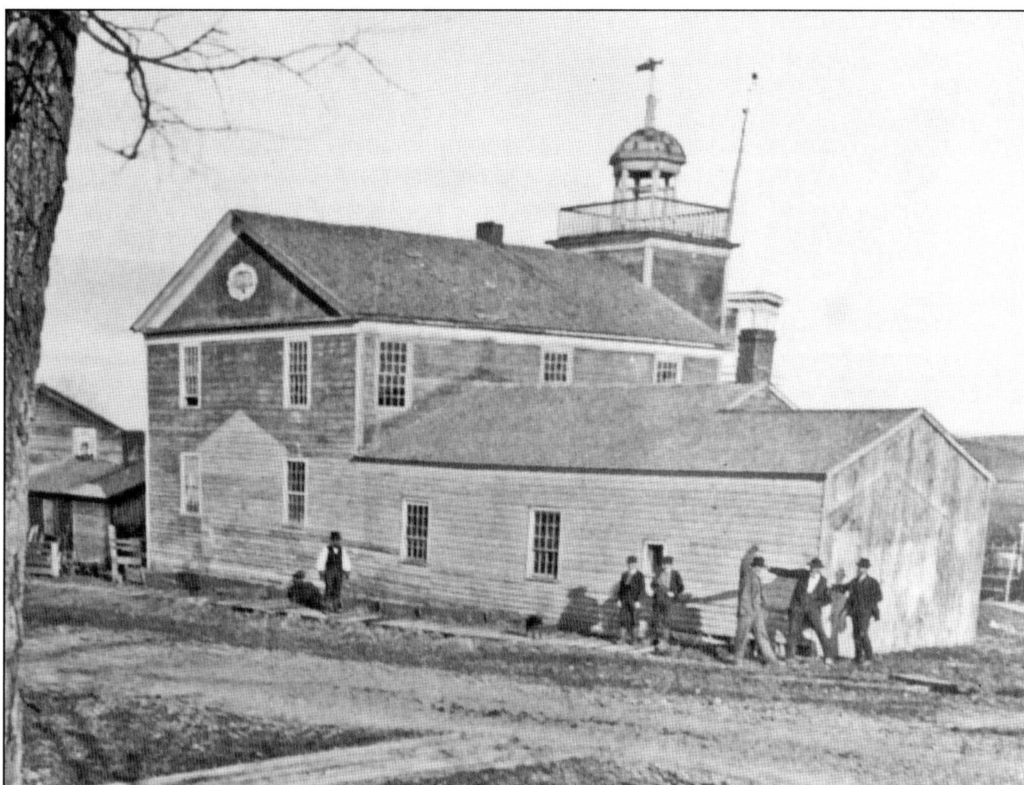

When the first village school (built in 1813) on Water Street became overcrowded, this two-story building was erected at Lake and Short Streets in 1816. Classes were held here for the next 16 years, while community meetings were held upstairs. Short Street is in the foreground, with Lake Street on the right. The steeple of the Methodist Episcopal church on Lake Street shows behind the building.

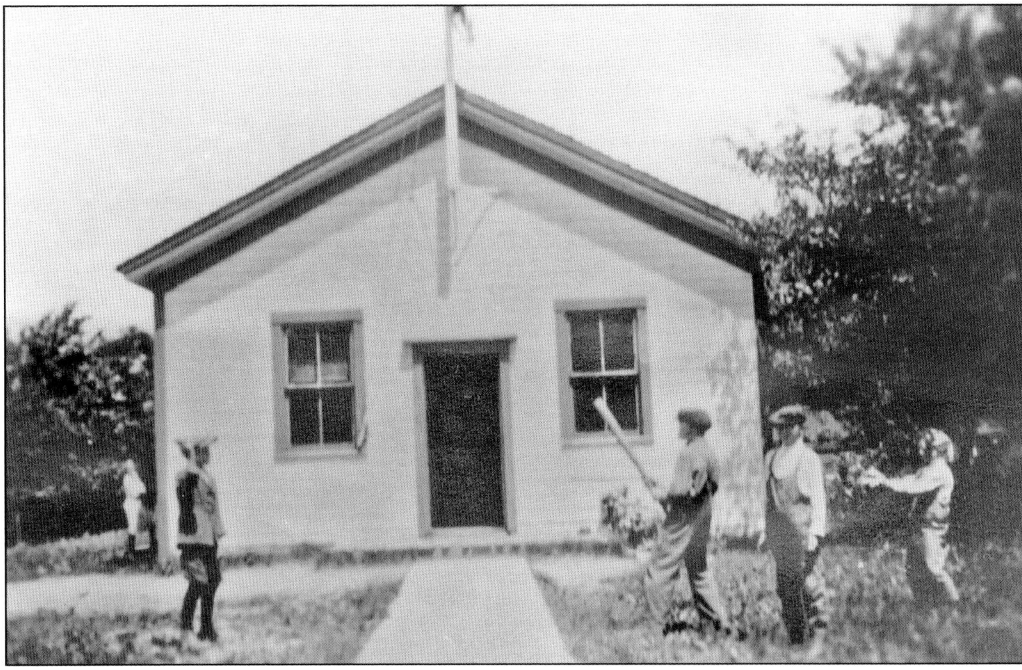

A log school was built in LaGrange in 1815, replaced later with a frame building. In 1880–1890, this structure, located across from the LaGrange Baptist Church, was constructed using some of the original frame building. After closing, the Covington Historical Society maintained the structure as a museum and gave it to the Wyoming Historical Pioneer Association. In 1998, it was moved to the Pioneer Museum grounds at Silver Lake.

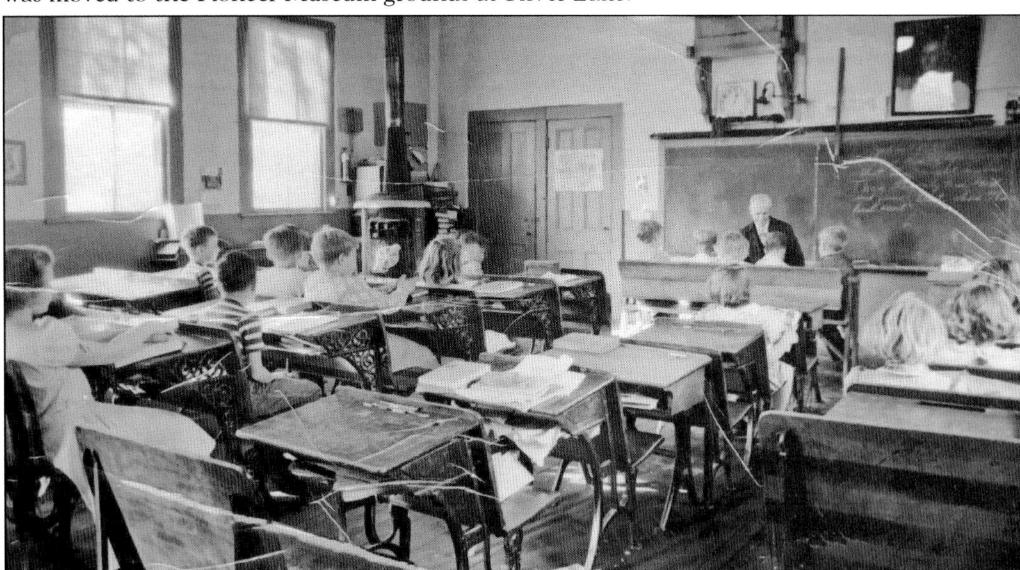

The LaGrange School served its community until 1958, when the last five students were sent to Perry Elementary School. This picture was taken about 1950, when students from the Altoft, Andrews, Cooper, DeMun, Dieter, and Kelly families attended. Mr. Harold Altoft, who taught here for 45 years, is teaching a class at the recitation bench in front, while others work at their desks. (Courtesy of the Altoft family.)

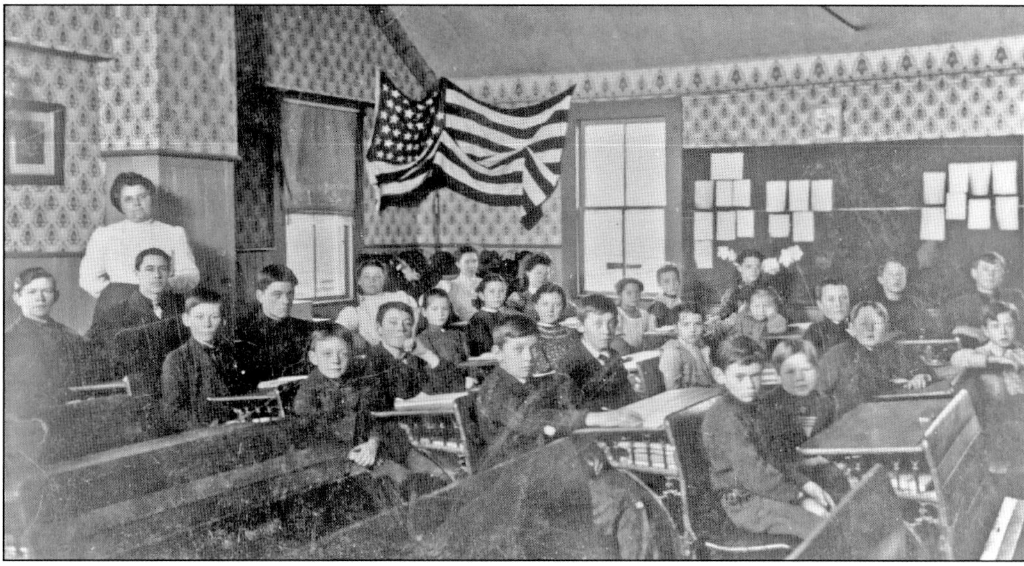

Perry District School No. 3 was located on the southwest corner of Simmons Road and Burke Hill Road. In 1904, Mrs. G. N. Avery was the teacher, and students with last names of Andrews, Auger, Benedict, Burbige, Conroy, Davis, McCaughan, Olton, Page, Paddock, Smith, Winter, and Wright posed for this picture.

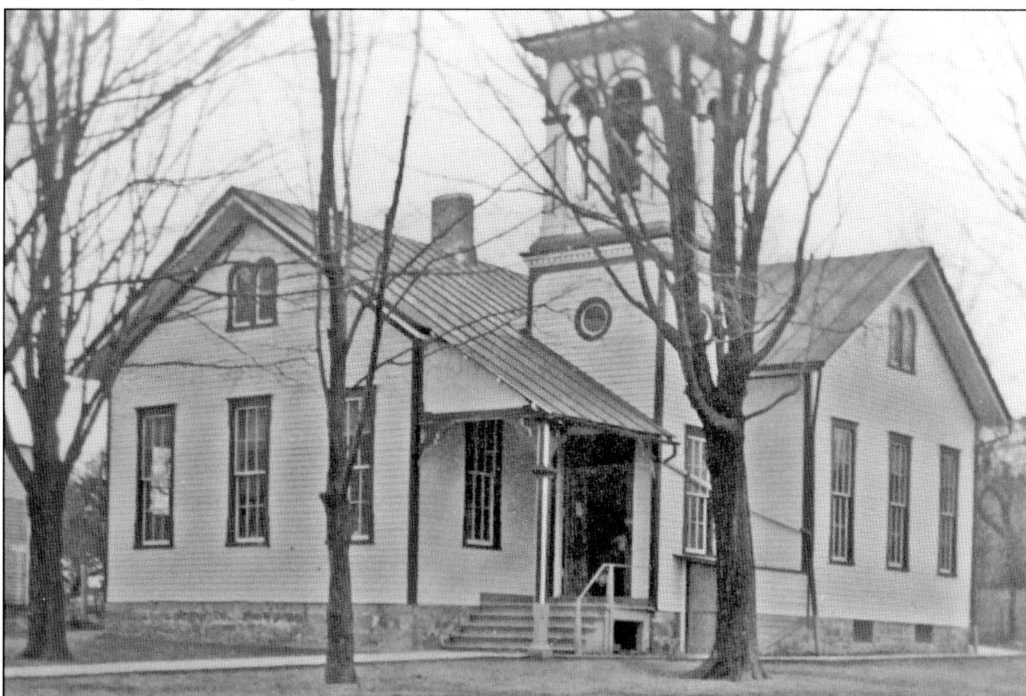

The first school in Perry Center was a log building constructed in 1813. This Perry Center School was built in 1869, when three neighborhood districts consolidated to form district 8. It was the largest rural school in the town of Perry and closed after the new Perry Central High School opened in 1955. It is located at the southwest corner of Routes 20A and 246 and is still used by the community today.

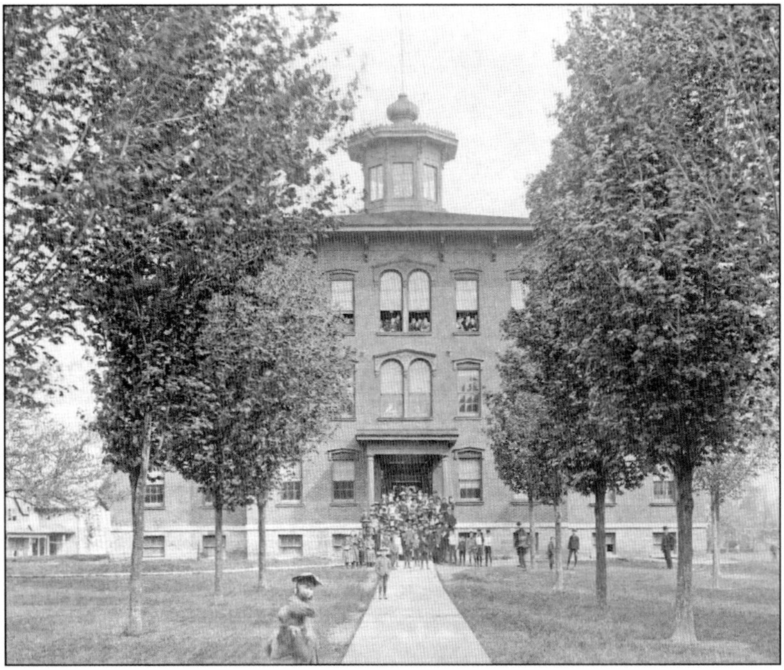

The Perry Academy building on Leicester Street became overcrowded, and in 1906 construction was started on a new school. Classes continued in the old building as the new school was built in front of it. The new school opened for classes in 1908, and this old academy building was torn down. (Henry Page Collection.)

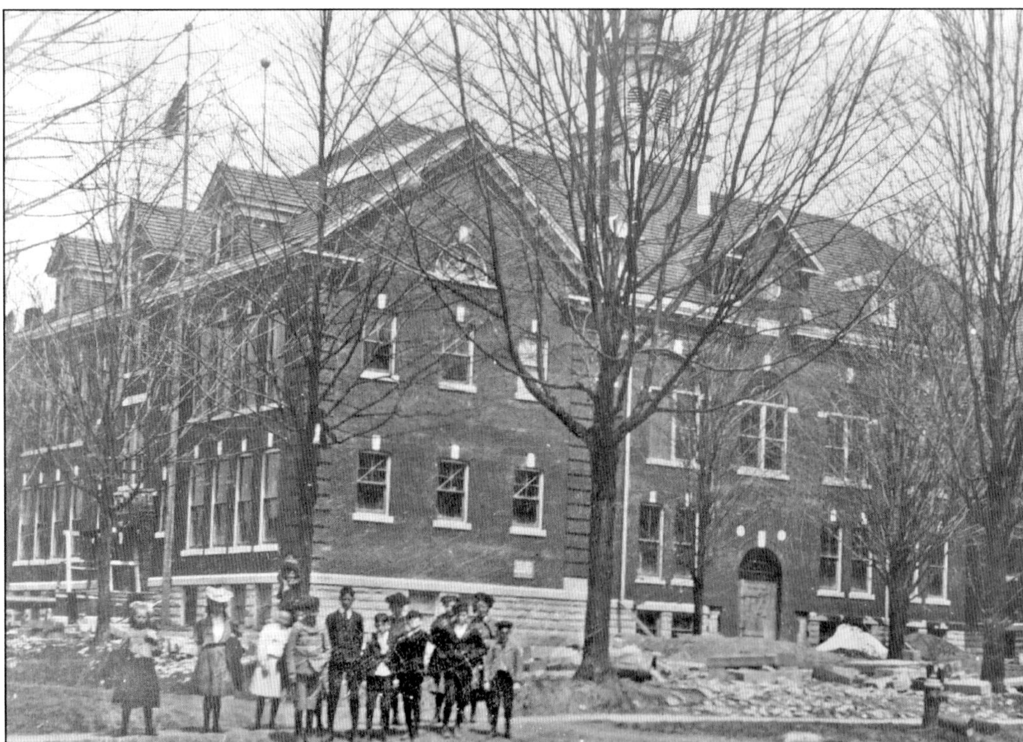

The new school was still being built when this picture was taken in 1907. The new building served all grades, like the previous school, and was also called Perry High School. An addition had to be added to this new building in 1923 because of overcrowding. More classrooms, an auditorium, and a gymnasium were added at that time.

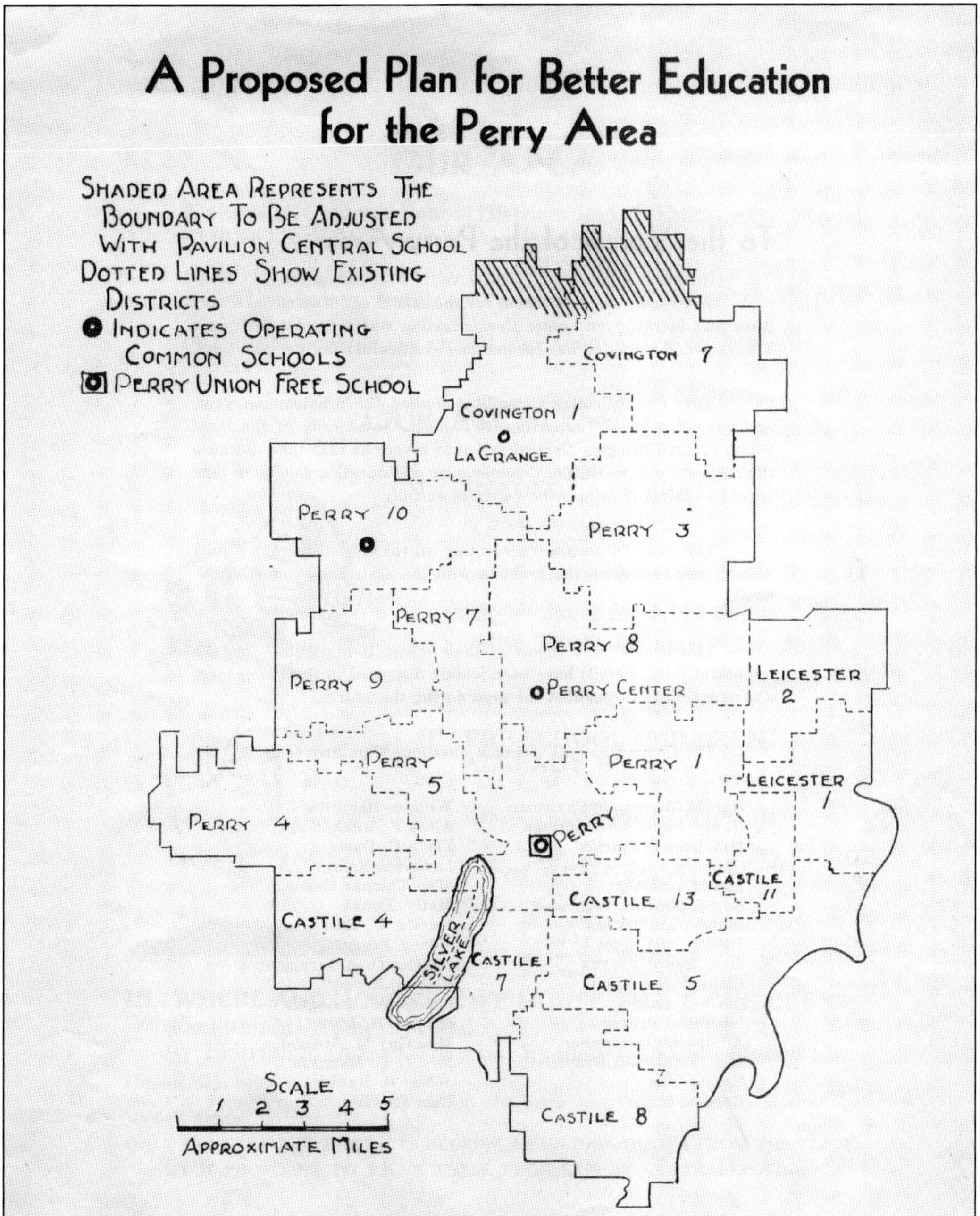

In 1950, this map was distributed to voters to explain centralization of the Perry district schools into Perry Central Schools. On the map, Perry Union Free School was the building on Leicester Street. The operating common schools were the Perry Center School (district 8), the Burke Hill School (district 10) at Burke Hill and Coe Roads, and LaGrange School (Covington 1). LaGrange was the last to close in 1958. (Henry Page Collection.)

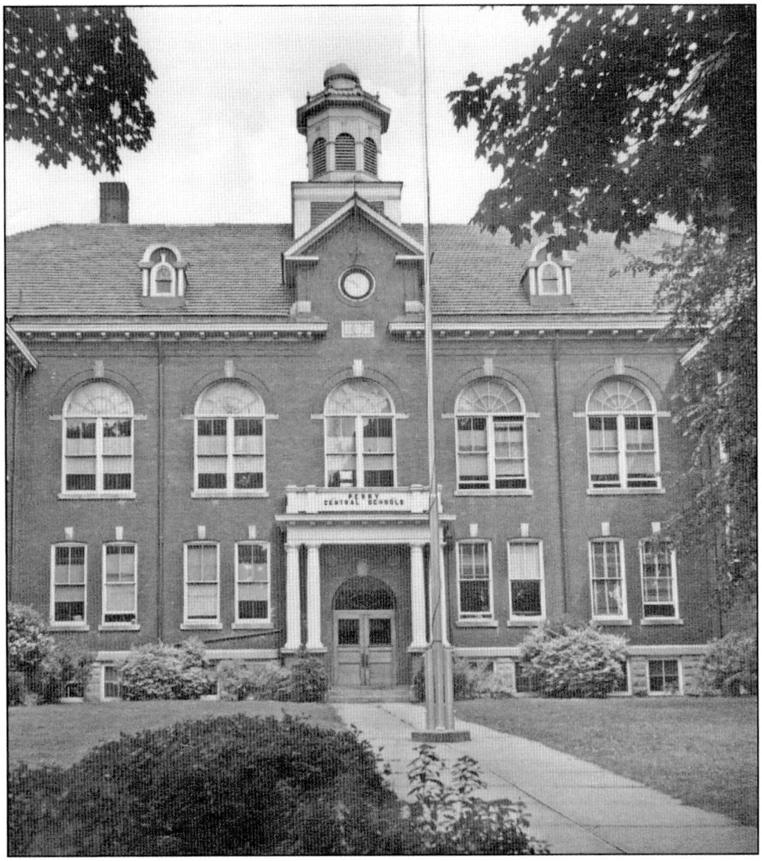

Perry Central Schools, so named after centralization, included all grades from most districts at the Leicester Street building. The school again became overcrowded, and in 1951, the Walkley Farm Equipment building on Dolbeer Street was purchased to use for classrooms.

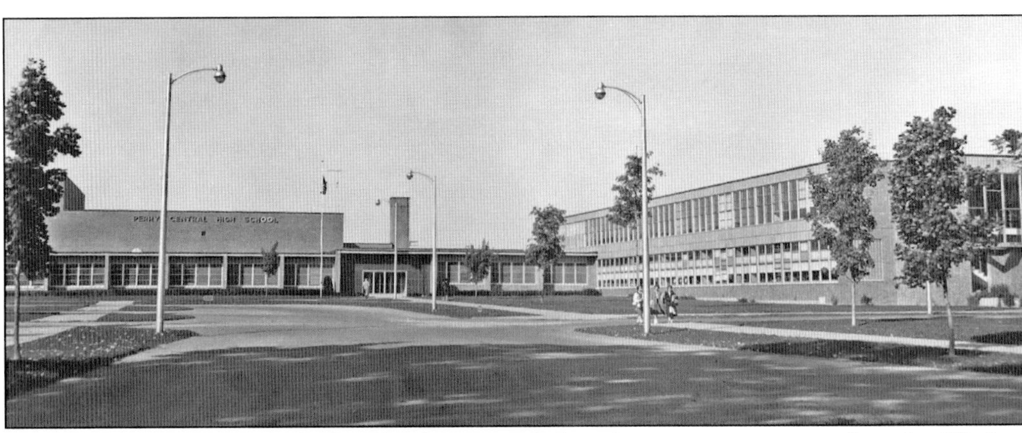

It was decided that a new high school was needed, and construction started at the Watkins Avenue site in 1953. Leicester Street building would become the elementary school. The new Perry Central High School opened for classes September 1955, but after a few years, more space was needed. In 1958, construction was completed on a second floor to the east wing.

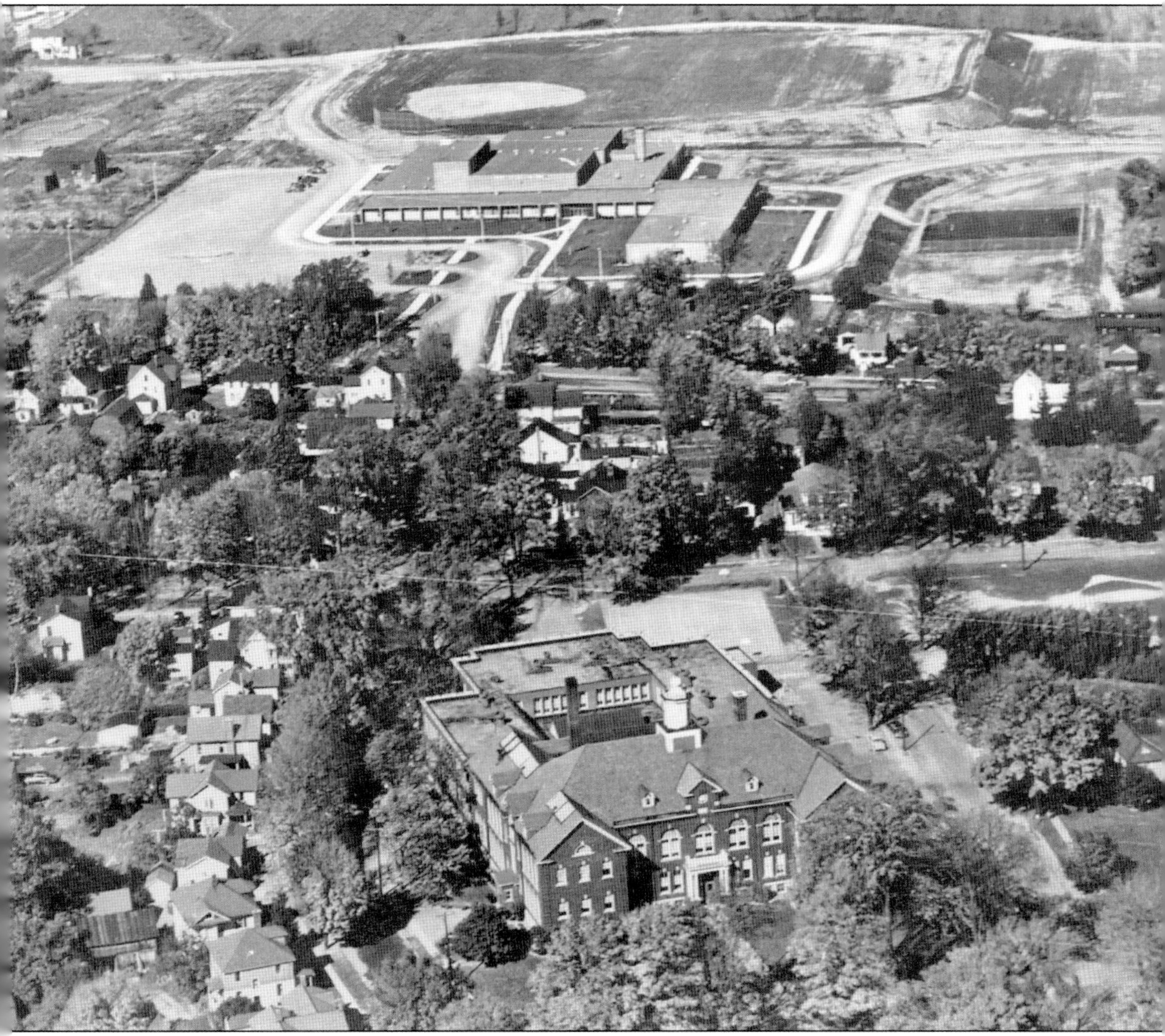

This photograph was taken by aerial photographer Henry DeWolf in 1956. The old building, Perry Elementary School, is shown in the foreground. The new high school with a one-story east wing and the athletic fields is at the top of the picture.

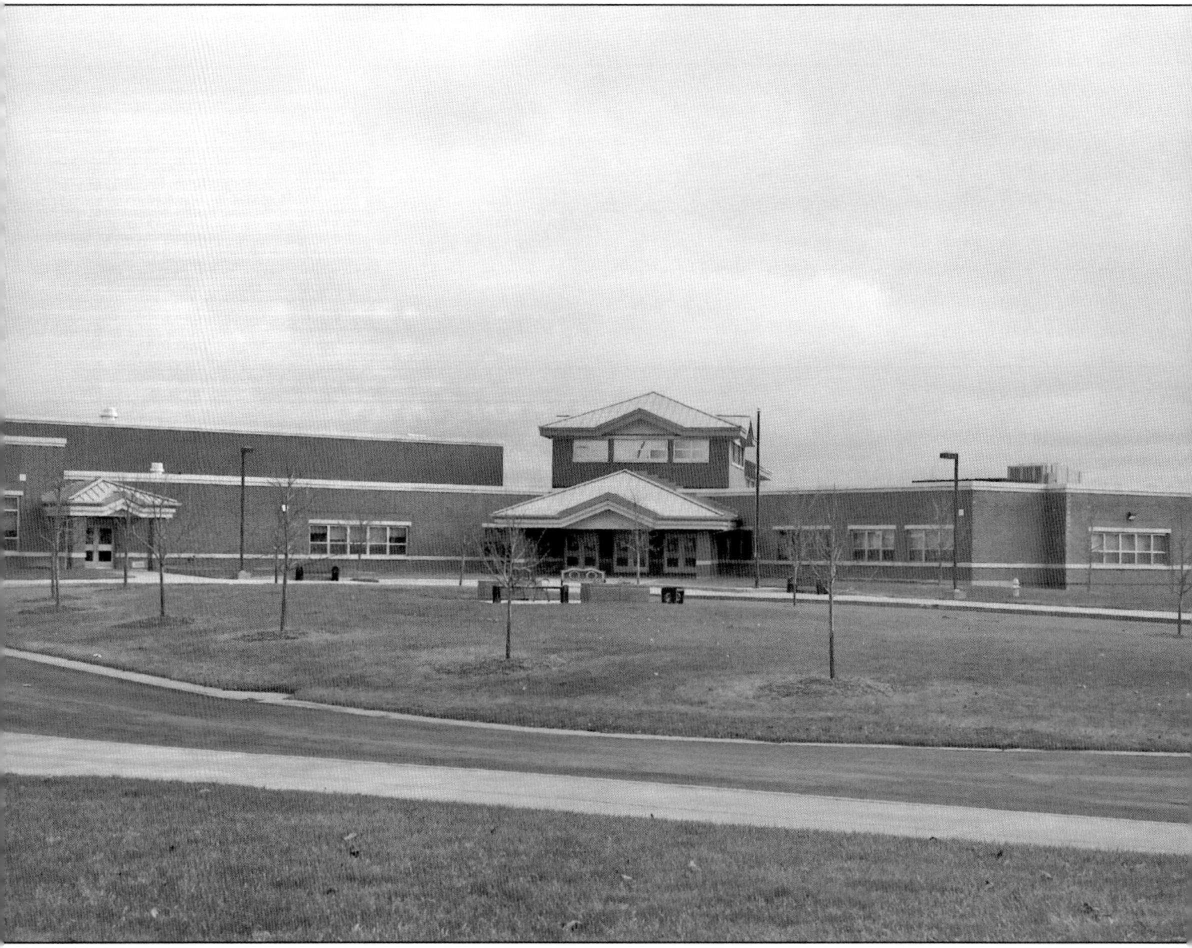

The new Perry Elementary and Middle School was completed in 2000 and included a stone inscribed, "Dedicated To The Youth of Perry." The old elementary building, now over 100 years old, served the community well for many years. It is now the Center on Leicester Street, with offices and apartments. (Photograph by Jennifer Nolan.)

Three

Silver Lake

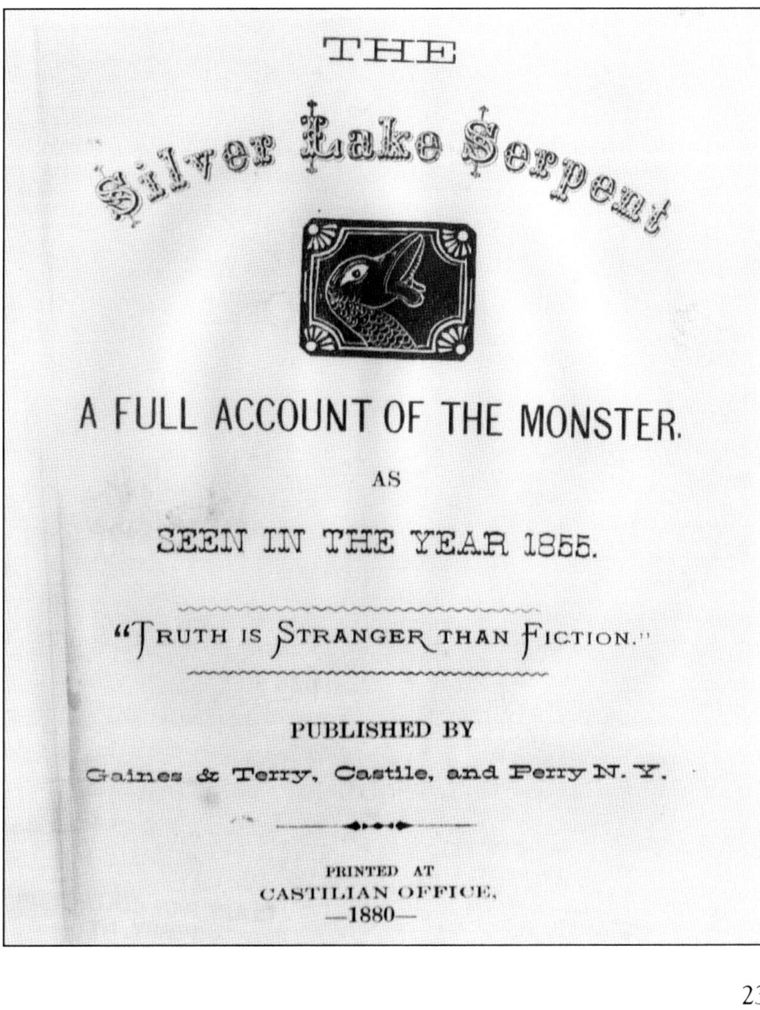
THE

Silver Lake Serpent

A FULL ACCOUNT OF THE MONSTER.

AS

SEEN IN THE YEAR 1855.

"TRUTH IS STRANGER THAN FICTION."

PUBLISHED BY

Gaines & Terry, Castile, and Perry N. Y.

PRINTED AT
CASTILIAN OFFICE,
—1880—

This booklet, printed 25 years after the event, contains information from the *Wyoming Times* about the Silver Lake sea serpent. On the night of July 13, 1855, four men and two boys were fishing on Silver Lake when what looked like a log rose up and moved towards them. Seeing a giant head and a tail lashing the water, they rowed frantically to shore. Other sightings occurred, and the story soon spread.

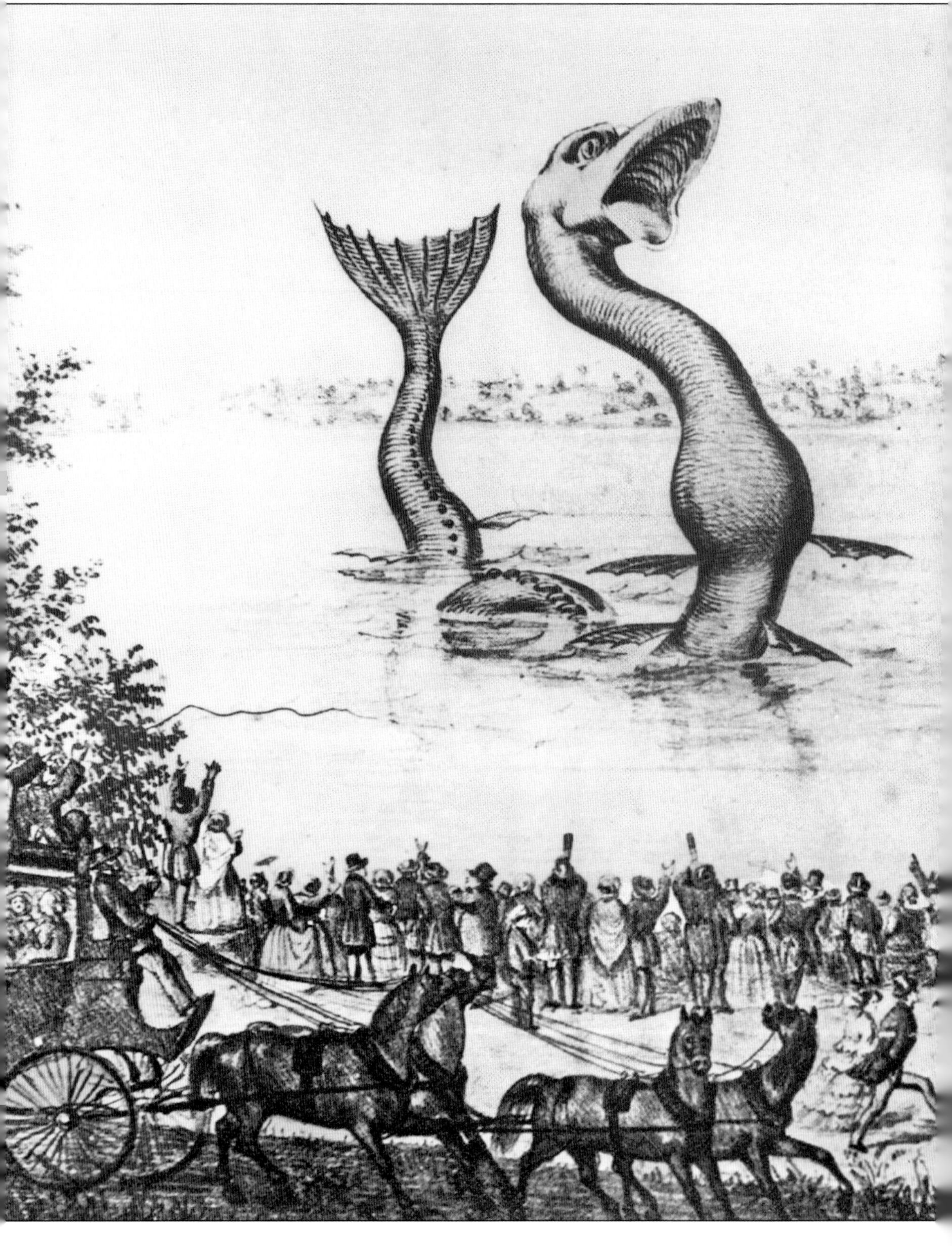

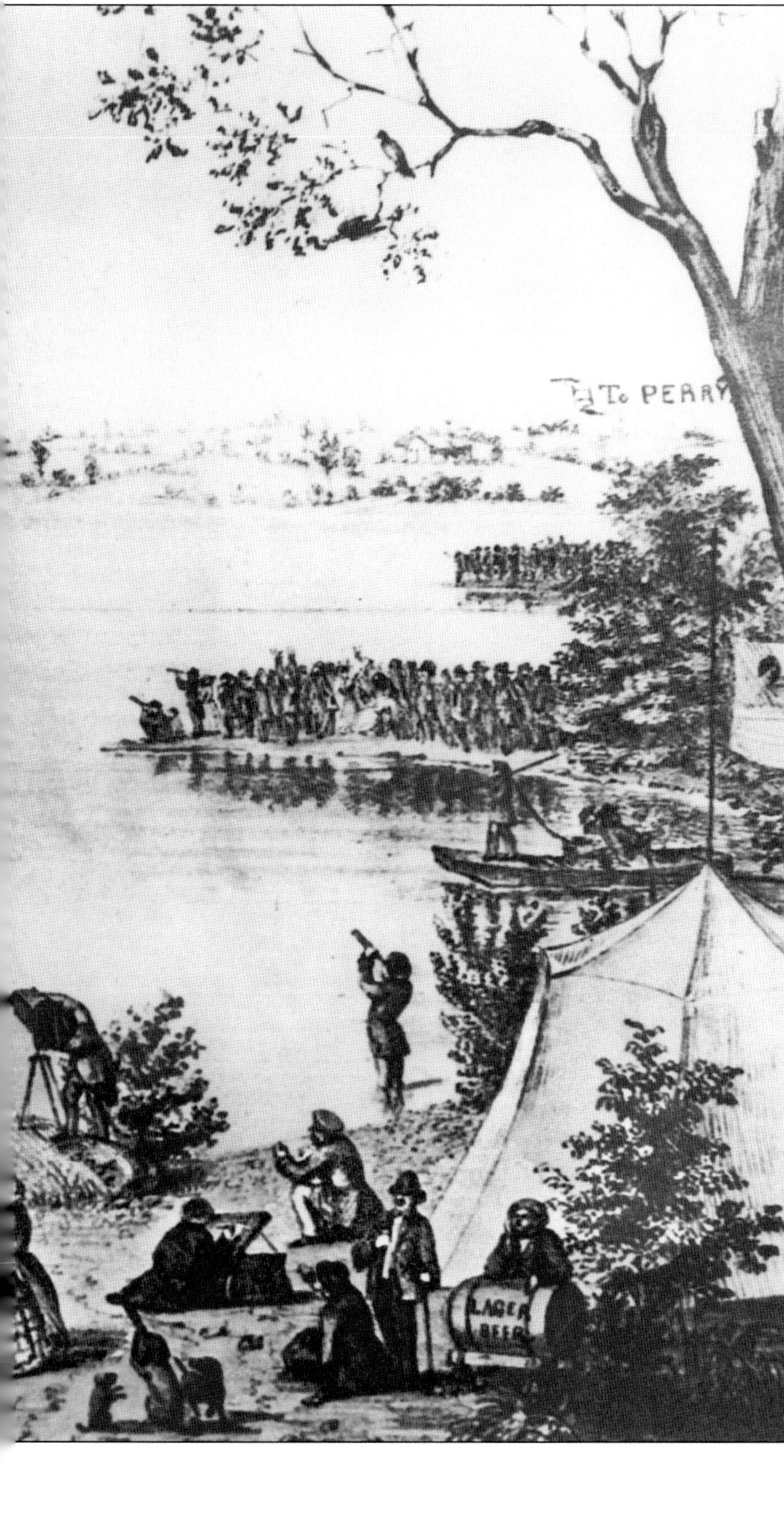

In July 1855, people flocked to the area to get a glimpse of the sea serpent. This illustration from the *Buffalo Daily Republic* depicts "the Monster Serpent of Silver Lake" and the crowds lining the shore. A boat containing an experienced whaler with a harpoon, one of the schemes to capture the creature, is on the right. The area was full of activity, and business boomed for several weeks, until the sea serpent appeared no more. The excitement slowly waned and the mystery remained unsolved. In 1857, the Walker House on Main Street was destroyed by fire. In the ashes were found the remains of the sea serpent. A. B. Walker, proprietor, had created a sea serpent out of canvas and coiled wire. Air pumped from large bellows inflated the creature, and ropes propelled it through the water, creating the drama that put Perry on the map in 1855.

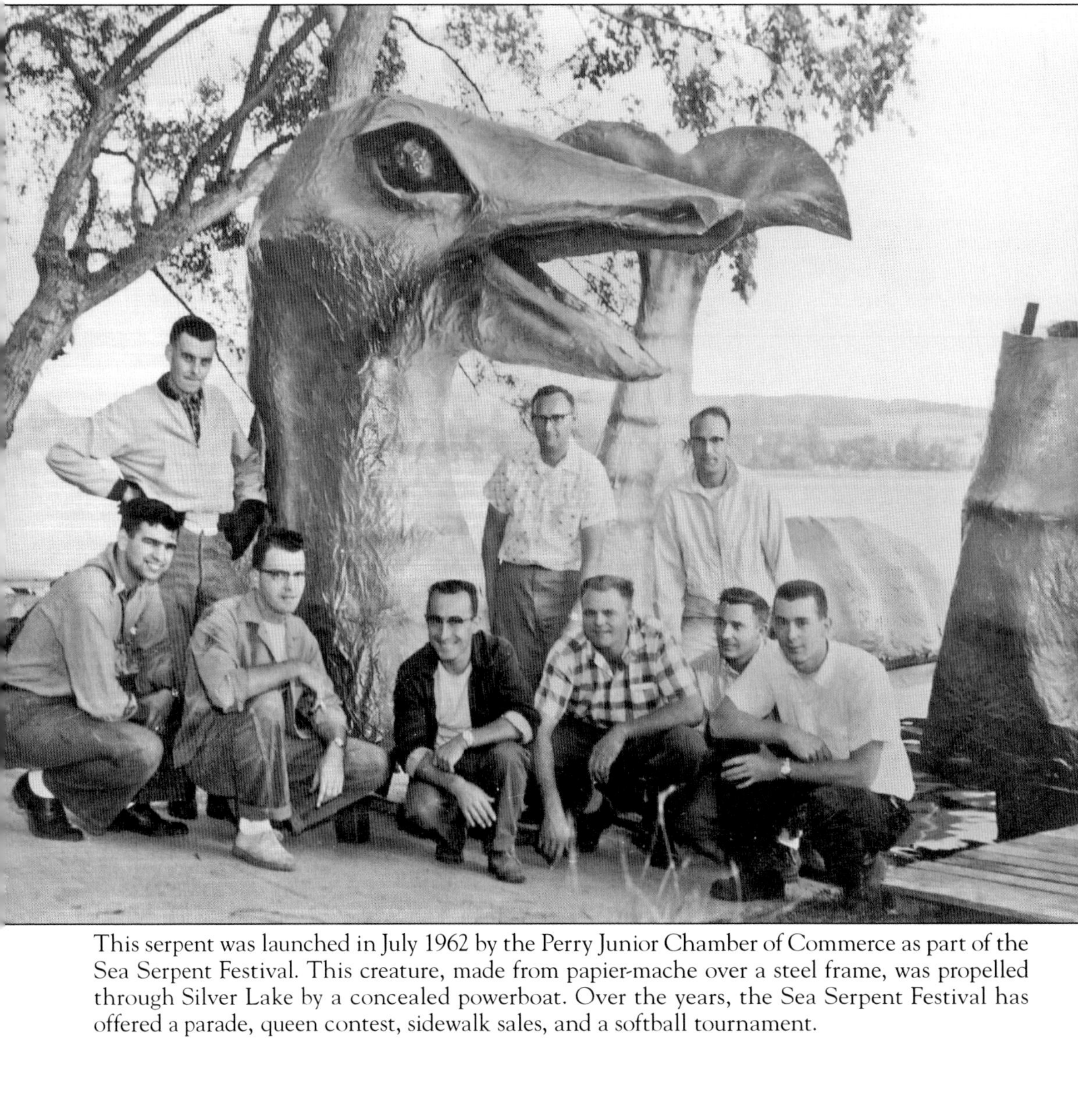

This serpent was launched in July 1962 by the Perry Junior Chamber of Commerce as part of the Sea Serpent Festival. This creature, made from papier-mache over a steel frame, was propelled through Silver Lake by a concealed powerboat. Over the years, the Sea Serpent Festival has offered a parade, queen contest, sidewalk sales, and a softball tournament.

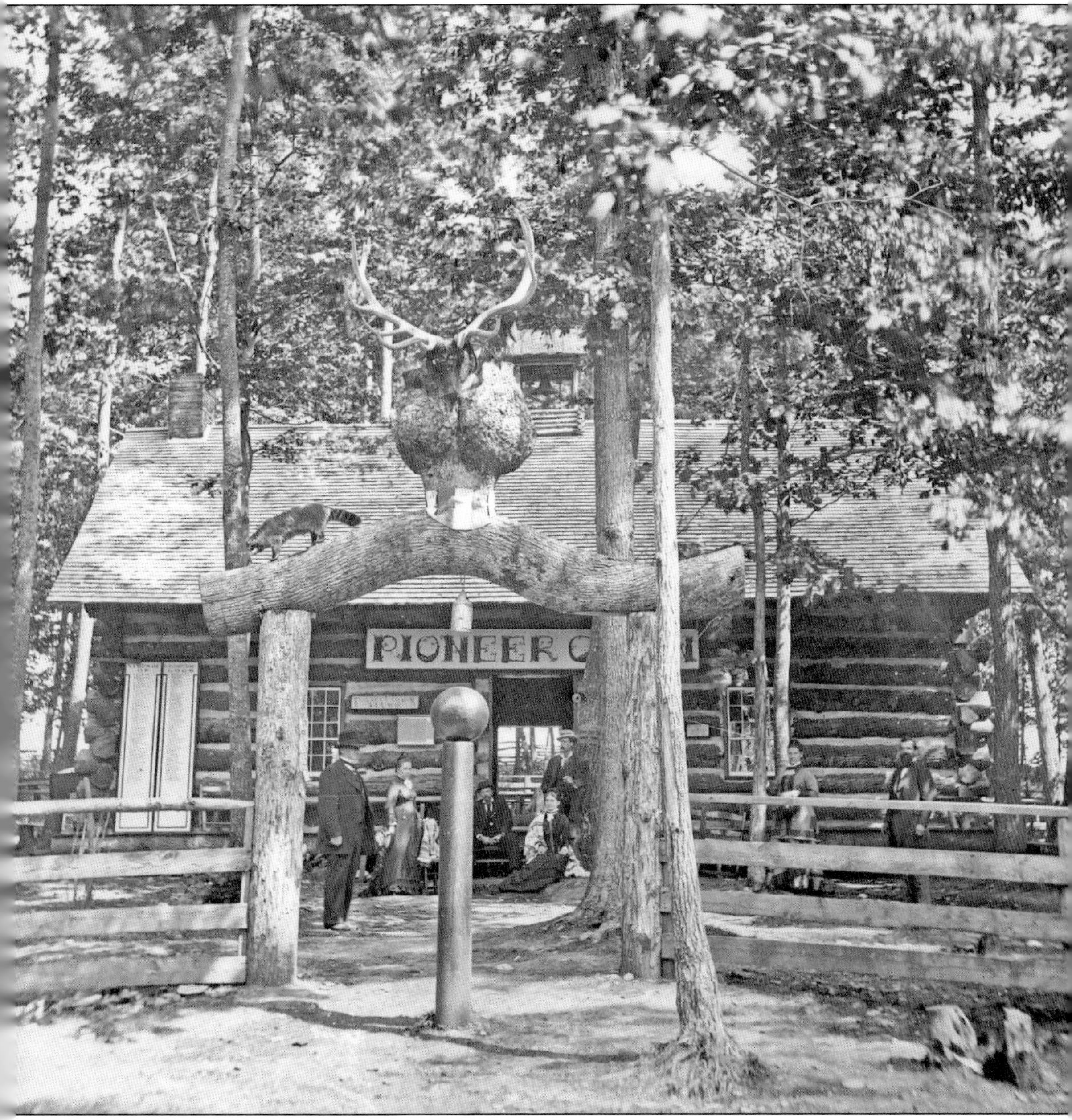

The Wyoming Historical Pioneer Association was incorporated in 1877 with the purpose of preserving relics, purchasing land for construction of a museum, and continuing the annual old folks picnic started in 1872. The Pioneer Cabin at Silver Lake was dedicated at the Pioneer Picnic in August 1878, with a crowd of 10,000 on the grounds.

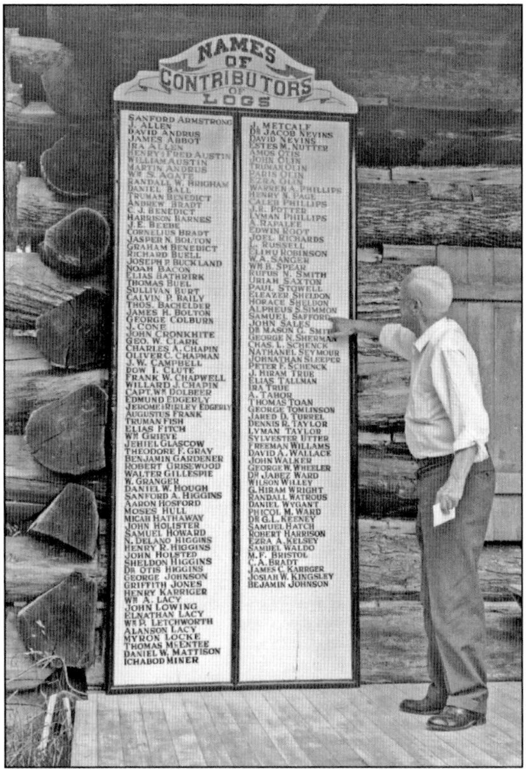

The Pioneer Cabin was built by volunteers with logs donated to commemorate the early pioneers. The list of contributors of logs has many names familiar to the area, including William Pryor Letchworth. This list is still at the cabin, and the relics collected are displayed in a museum building added in 1992. (Henry Page Collection.)

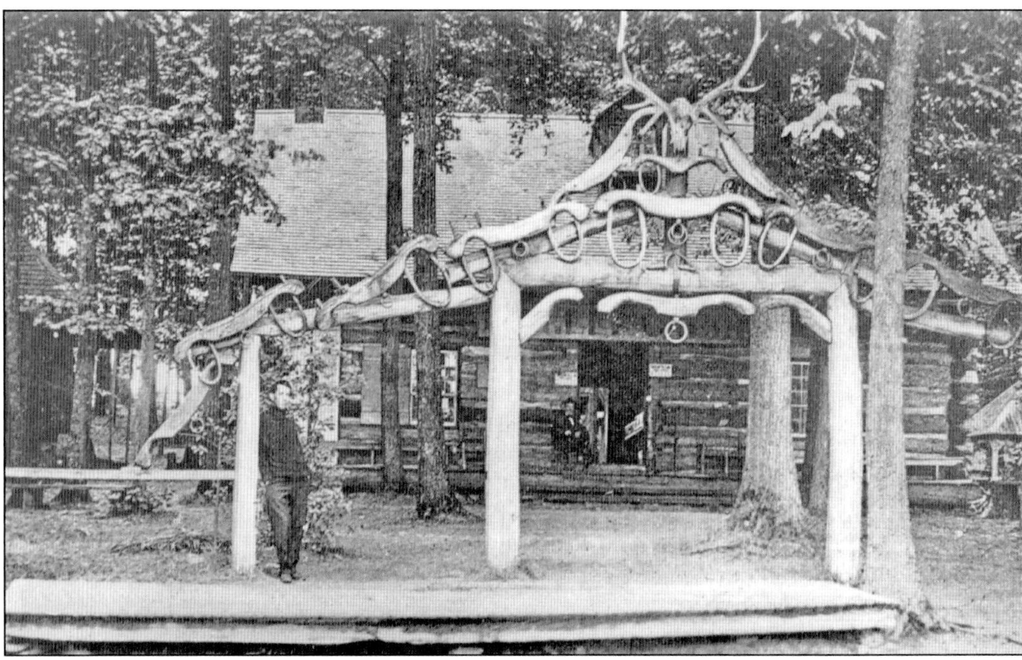

A later image of the Pioneer Cabin shows a different entrance. The picnic area and the auditorium are to the right. The "Indian Council Tree" is on the left. In 1998, the LaGrange School was moved to the Pioneer Museum grounds. This was placed south of the cabin, along with an early church building added in 2005.

The hollow base of the "Indian Council Tree" was moved to the Pioneer Cabin grounds in 1882 and preserved on a platform with a roof. This tree had served as a landmark for Native American and pioneer travelers on a trail near present Route 63 in Pavilion. It was a nearly 2,000-year-old buttonwood, or eastern sycamore, with a circumference of 50 feet.

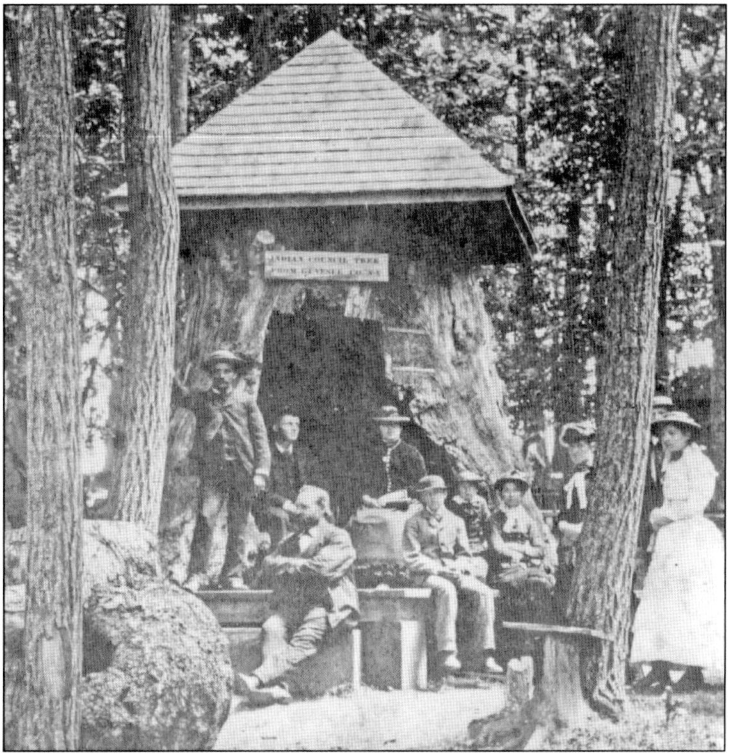

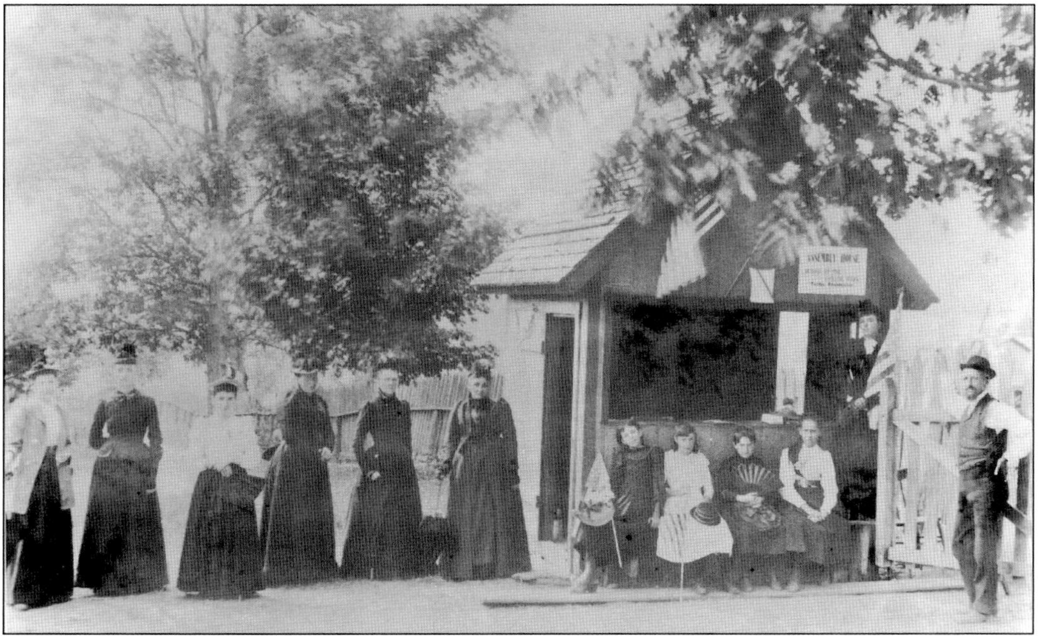

The Silver Lake Temperance Assembly operated by Mead and Stearns met on grounds south of the Pioneer Cabin. An open-air auditorium was built and was made available for the annual Pioneer Picnic. In 1892, this property was added to the Pioneer grounds. At the 1899 Pioneer Picnic, Gov. Theodore Roosevelt spoke here to about 25,000 people. The auditorium was destroyed by fire in 1931. (Henry Page Collection.)

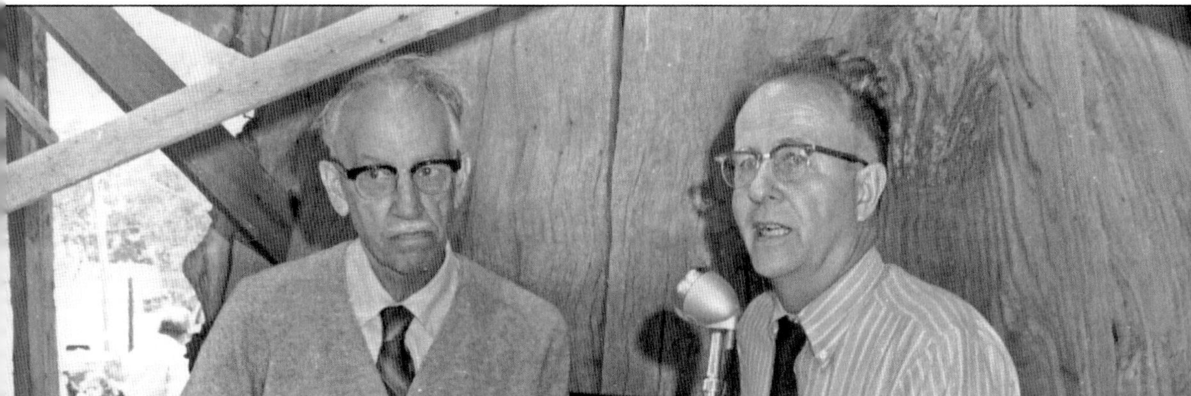

Henry Page was honored for 45 years as treasurer of the Wyoming Historical Pioneer Association at the centennial meeting in 1972. The Page family had served the association since it began. Clark Rice, at right, was elected president at this time. Rice was the photographer and Page the researcher; both contributed to the preservation of the history of the Perry area. (Henry Page Collection.)

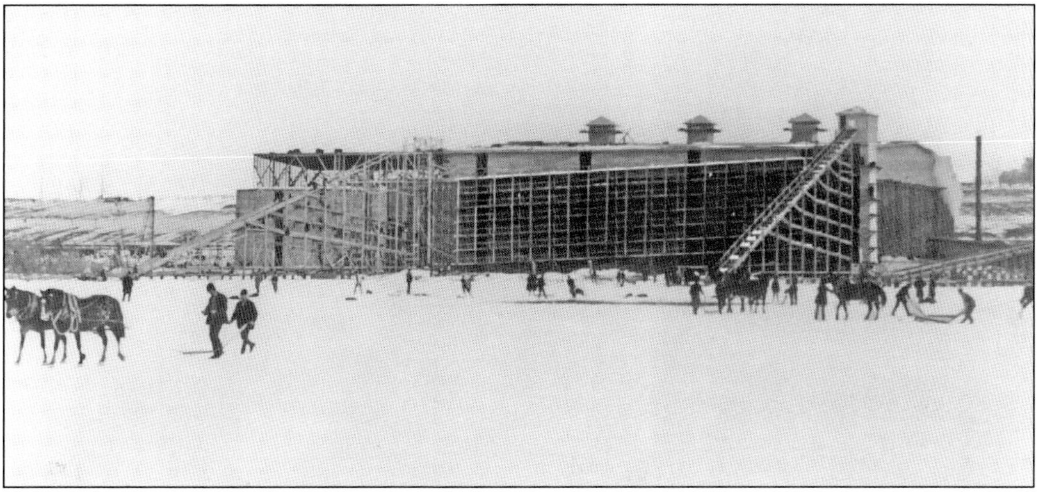

Before electric refrigeration, blocks of ice were cut in winter, stored in insulating sawdust, and used in warmer weather. The Silver Lake Ice Company was on the east shore of the lake with a capacity of 60,000 tons. It was torn down in 1925. To start the ice harvesting, men and a teams of horses cleared snow from the ice with 6-foot scoops.

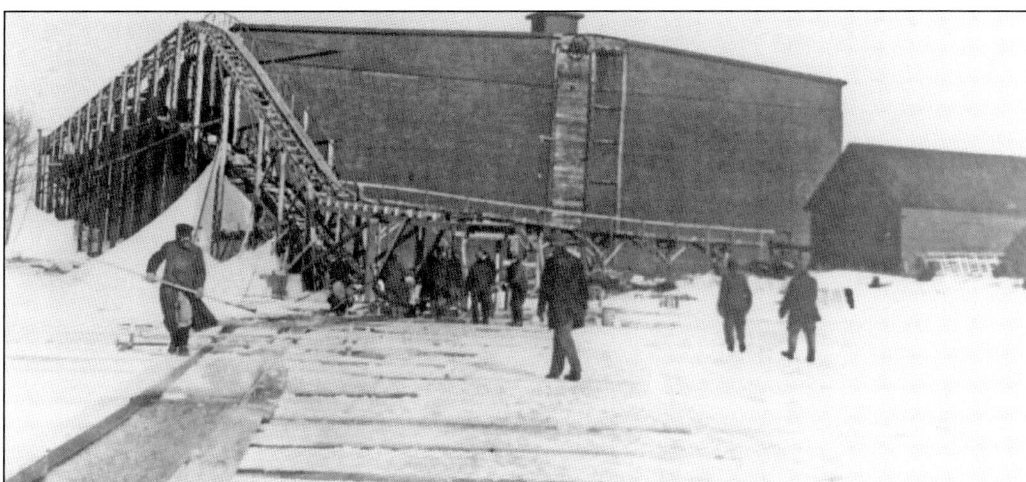

The lines on the ice were marked for cutting, with one man leading the team and another riding on the plow. The next step was to cut the ice along the lines with an ice saw. The blocks of ice then had to be separated and floated through channels to the conveyor with a pole or hook.

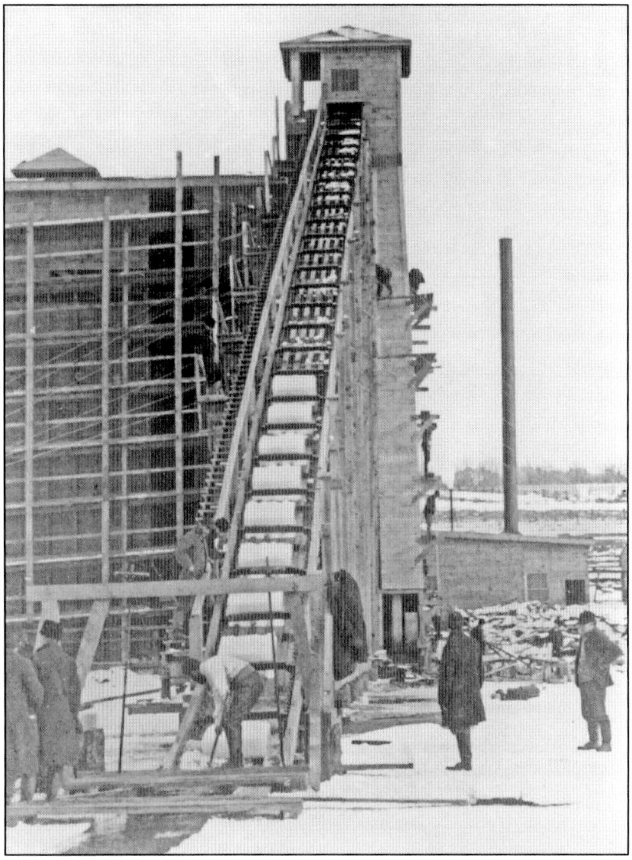

At the icehouse, the ice was lifted onto the conveyor and sent for stacking within. Space was left between the outside edge of the ice and the wall of the icehouse, and also at the top, to be filled with sawdust for insulation. Silver Lake's spring-fed water made excellent clear ice, which was in great demand and shipped to many large cities.

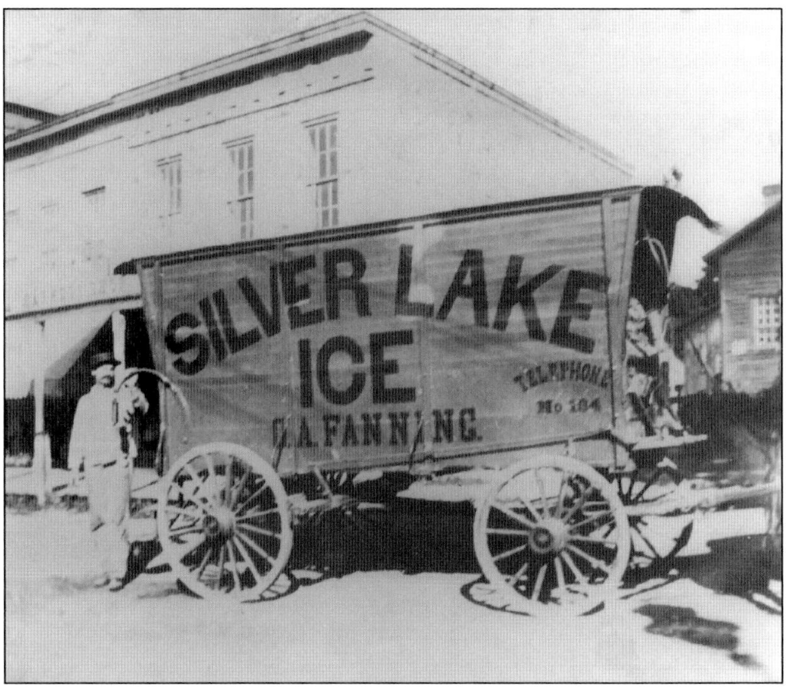

The Fanning Company had a small ice conveyor at the lake that loaded ice onto railroad cars to move to the 3,000-ton icehouse next to the coal trestle at South Center Street. In warm weather, this wagon would deliver ice to customers in Perry. A 25-pound ice block would last one day in the ice box. The ice business was discontinued in 1943.

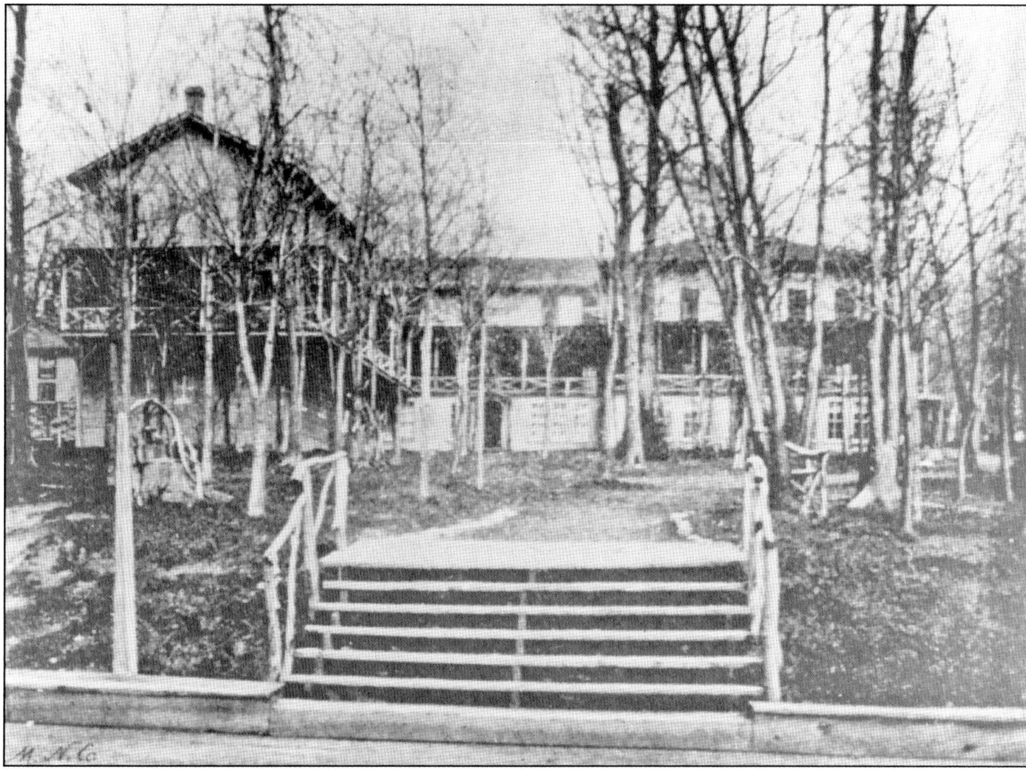

After the Walker House on Main Street burned in 1857, A. B. Walker moved to Canada, but returned in 1868 to build a new Walker House on the old Main Street site. A third Walker House was built at the lake after the opening of the railroad for passenger service in 1872. He ran both hotels for a number of years, until his daughter and son-in-law took over at the lake.

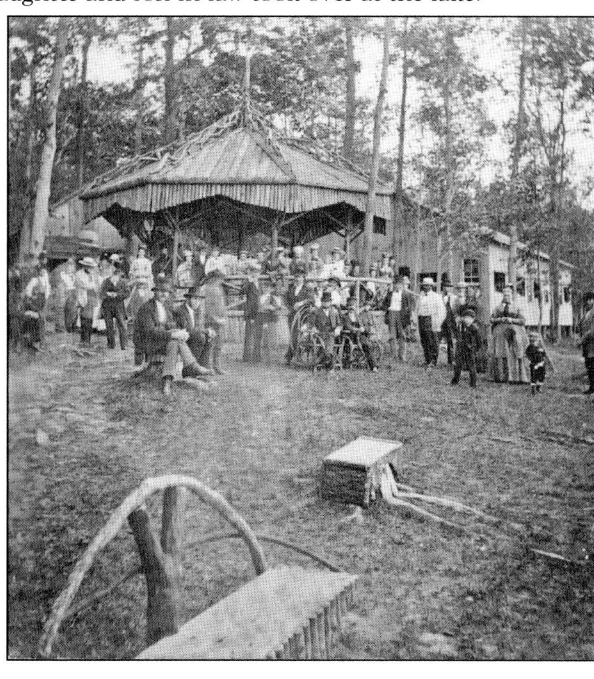

The Walker House was built between the lake and the Pioneer Cabin. This is identified as the Walker Dance Hall, on the right, and the pavilion for refreshments, both located in front of the Silver Lake Walker House. Perhaps it was at Pioneer Picnic time when this area was crowded with people. (Henry Page Collection.)

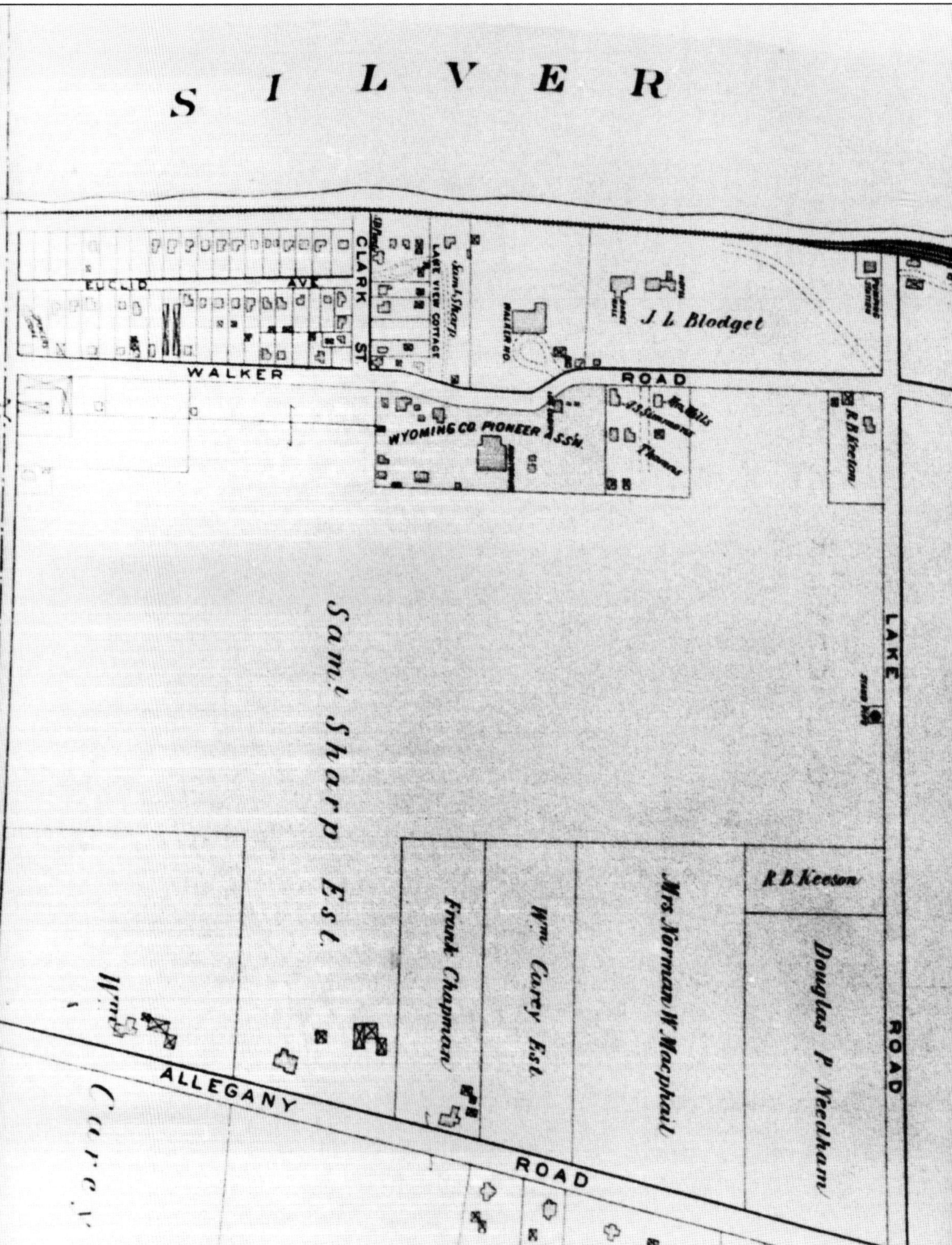

S I L V E R
CLARK ST
EUCLID AVE
WALKER ROAD
Saml Sharp
LAKE VIEW COTTAGE
J. L. Blodget
WYOMING CO PIONEER ASS'N
R.B. Keeson
Saml Sharp Est.
LAKE ROAD
R.B. Keeson
Frank Chapman
Wm Carey Est.
Mrs Norman W. Macphail
Douglas P. Needham
ALLEGANY ROAD

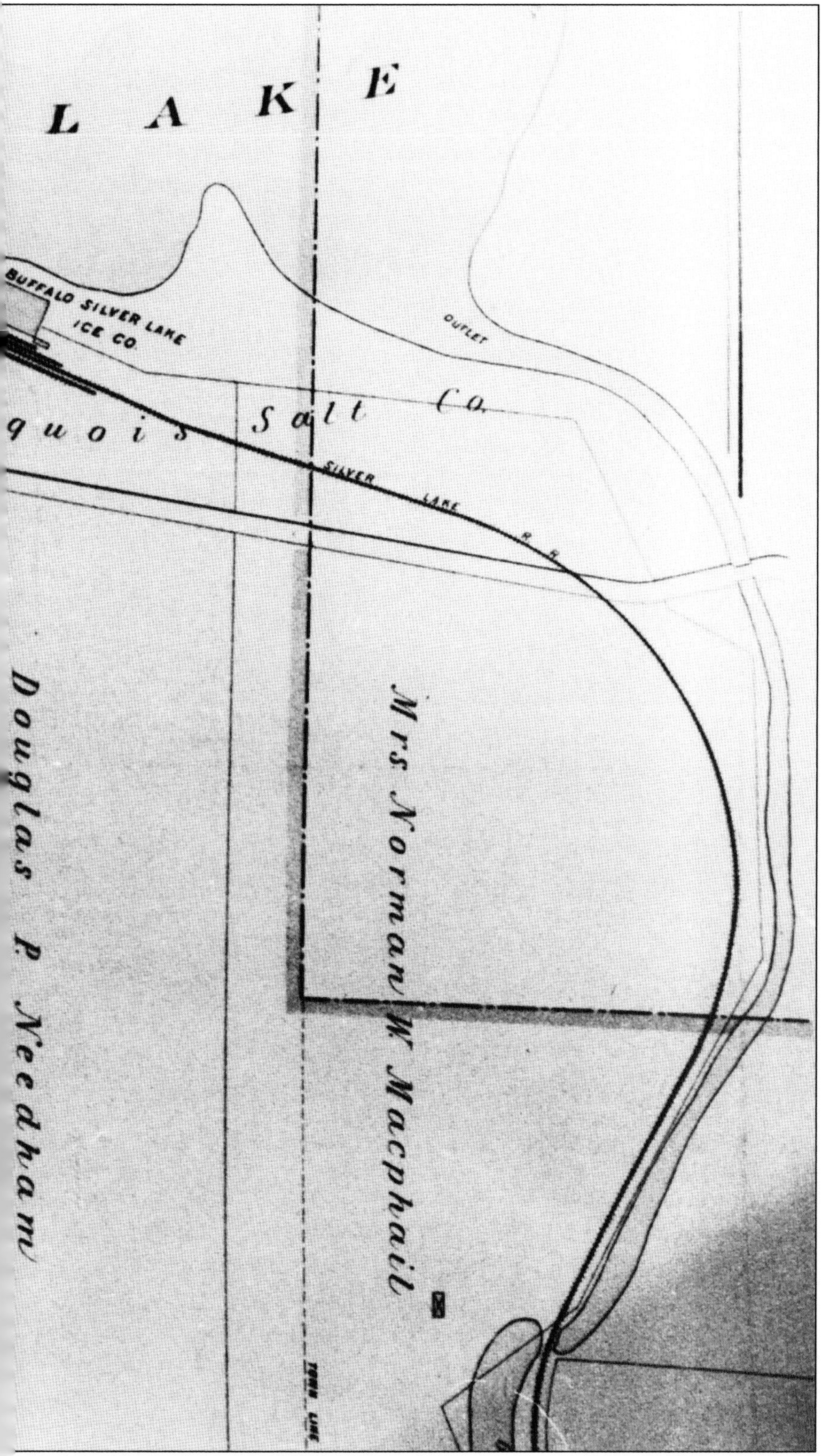

This 1902 map shows the Buffalo Silver Lake Ice Company between the east shore of Silver Lake and the Silver Lake Railroad. Lake Road, which is now Standpipe Road, has the water-pumping station at the lake and the standpipe halfway to Allegany Road (Route 39). At the bend of Walker Road is the property of the Wyoming Historical Pioneer Association with the Pioneer Cabin and auditorium labeled. Across the road is the Walker House, built at the lake after the railroad opened.

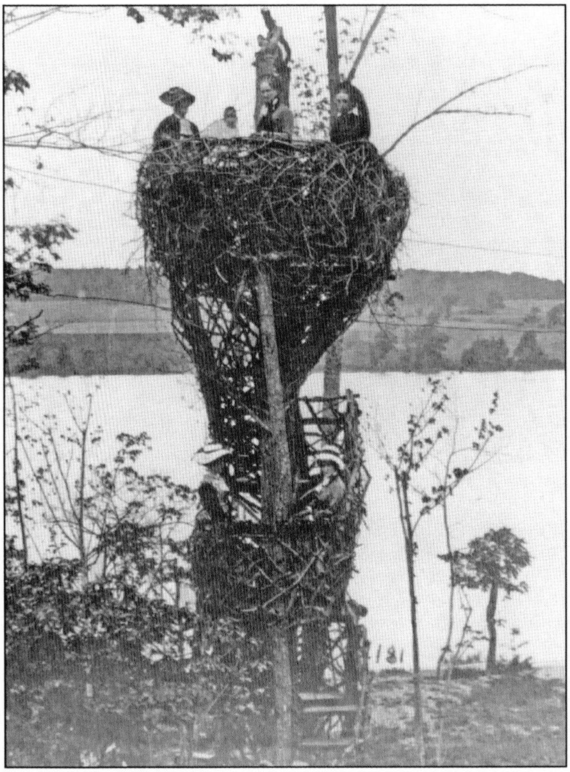

This is the Crows Nest, one of the entertainments for guests of the Walker House. It provided a great view of the lake. An old tourist poster advertised, "If you are tortured with Hay Fever come to Silver Lake and secure perfect relief. By Nature's own Restorer- The Pure Lake Air, and Rest found at Walker's."

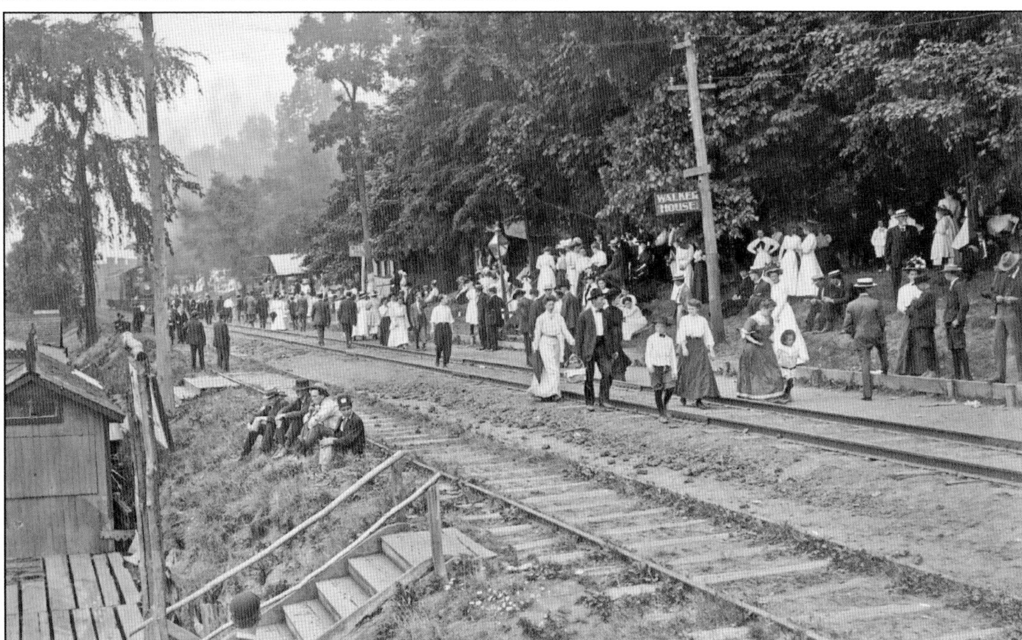

Crowds at Silver Lake, probably on Pioneer Picnic Day, are on the railroad tracks that were between the lake and the Walker House, which is up the hill to the right. On Pioneer Picnic Day, all day, trains ran back and forth from the Perry train station on Center Street to the lake for 5¢. People would carry their picnic lunch up the hill to the Pioneer grounds on the other side of Walkers.

Boating was a popular activity at Silver Lake with people renting the small sailboats or taking a tour of the lake on a steamer. This steamer was a side-wheeler, the *Nellie Palmer.* It was built in 1864 and named for the granddaughter of the largest contributor. After several years on the lake, the steamer burned at her dock.

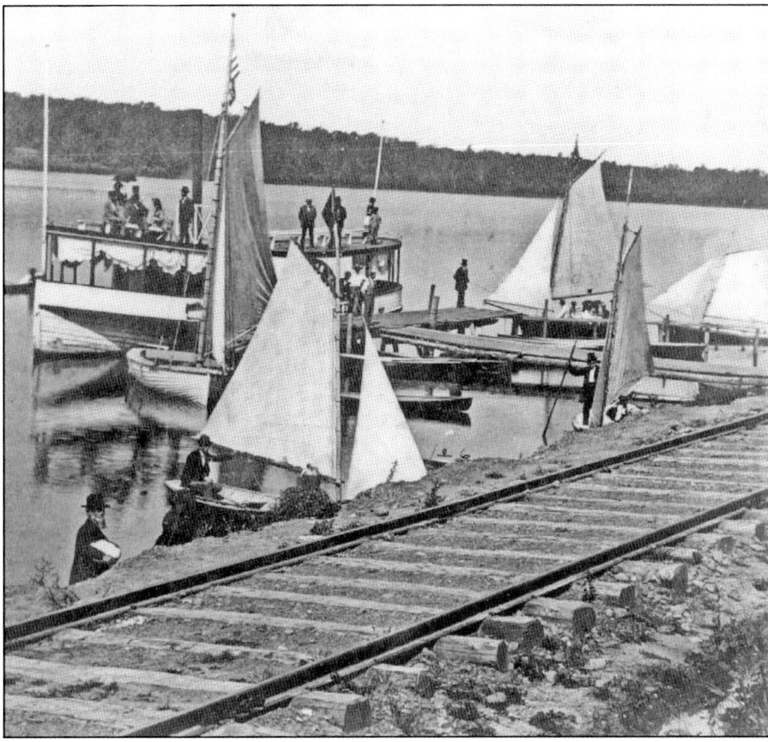

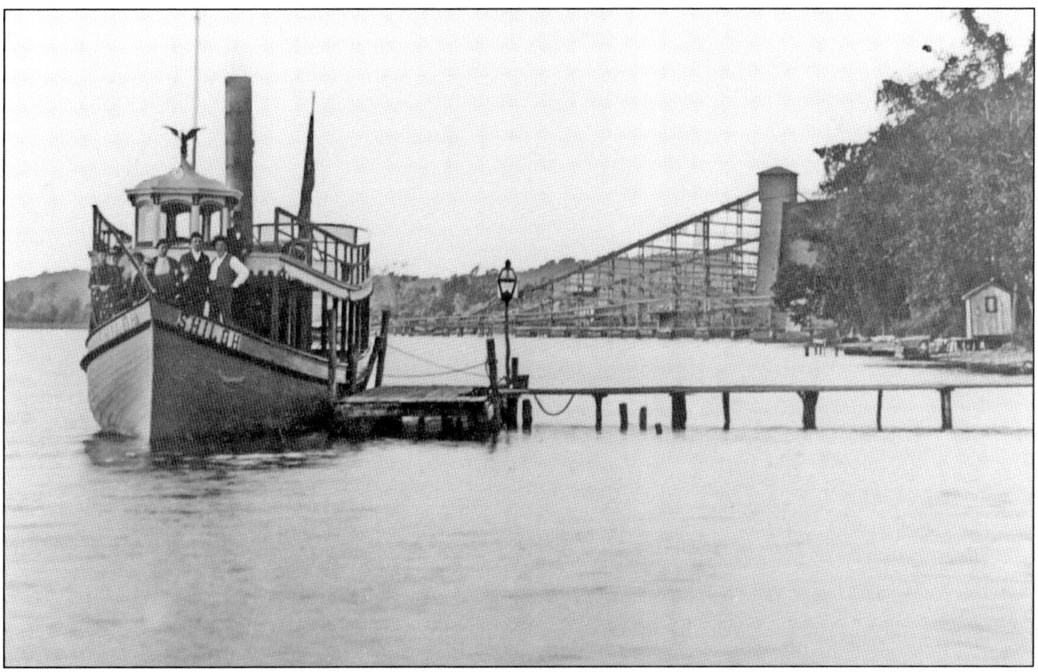

This steamer was the *Shiloh*, named for a popular cure made in LeRoy. The first *Shiloh* burned in 1884, and the second smaller steamer, pictured here, was launched the next year. The second *Shiloh* was declared unsafe, was beached, and burned in 1900. This picture shows the Silver Lake Ice House in the background.

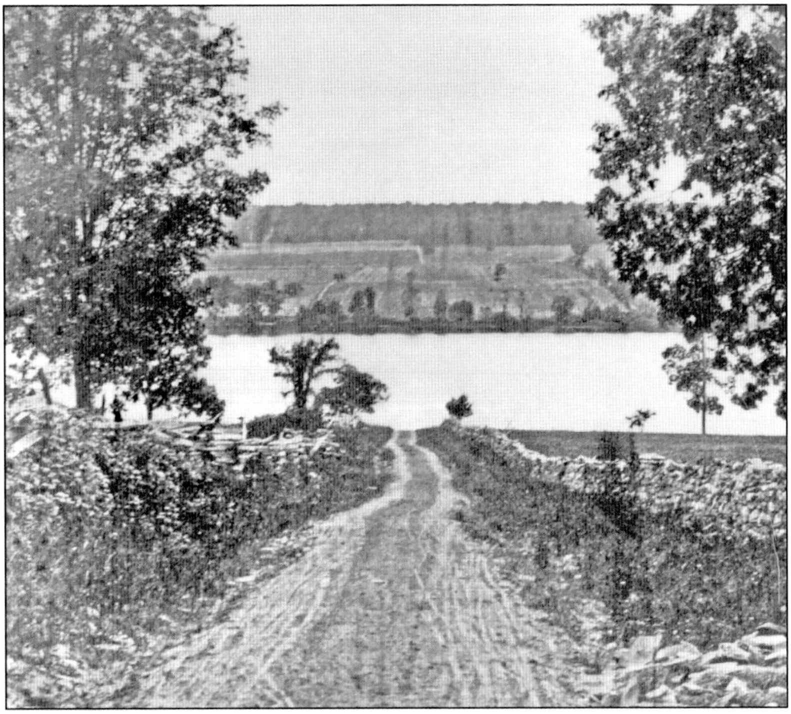

This was called Lake Road, now Standpipe Road, looking west towards Silver Lake. Later the pumping station would be at the waterfront on the left, the Silver Lake Ice House at the Davis Tract to the right. The cylinder-shaped standpipe would be on the left foreground, where the water tower is today.

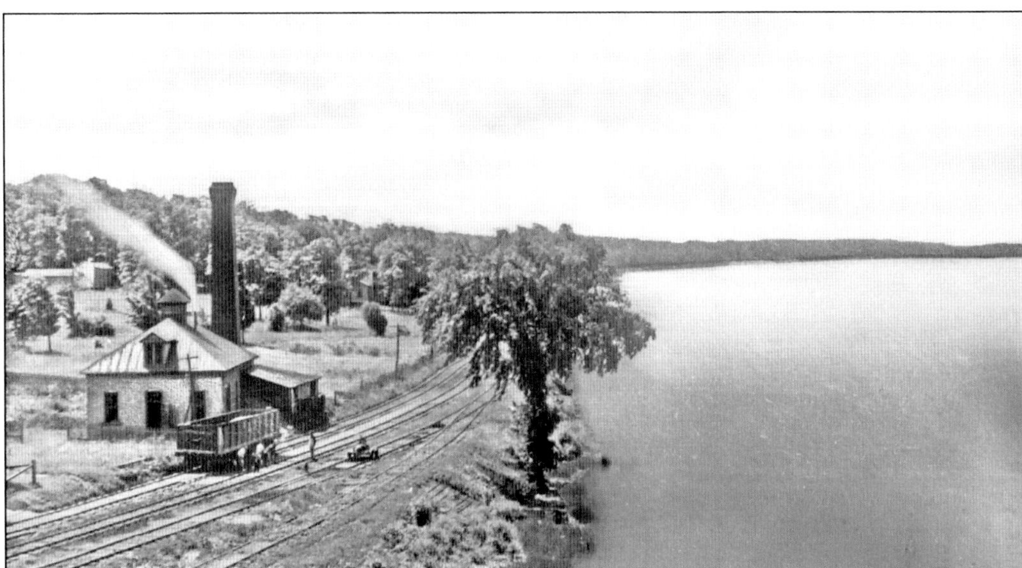

A water system was needed not only for clean water for the village, but for fighting fires. In 1896, the system was started with the steam-powered pumps taking water from the lake. This water-pumping station was on the east side of the Silver Lake at Standpipe Road. It was replaced with a new one in 1954. (Photograph by A. L. Remington.)

Four

Churches

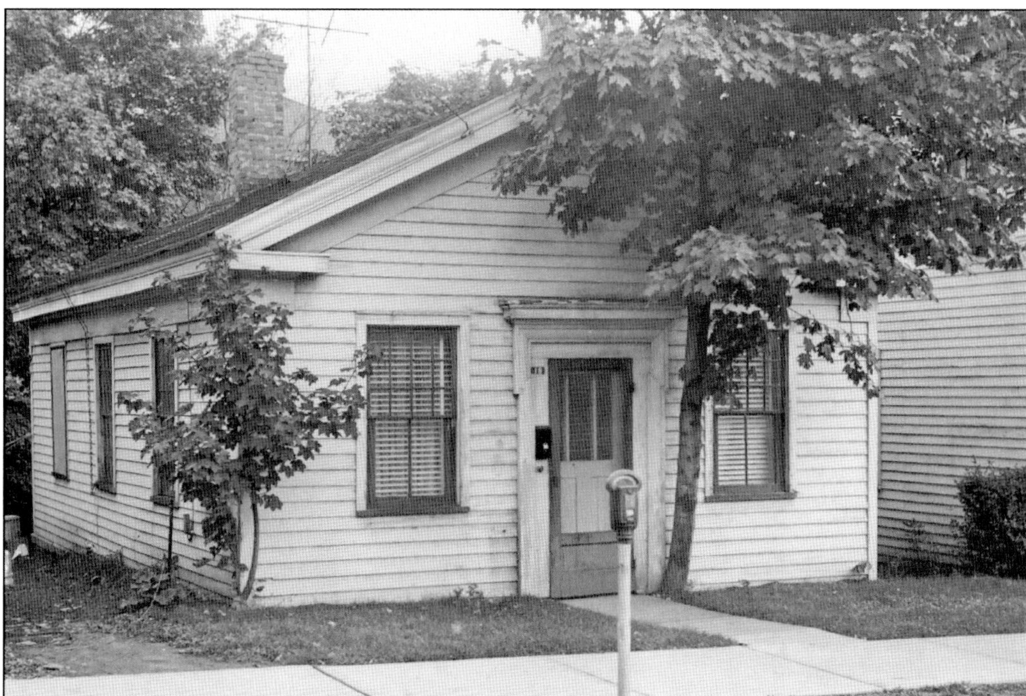

This building shown at 18 Covington Street served as the first Presbyterian church from 1834–1839. The Catholic church bought it in 1859 and used it until 1873. It was also used as a private school, a residence, and for many retail ventures. Betty Rice donated this building to the Wyoming Historical Pioneer Association. In 2005, it was moved to the Pioneer Museum grounds at Silver Lake and restored to depict early church days.

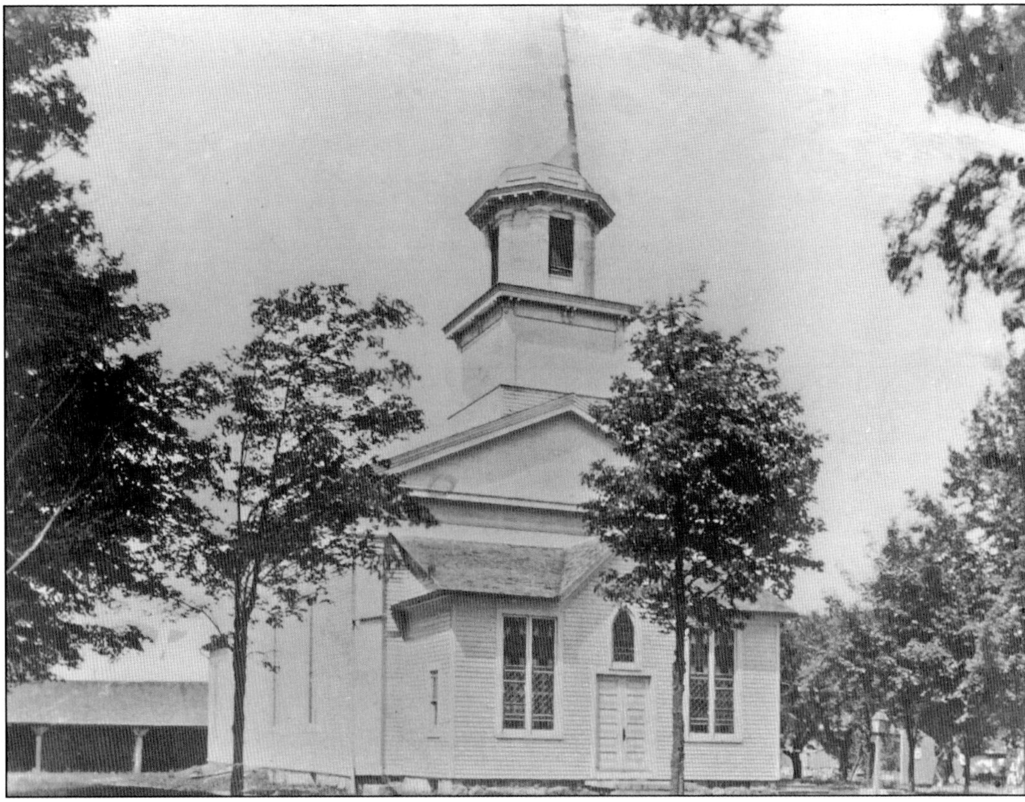

The first church society formed in the town of Perry was the Congregational church at Perry Center in 1814. Presbyterians also worshiped here until they formed their own society in the village in 1834. The church building was constructed in 1830, with major changes and a rededication in 1900. This picture, showing barns to the left, was taken before 1916.

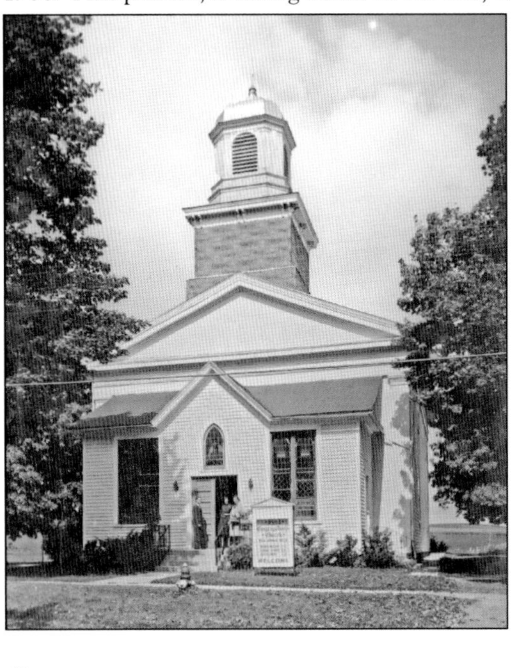

In 1964, the First Congregational Church in Perry Center had a 150-year celebration. This picture was probably taken then, when Rev. John Beck was minister. After the steeple was destroyed by lightning in 1916, it was decided not to replace the spire, but to retain the middle section with a new rounded top. Today, a new spire has been added.

The First Baptist Society of Perry was formed in 1816, worshiping at first in homes, later in the village school. In 1830, the original meetinghouse was built on Main Street, and in 1849, was enlarged to double the size, as shown here. The horse barns are seen at the rear of the lot backing up to Leicester Street.

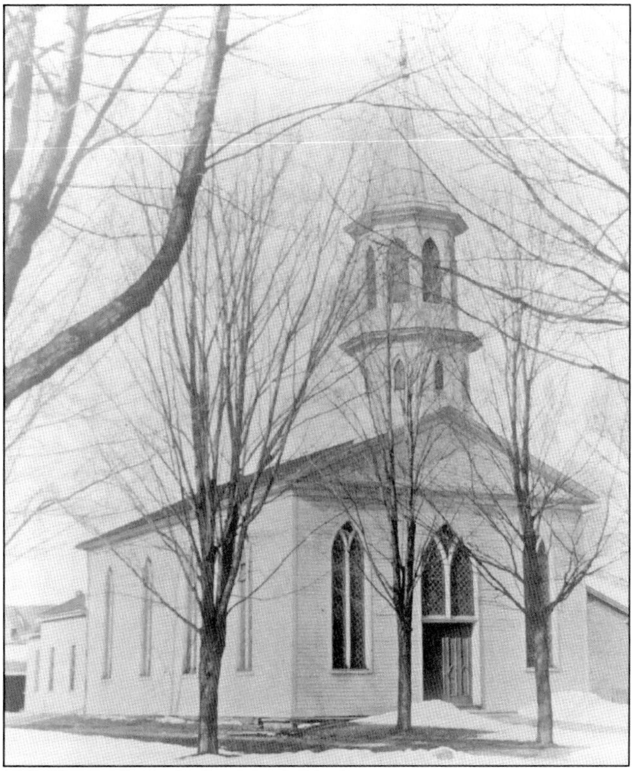

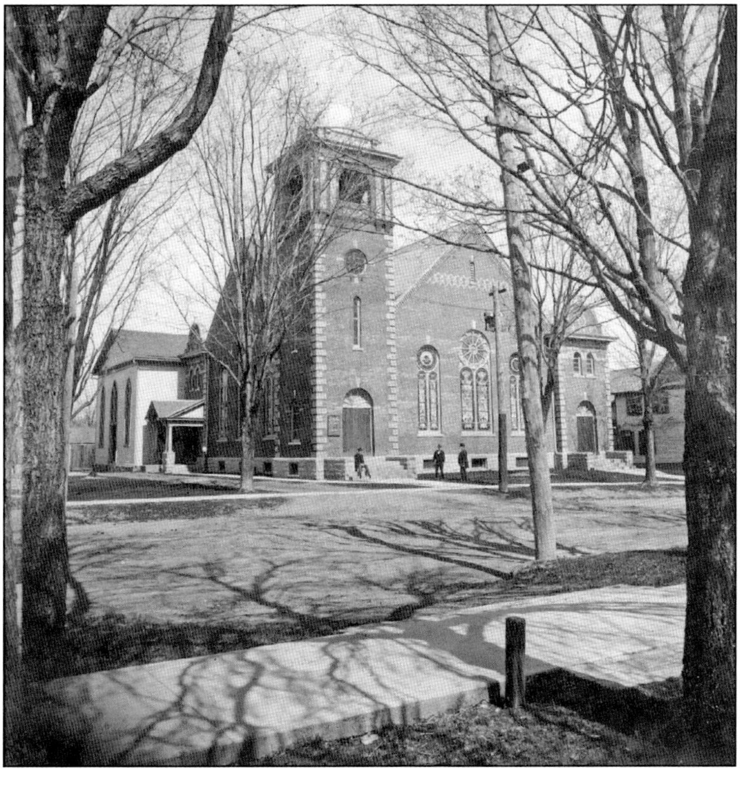

The First Baptist Church started construction in 1900 on this new brick building with two entrances facing Main Street. At that time, the old church structure was moved to the rear of the lot and turned 90 degrees. It was used as a Sunday schoolroom and annex and was remodeled in later years. The parsonage to the right of the church was built in 1886. (Henry Page Collection.)

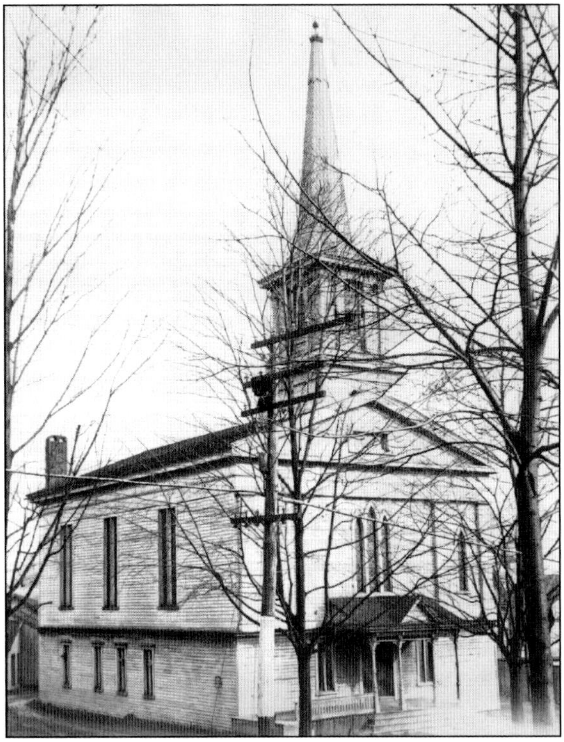

The third church building of the Methodist Episcopal Church, which had organized in 1816, was constructed in 1840, facing east on a street running between Lake and Covington Streets. In 1883, the building was turned to face Lake Street, and elevated with a basement built underneath. This picture is the renovated church building on Lake Street.

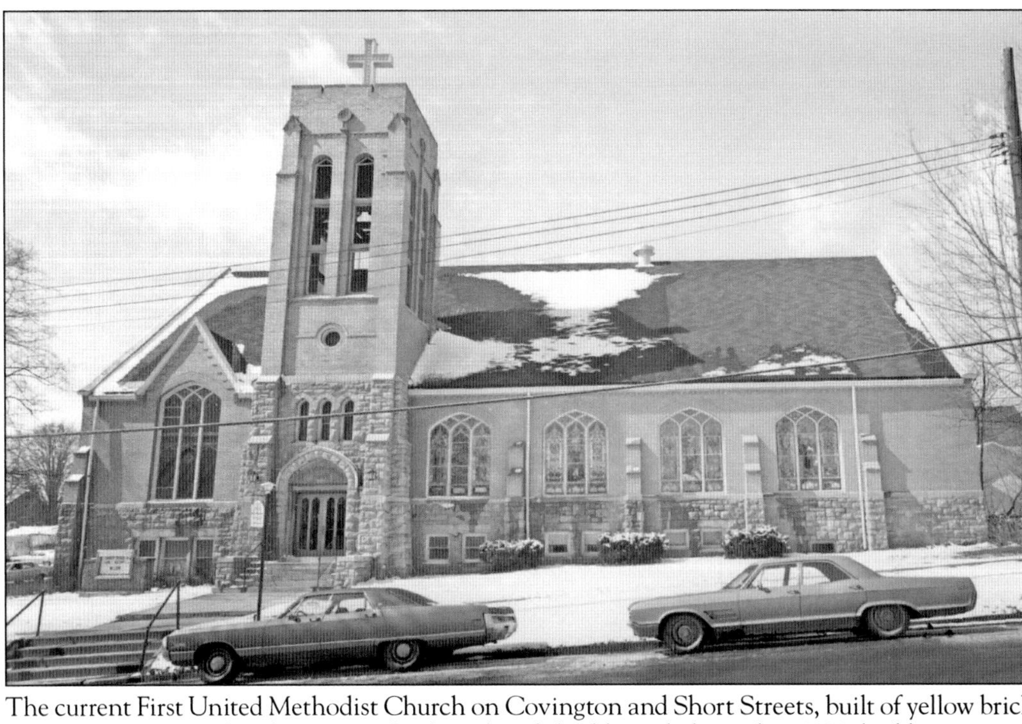

The current First United Methodist Church on Covington and Short Streets, built of yellow brick and stone, was completed in 1907. The first church building, dedicated in 1824, had become too small and was sold to the Universalist society. The second larger edifice was built in 1832 and burned six years later. This is the fourth Methodist church.

The first church building of the Universalist society, formed in 1831, was bought from the Methodists in 1833 and moved. A new church building, with a tall steeple at the center, was completed in 1852 at the southeast corner of St. Helena and Main Streets. The oil lamp on the corner indicates the date of this picture to be between 1877 and 1892.

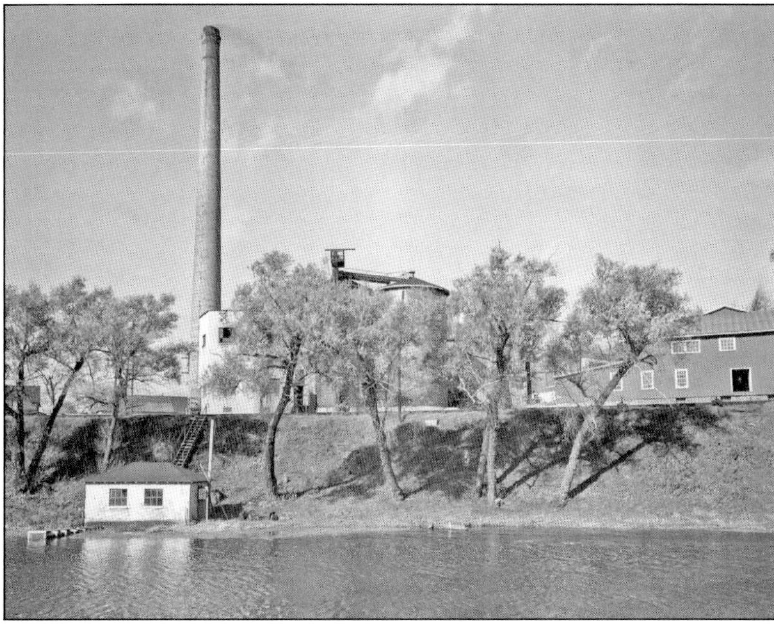

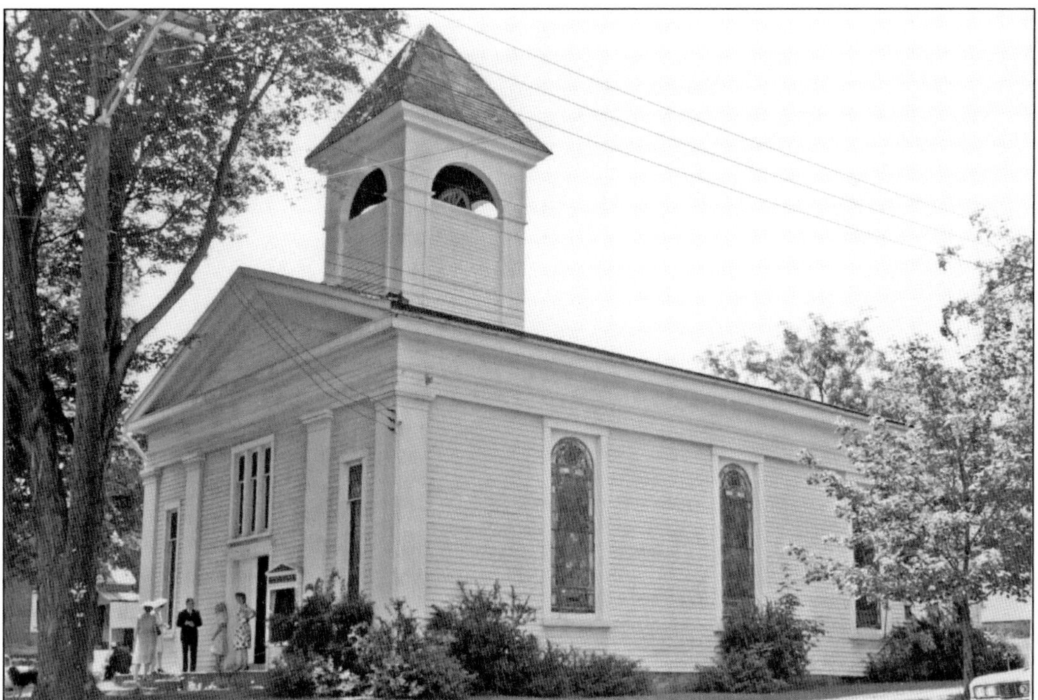

In this 1957 picture, the First Universalist Church no longer has the two rounded columns in front, the steeple has been changed to a bell tower on the right side, and the windows have been replaced. The church closed in 1968. It became the Perry Athletic Club with the bell tower removed, windows and front door covered, and the exterior sided in gray with white trim.

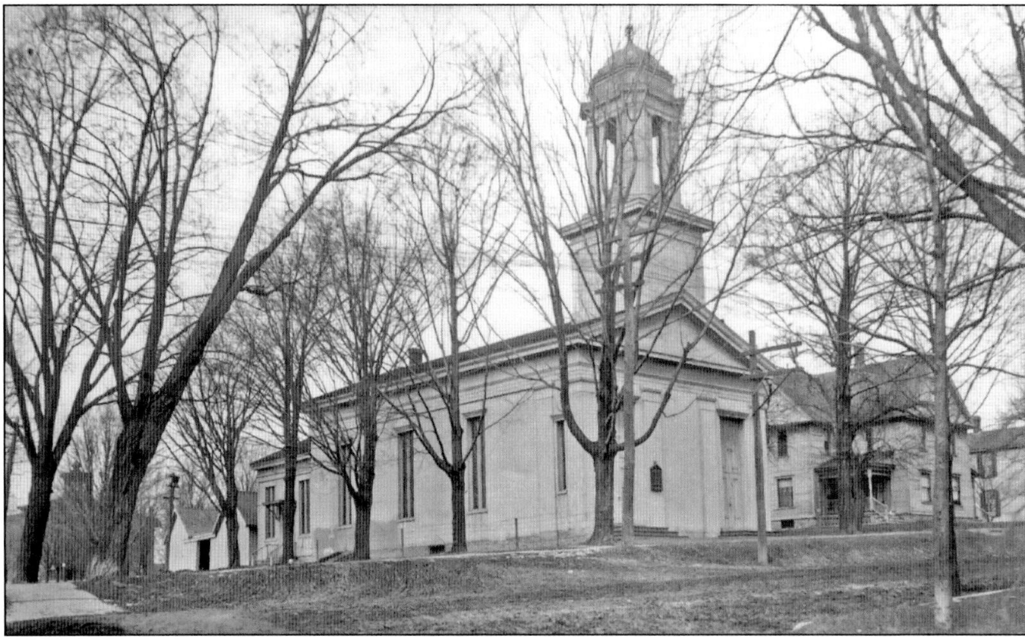

The second church building of the Presbyterians was constructed on the corner of Church and Main Streets, opening in 1839. This was made of bricks and painted white, with a chapel and Sunday school in the back. The horse barns are farther back along Church Street, and the Perry Academy on Leicester Street is in the background to the left.

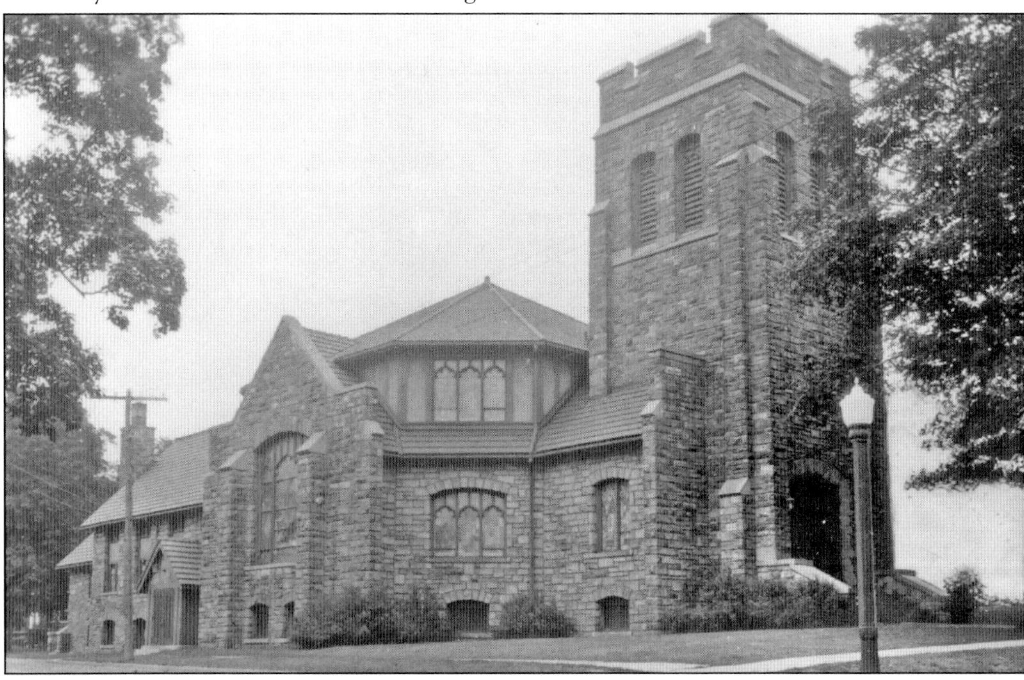

The last service in the second Presbyterian church was in July 1909. The Presbyterians worshiped with the Baptists during the construction of their new church. In 1911, the third church building, constructed of stone, was completed and became Brick Presbyterian Church. A carillon of bells, added in 1969, serenades the village twice a day.

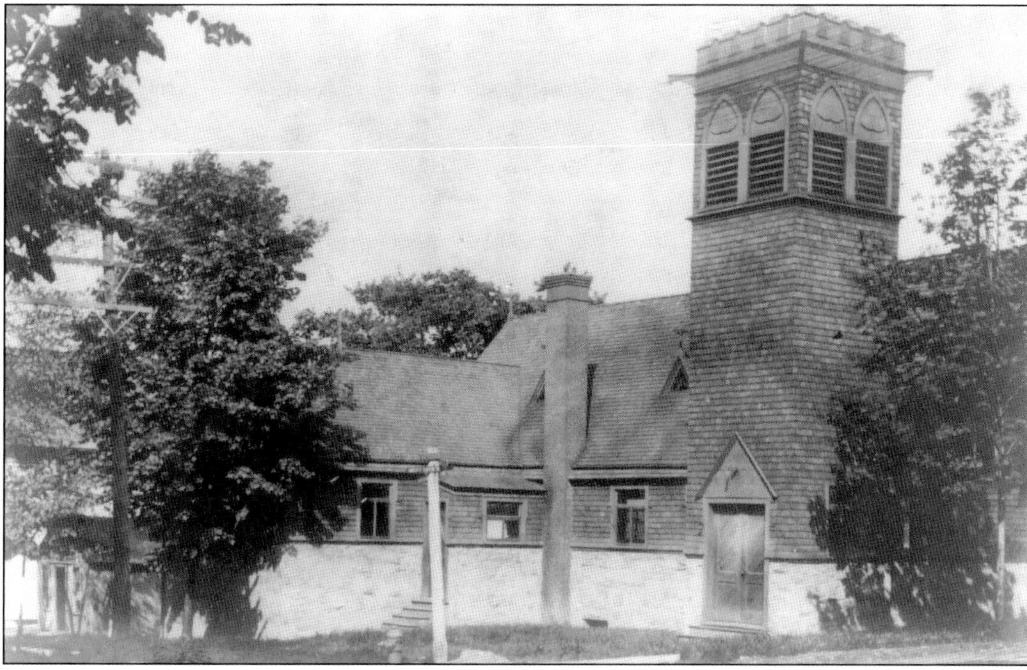

Episcopal church services were held in Perry as early as 1845. In 1875, the Episcopalians were conducting services in a little chapel on Main Street where Borden Avenue is now. They met in the Universalist church from 1897 until the Holy Apostles Episcopal Church opened in 1899 across the street at the northeast corner of St. Helena and Main Streets.

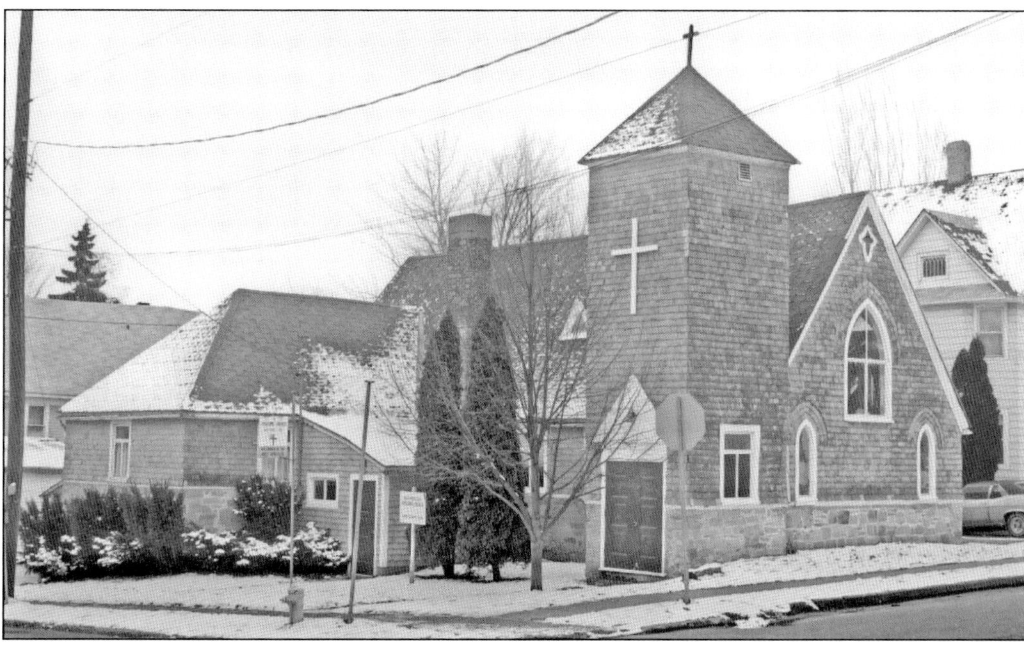

This more recent picture of the Episcopal church shows some of the exterior changes that have occurred to the building. Today the church has the Episcopal red door. The very small but active congregation also runs a thrift shop on Main Street. For a recent open house, this Episcopal church called itself "the little church that could."

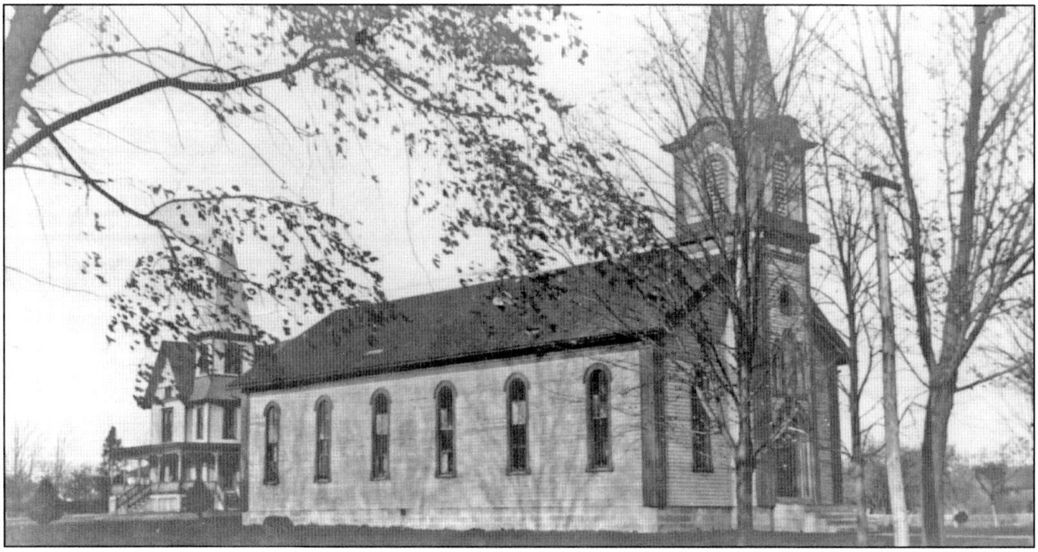

The first Catholic Mass was celebrated in Perry in 1848. The first Catholic church building, used from 1859–1873, was the Covington Street building once used by the Presbyterians. This wooden St. Joseph's Roman Catholic Church, pictured above, opened in 1873 on Leicester Street. The rectory was built behind the church, facing Park Street and the Perry Academy.

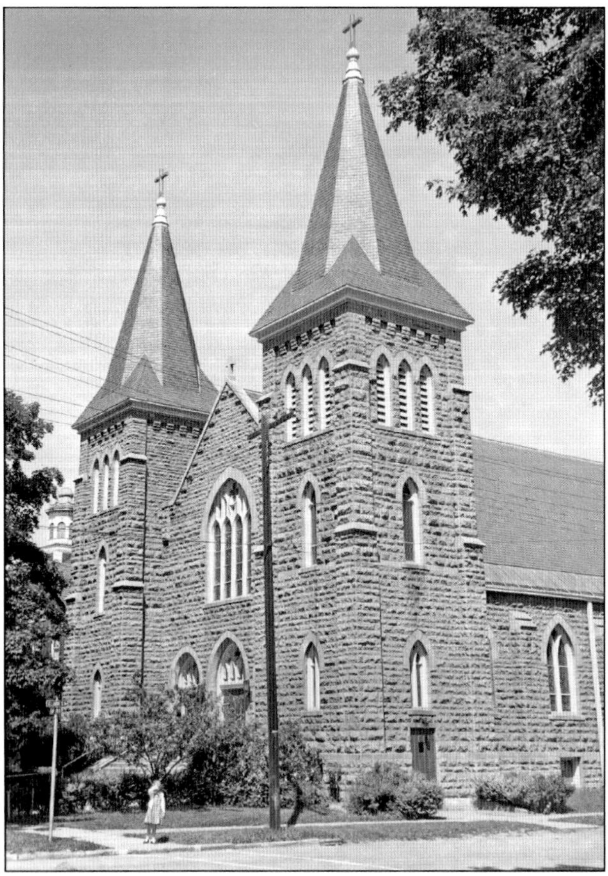

This third Catholic church, completed in 1908, was constructed of marble with twin towers. The old wooden structure had been moved north of the rectory during construction and was demolished after being used as a hall for several years. A new rectory replaced the old. The cupola of the elementary school shows at the left.

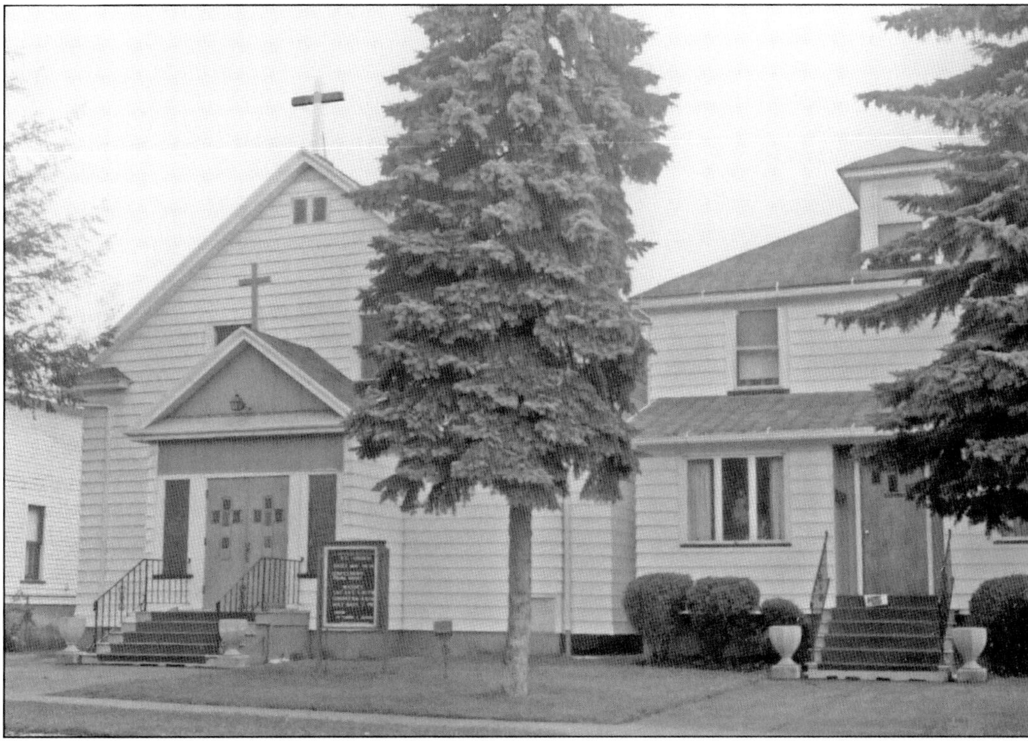

St. Stanislaus Kostka Roman Catholic Church was established in 1910 to serve the Polish immigrants who had come to work in the mills. This church building on Water Street, with the rectory to the right, was built in 1912. This church was closed recently but has joined with the congregation at St. Joseph's for worship as St. Isidore's Parish.

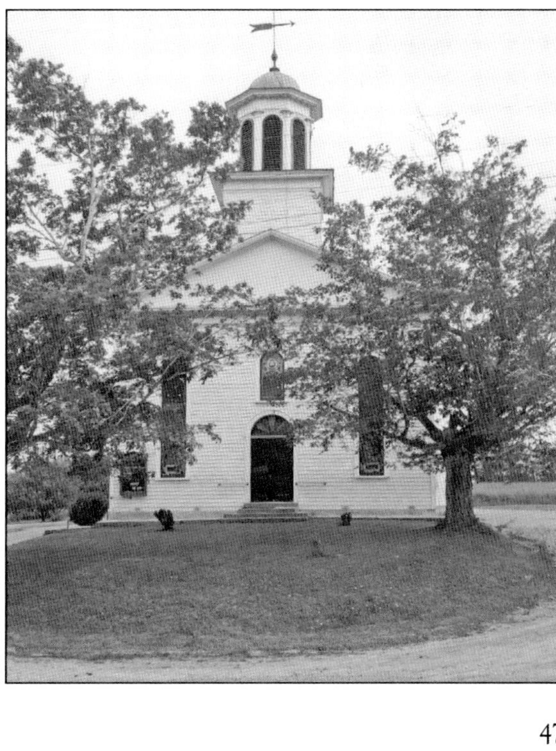

LaGrange Baptist Church celebrated 150 years in 1975 with this picture appearing on a brochure. This society formed in 1825 as the Baptist Church of Covington and Perry, meeting in a barn and later the LaGrange School. Located on the south side of LaGrange Road, west of Route 246, this church was constructed in 1835 with alterations in 1869 to its appearance here.

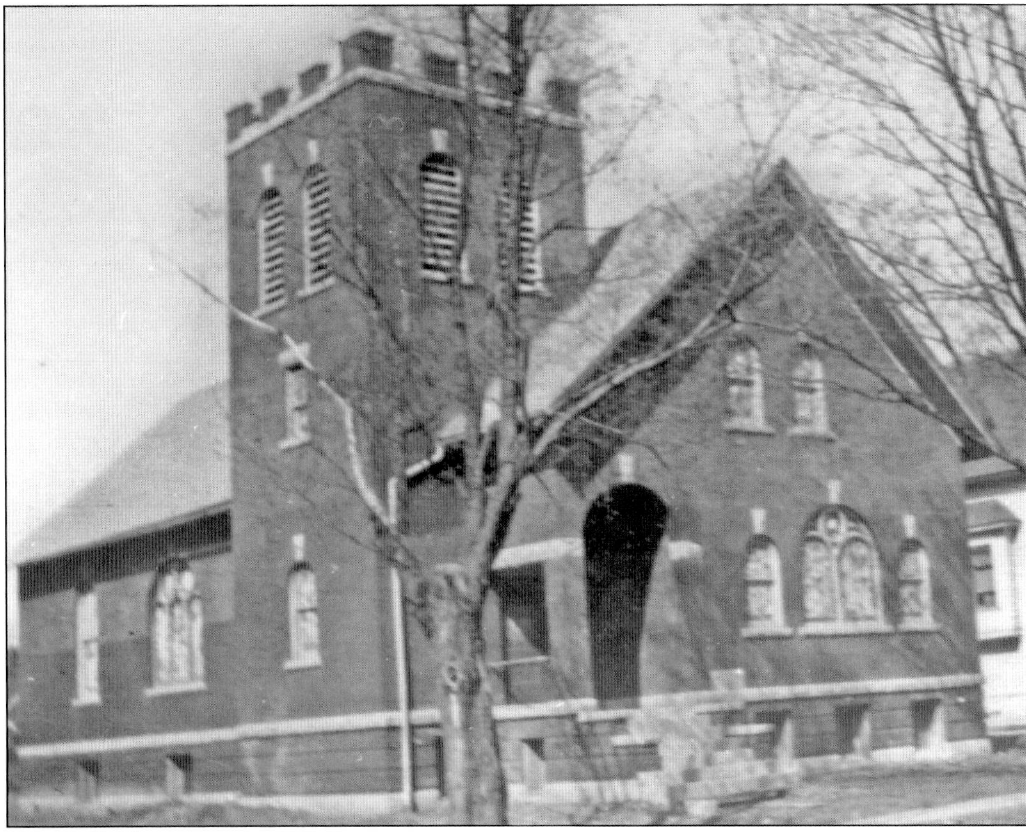

The Free Methodist Church was established in 1860. A church building was erected the next year at the southeast corner of Gardeau and Main Streets, with the parsonage adjoining. In 1862, a group from a small Burke Hill church society joined the congregation. A new parsonage and land were purchased in 1915 on Church Street across from the Presbyterian church. The new First Free Methodist Church was built in 1916. In 1976, the name was changed and was rededicated as the Coleman Memorial Free Methodist Church named for Bishop George Coleman who had grown up in the Perry church and gone on to serve the denomination. Below is the interior of this church.

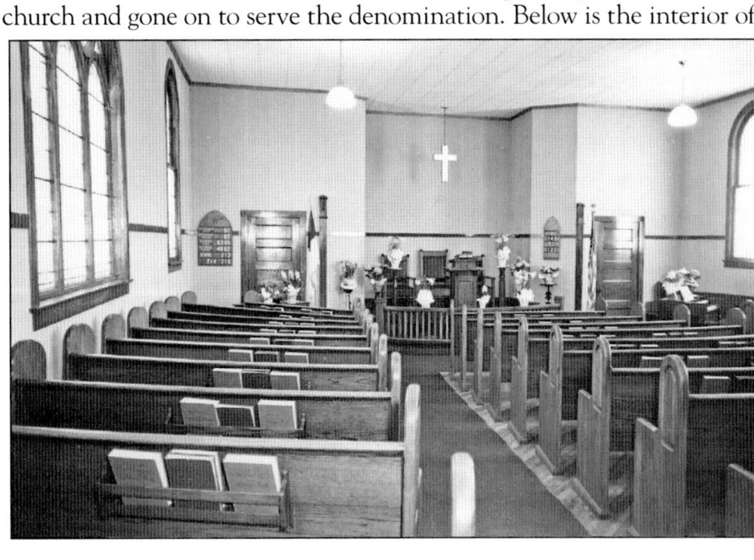

Five

Main Street

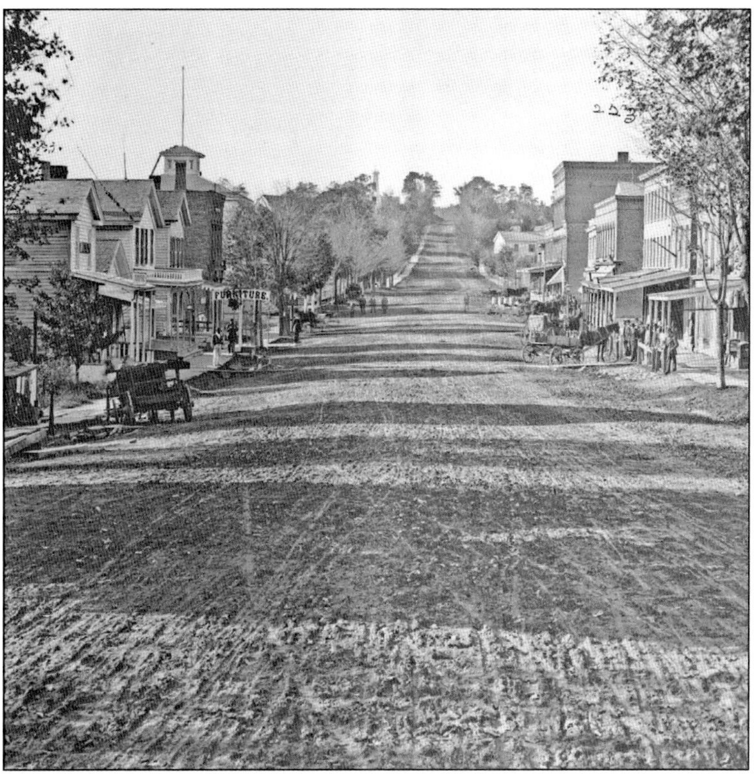

This is Perry's North Main Street, both east and west sides, looking south from where the Masonic Temple is today. The time period is between 1869, when the second Walker House with the cupola on the left was built, and 1891, when the three-story Smith (later Montesano) building on the right burned. The Universalist church steeple is in the background on the left. The white frame building in the background to the right is at the corner of Main and Mill Streets and would become Ireland's hardware store.

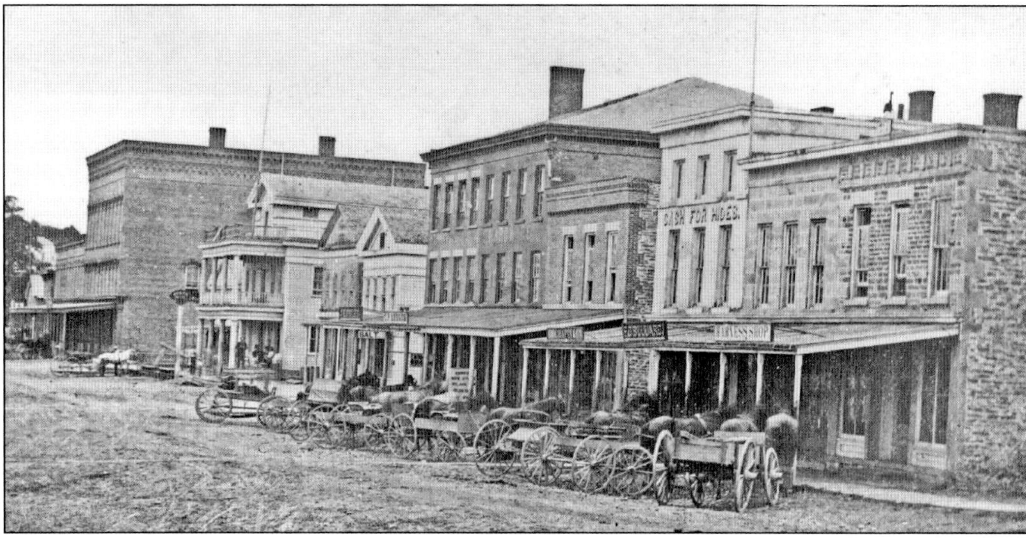

This is the west side of North Main Street about Civil War times. The harness shop at the right became L. G Abbott's (a jeweler) later the Perry Liquor Store, and now Shear Pleasure. The brick Bailey-Roche building at the north corner of Covington Street had a hardware store. The two frame buildings south of Covington Street, along with village and town records, burned in 1866. The National Hotel with two porches was next, then the frame Garrison building, Lake Street, and the three-story Smith building.

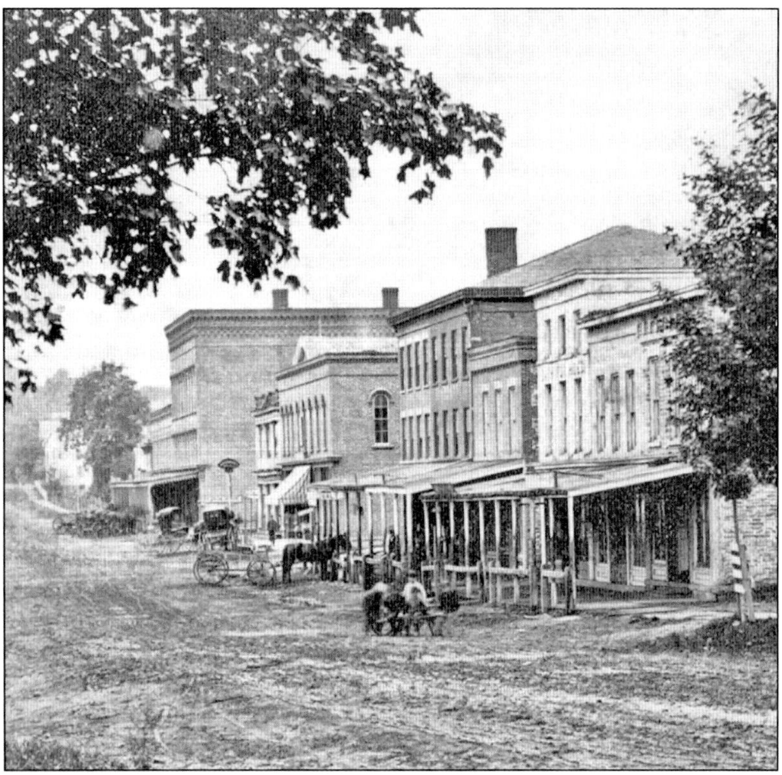

This is the same view as above, but the two frame structures at Covington Street were replaced in 1867 by the brick Cole building at the corner with Cole Shoes, today housing an empty restaurant and Hart's Insurance. The frame Wygant bookstore was replaced with a brick building, which later became a drugstore and is now part of the Family Furniture Store. (Henry Page Collection.)

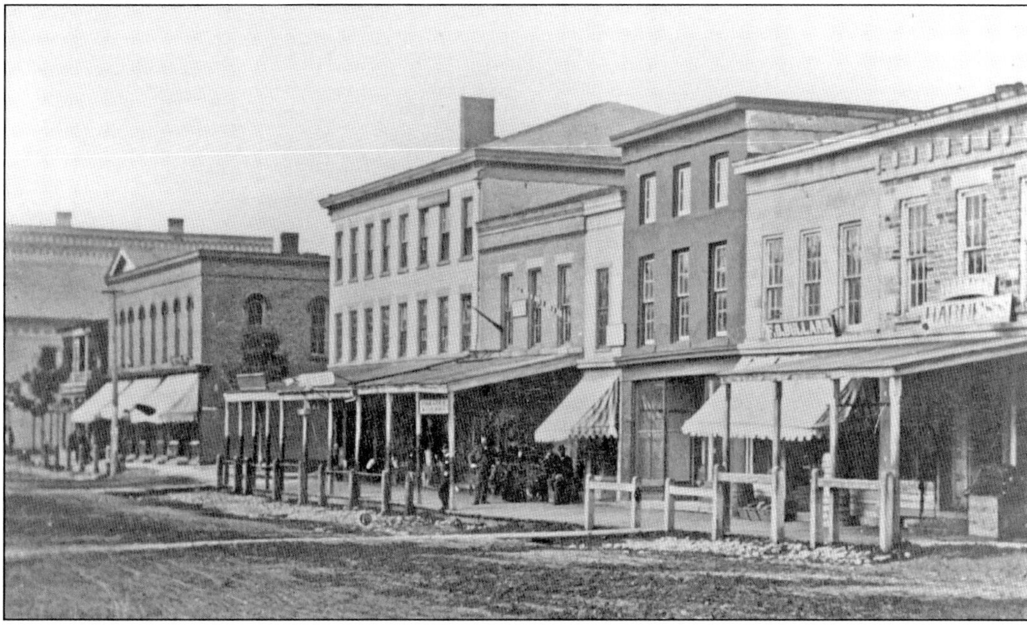

This is the same view of Main Street, but a small little building with an awning has been added between the one that no longer says "cash for hides," and the building to the south. This would become a shoe store and eventually the Hole In the Wall Restaurant, which later expanded into the White building to the south. Today it is empty.

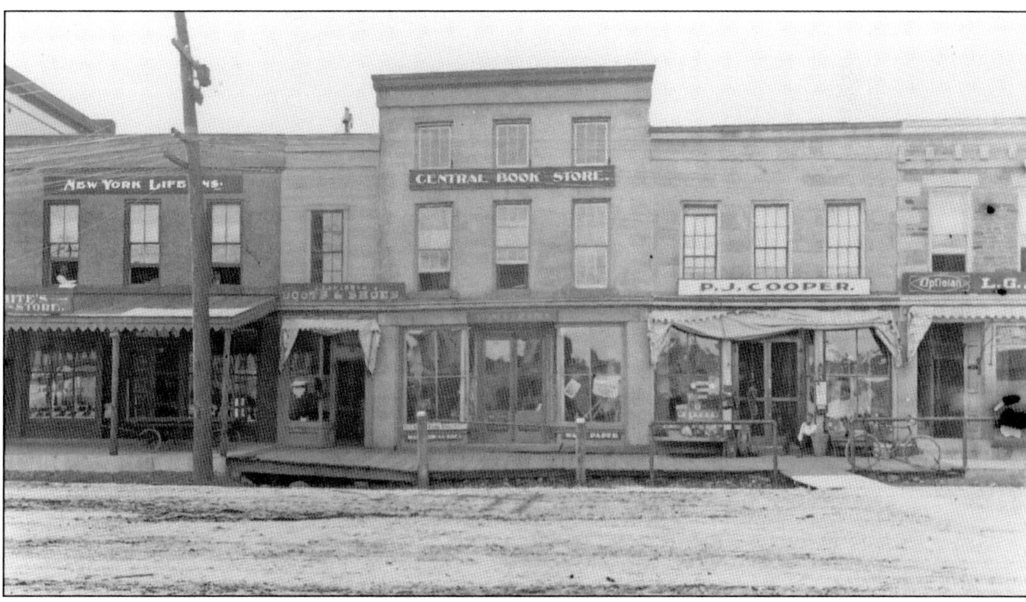

The P. J. Cooper store became the P. S. Armstrong grocery store and later the Villa Capri restaurant, now vacant. Jenckes' Central Book Store moved to the section of the Cole building that is now Hart's Insurance. The space became Coburn and Brooks restaurant in 1902, later Lawton's, then a health food store, later the fourth location for J and C Luncheonette, now empty.

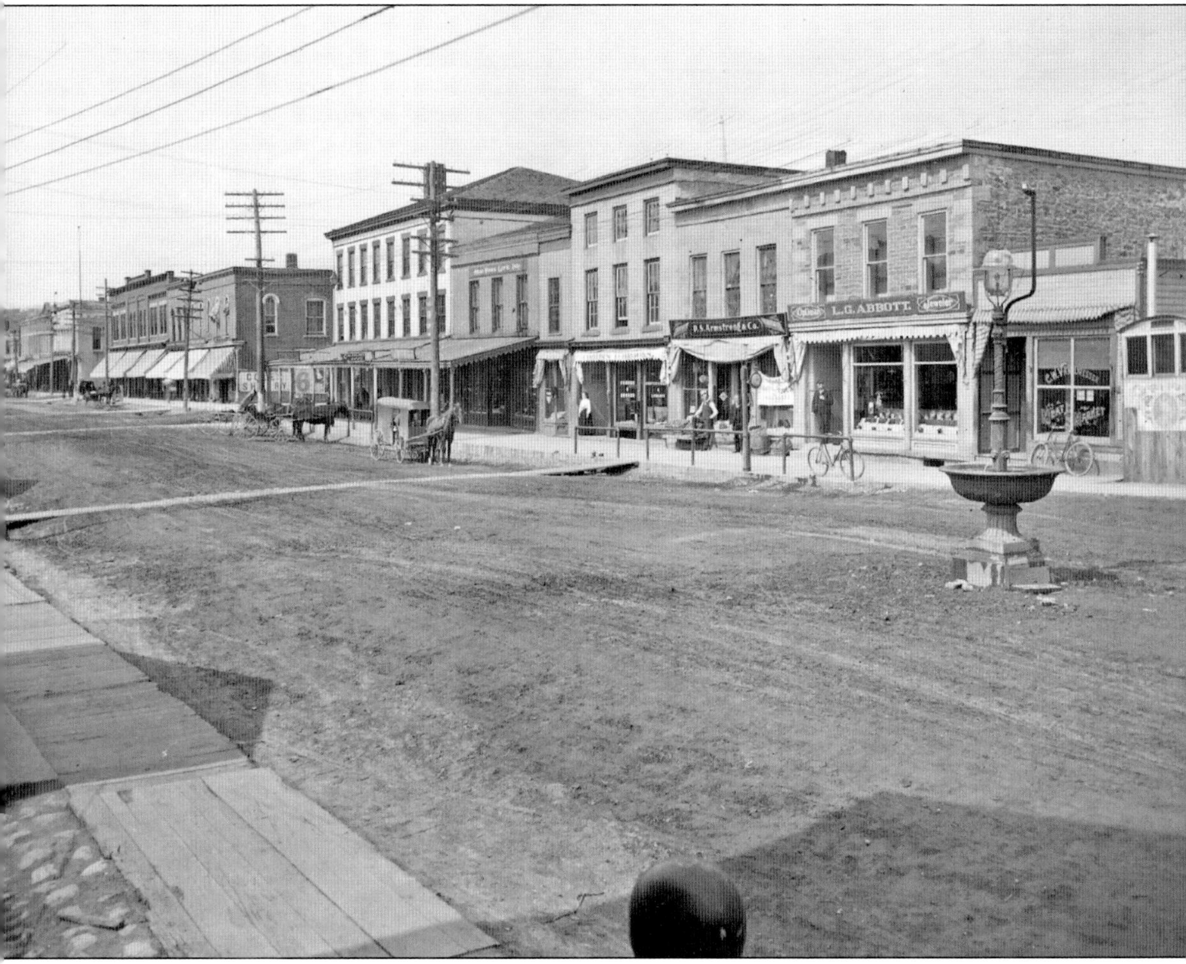

The water trough was installed in 1896, and another on South Main at the outlet. Starting on the right, the buildings are the Lunch Car (does not exist today), Vandresser Meat Market, L. G. Abbott (jeweler), Armstrong (groceries), Coburn and Brooks (restaurant), Sherman (shoes), White's Shoe Store, probably a hardware store, and Hatch and Roche Grocery. Across Covington Street is Cole Shoes, the second awning is Jenckes' bookstore, then J. H. Owen (druggist), the next two are Wise (dry goods), and the grocery of John Garrison is next to Lake Street.

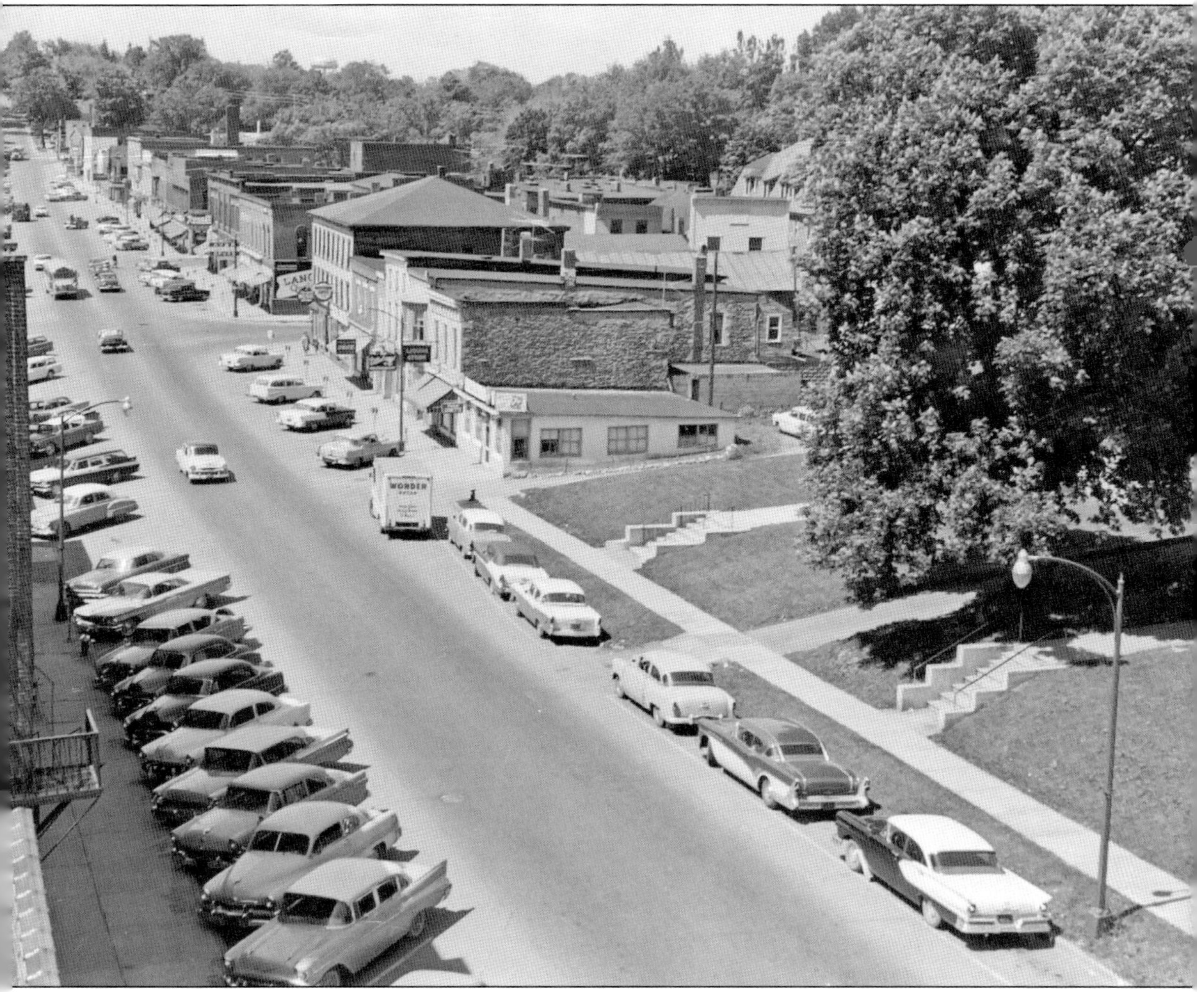

This is the west side of Main Street taken from the top of the village hall in the late 1950s. The edge of the Robeson plant is on the left foreground. The second set of steps on the right leads to the Masonic Temple behind the trees. The first building on the right that was a meat market has become a restaurant. Today it is Sky High Ink. The liquor store is next, then Villa Capri, an unknown store, the Hole in the Wall Restaurant, Peddle's Western Auto Store, and Decker's Music Store. Lanckton's shoe store is in the Cole building on the south corner of Covington Street. The Rexall sign is at the drugstore in the Garrison building at the corner of Lake and Main Streets.

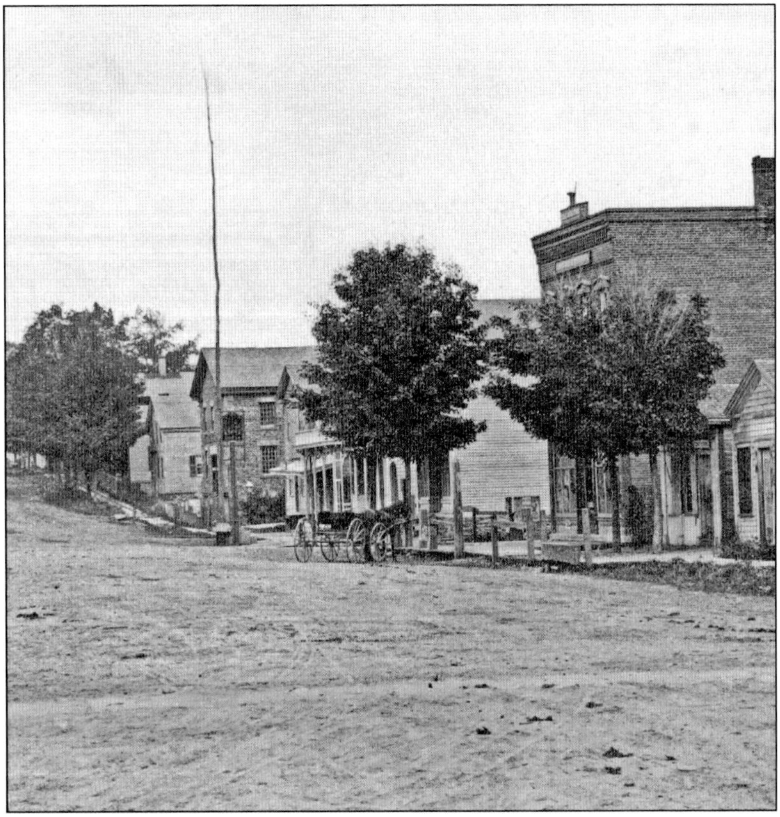

This is east side of North Main Street looking north. The two frame buildings on the right, occupied by the post office and Dr. Traver, were located where Borden Avenue would later be. The brick Watson building is next, the empty lot would become the Caswell block. Next is the Cole Hotel and Bolton's meat market with a "liberty pole" in front. The next building is a cabinet shop, then the cobblestone foundry.

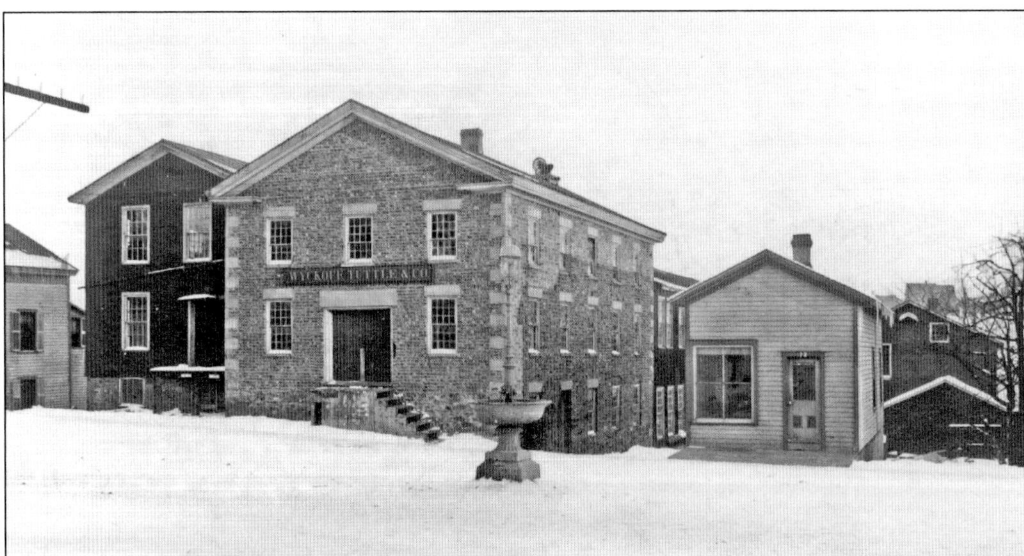

The cobblestone building was constructed by the community after Mr. Hick's foundry burned about 1839. It became the Perry Steam Furnace, under different owners Perry Iron Works, and in 1885, Wyckoff, Tuttle, and Company, the manufacturer of mowers and reapers. This became the Robeson Cutlery Company in 1898. The walls of the cobblestone building had to be replaced in 1952.

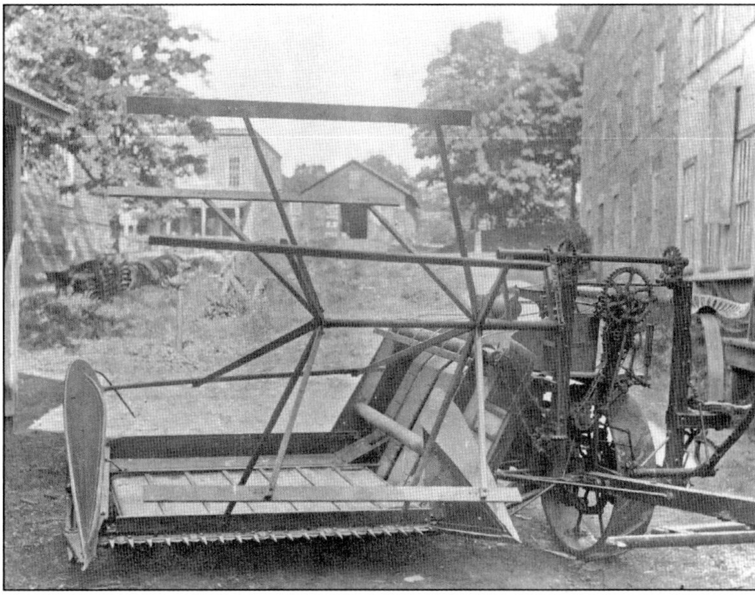

This is one of the products built by Wyckoff, Tuttle, and Company, in a photograph taken between the cobblestone building on the right and the frame office on the left. Across Main Street on the left is the harness shop, later the liquor store, and a blacksmith shop where later Vandresser's meat market would be.

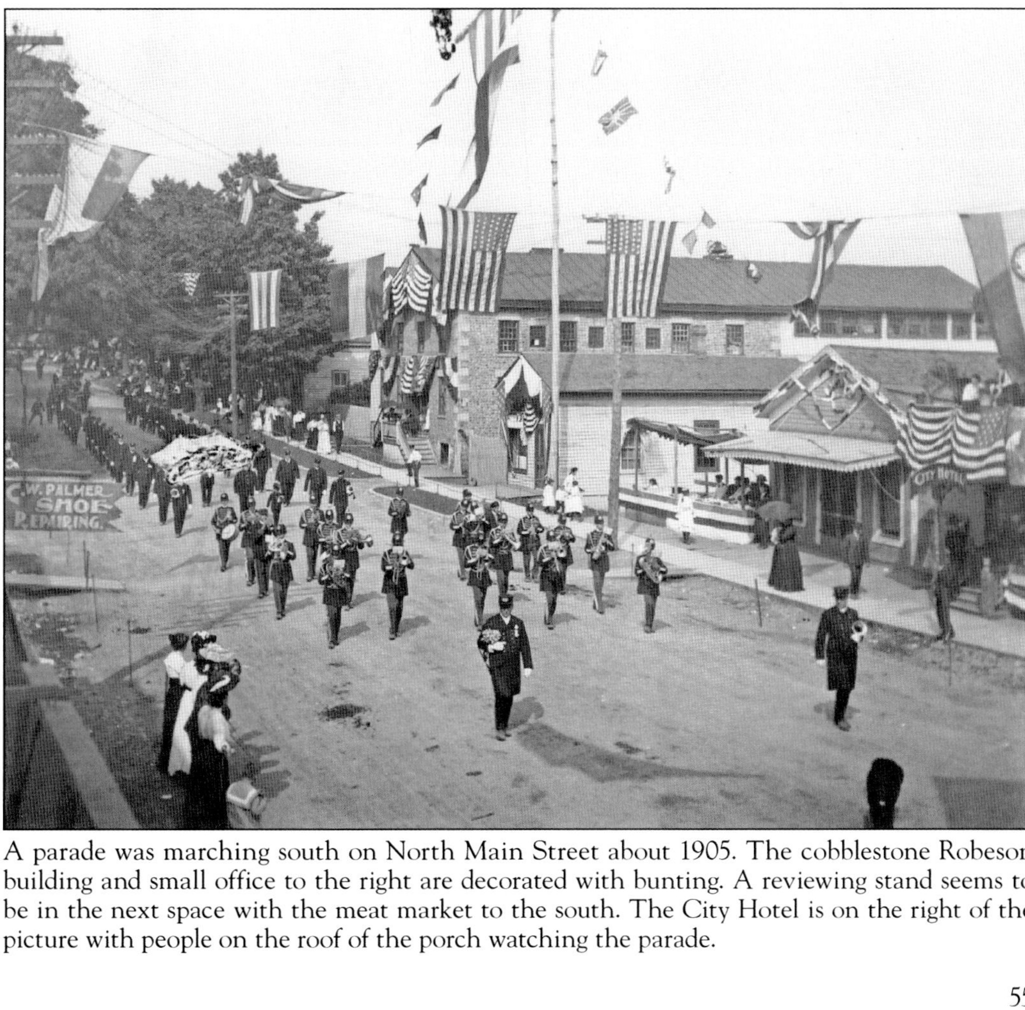

A parade was marching south on North Main Street about 1905. The cobblestone Robeson building and small office to the right are decorated with bunting. A reviewing stand seems to be in the next space with the meat market to the south. The City Hotel is on the right of the picture with people on the roof of the porch watching the parade.

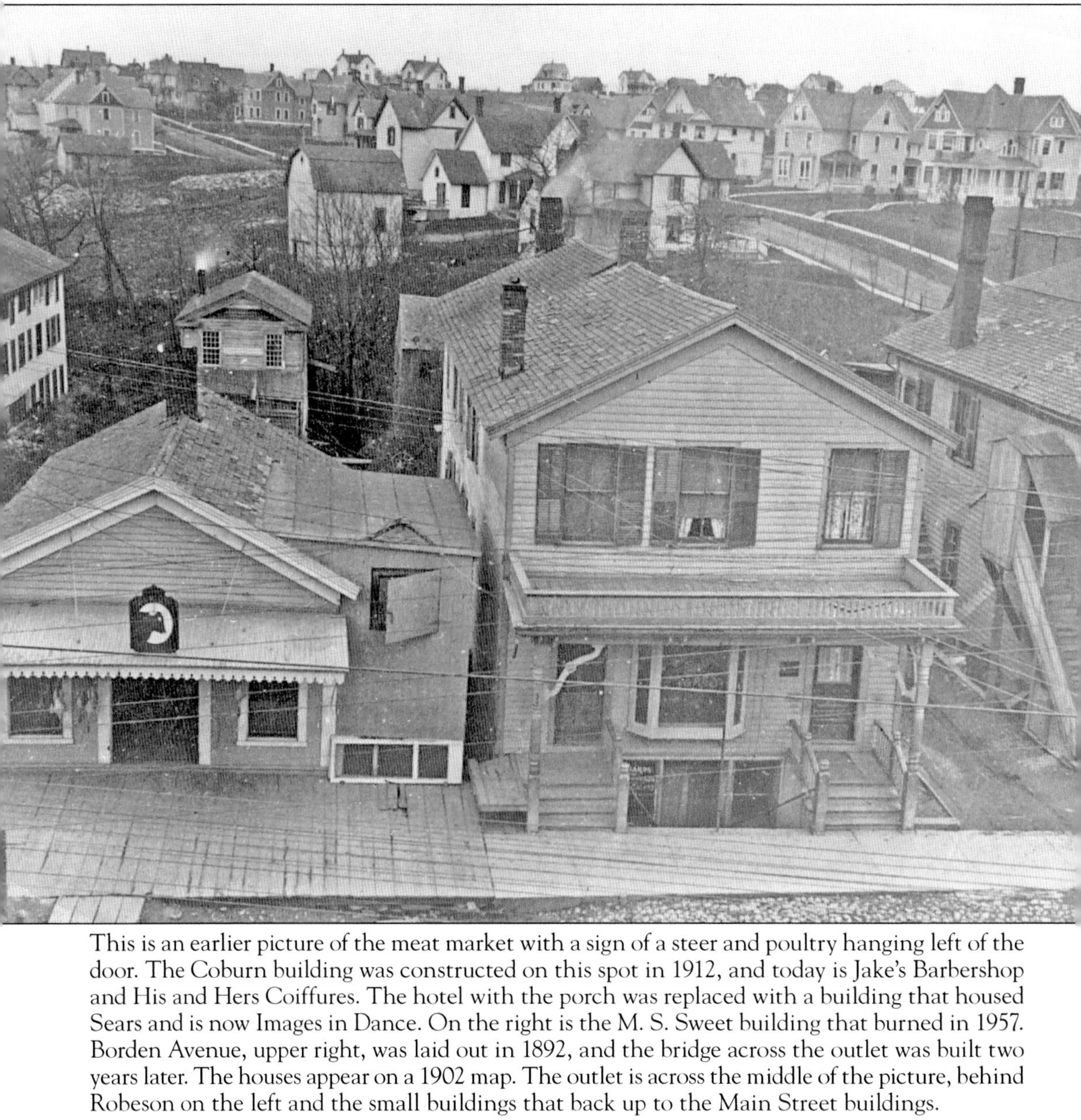

This is an earlier picture of the meat market with a sign of a steer and poultry hanging left of the door. The Coburn building was constructed on this spot in 1912, and today is Jake's Barbershop and His and Hers Coiffures. The hotel with the porch was replaced with a building that housed Sears and is now Images in Dance. On the right is the M. S. Sweet building that burned in 1957. Borden Avenue, upper right, was laid out in 1892, and the bridge across the outlet was built two years later. The houses appear on a 1902 map. The outlet is across the middle of the picture, behind Robeson on the left and the small buildings that back up to the Main Street buildings.

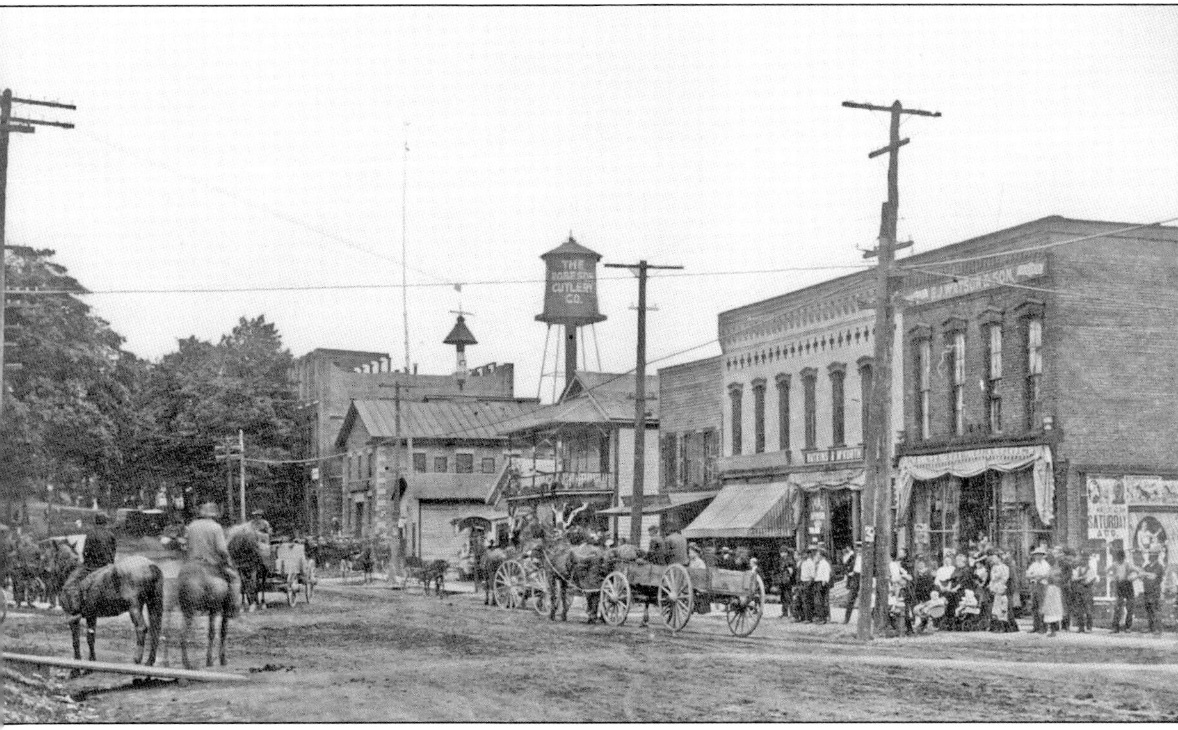

The three-story brick Robeson Factory at the north end of Main Street was nearing completion in 1907. A crowd of people is standing at the corner of Borden Avenue and Main Street in front of the Watson (originally Higgins) building that housed a drugstore. The Caswell building was occupied by Watkins and McKurth grocery and a shoe store. The M. S. Sweet building is next, then the hotel, and the meat market next to the four Robeson buildings with a water tower. An electric arc light installed in 1892 hangs across the intersection.

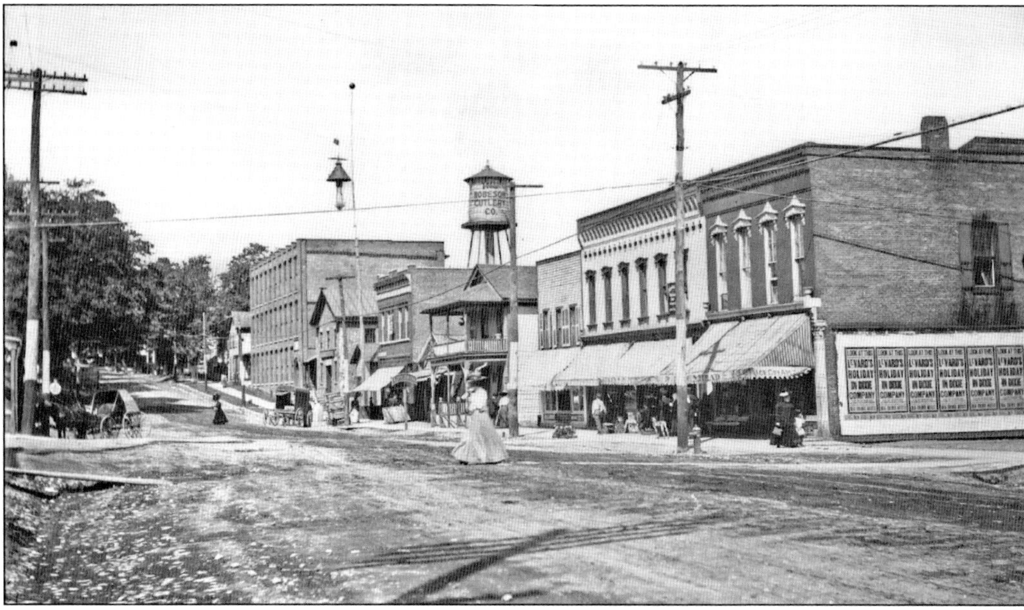

This picture was taken after the completion of the three-story Robeson building. The Watson building on the corner has changes to its facade. New to this section is the brick Kingston building, between the meat market and the small frame office of Robeson. Built in 1908, later it was J and C Luncheonette, then Walt's clothing store, and today is Go4ItGraphics.

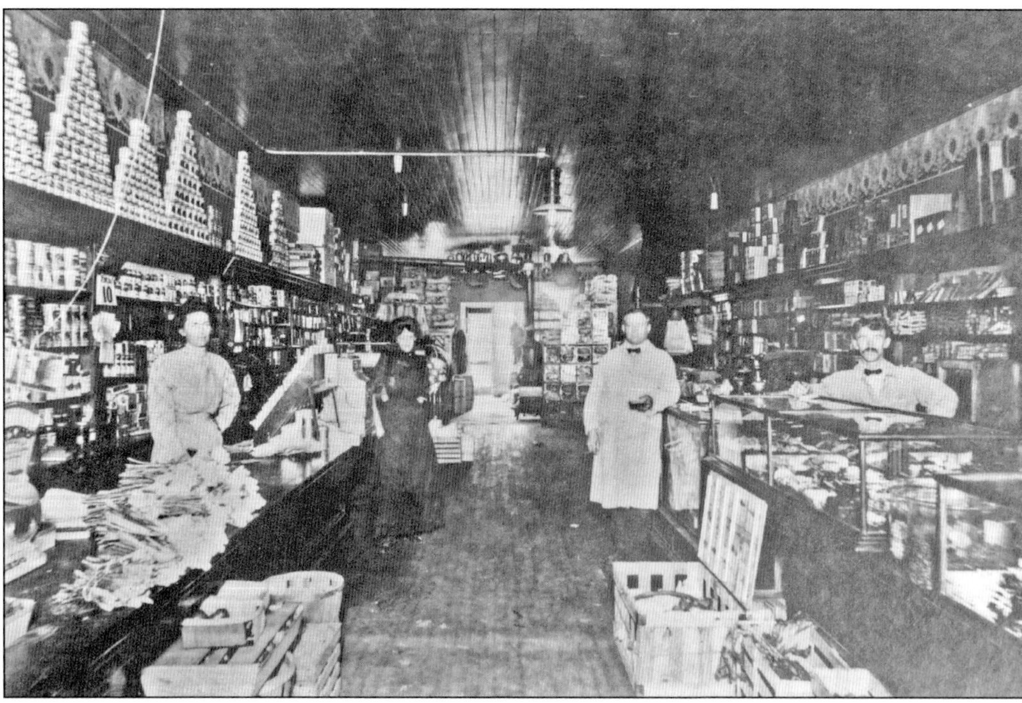

In 1908, this picture was taken of the interior of the Watkins and McKurth grocery located in the Caswell building, the second store north of Borden Avenue. Frank McKurth is second from the right. This store closed prior to 1915, and in 1917, the partners built a garage on Covington Street for their Ford agency.

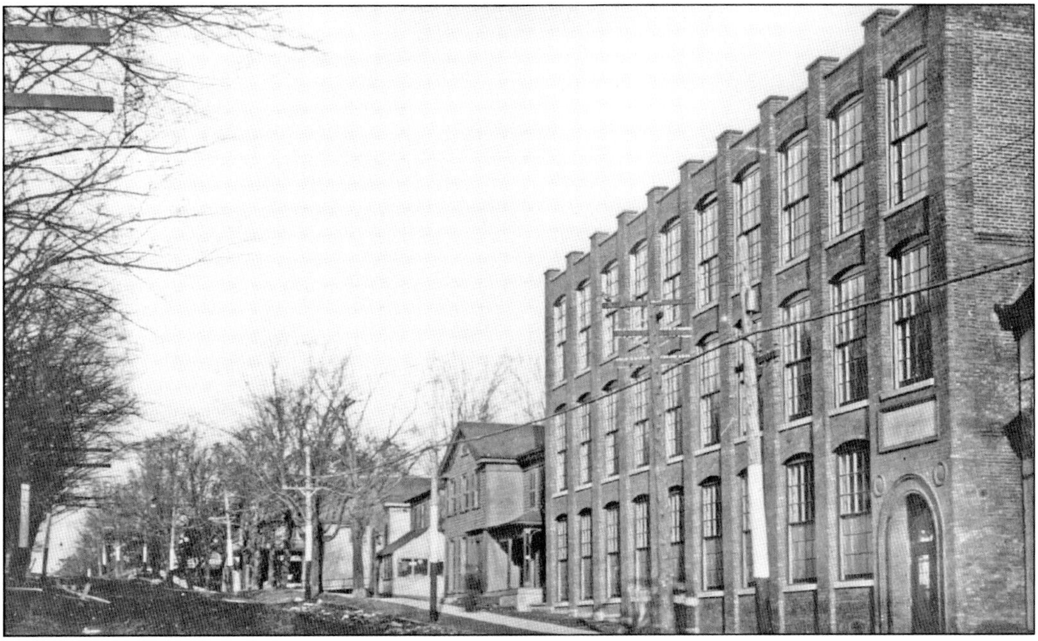

This shows the three-story Robeson building between 1906 and 1914. A frame house is to the left, next is a small white store in front of a residence. The Free Methodist Church is at the corner of Gardeau and Main Streets and would move to its new building in 1916. Across Gardeau Street is a frame store, later the site of a gas station, now an empty lot. (Henry Page Collection.)

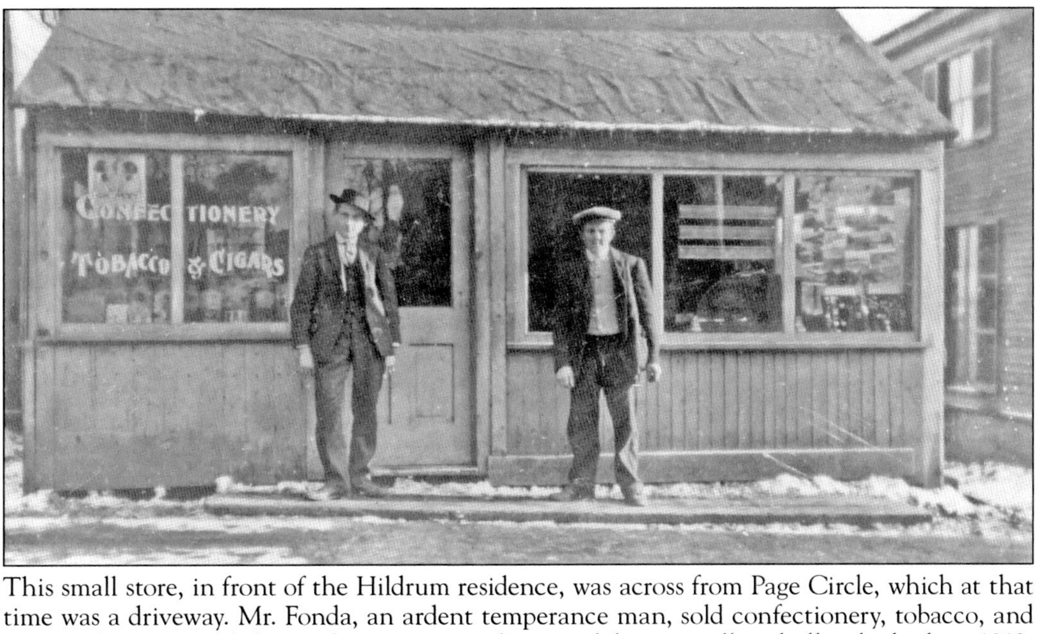

This small store, in front of the Hildrum residence, was across from Page Circle, which at that time was a driveway. Mr. Fonda, an ardent temperance man, sold confectionery, tobacco, and cigars. This store and the residence were on the site of the new village hall to be built in 1912, when the village and fire department decided to combine facilities. (Henry Page Collection.)

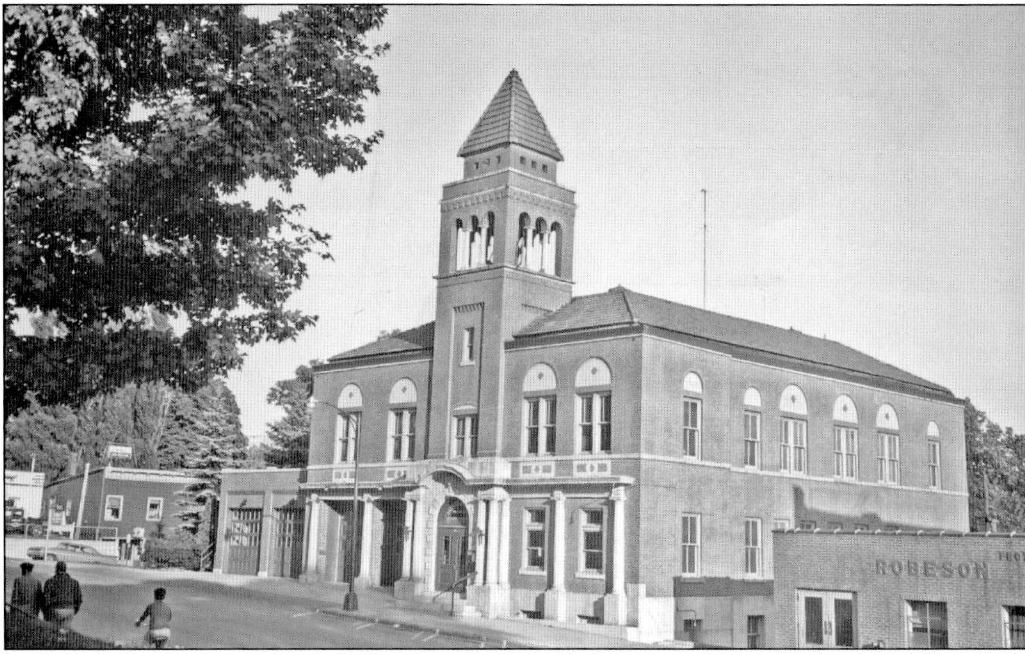

This is the village hall in a photograph taken in the 1950s, after two more bays for fire trucks were added to the original building. The fire department had outgrown its building on South Main Street, which also housed the jail in the basement. The village offices were in rented space. In 1913, the village hall opened with all village services in one building.

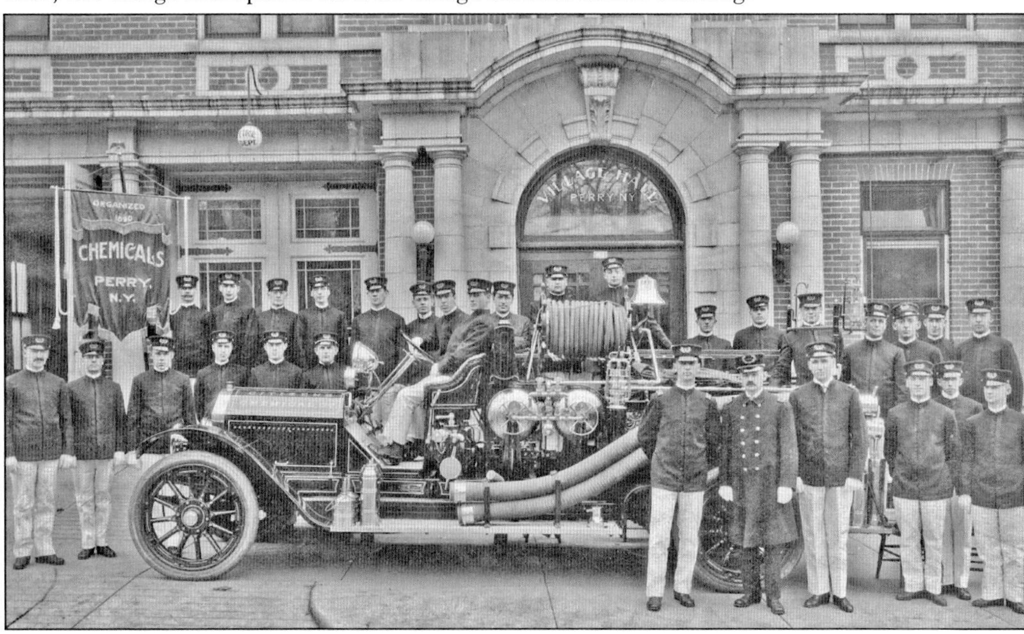

The Citizens Chemical Company posed for this picture in front of the village hall in 1916. Myron Kershaw, in the front row in dark pants, was the chief. To the left of him is Frank D. Roberts, pharmacist and author of *History of the Town of Perry, New York*. Dr. Frank M. Crocker, top row on the right, drew the map of the Gardeau Reservation used in the beginning of this book. (Henry Page Collection.)

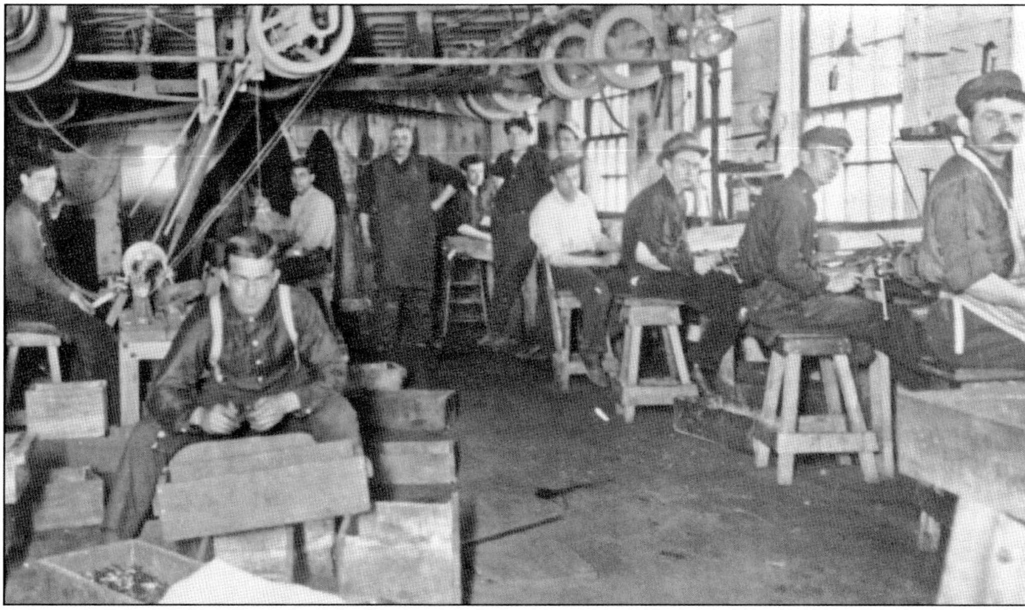

Robeson Cutlery Company moved to Perry from Camillus, New York, in 1898. It started with about 35 employees, and by 1914, it had a workforce of about 400. At that time it was one of the three largest cutlery factories in the country, producing an excellent product.

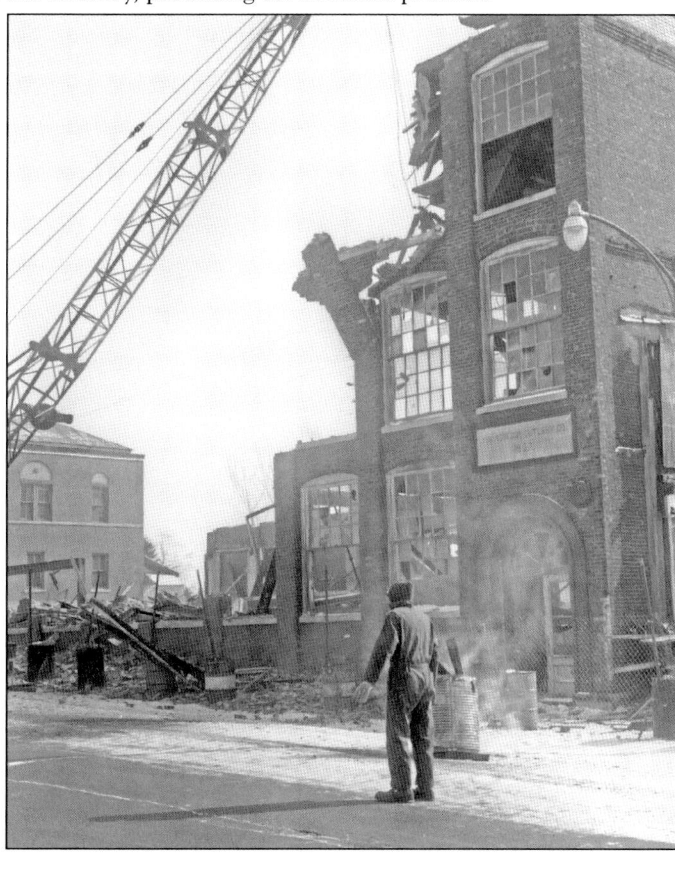

In 1980, The Robeson Company buildings on Main Street were demolished. The space was filled with a plaza and the new Perry Post Office. The post office was built next to Frank's Electric building, which was an altered Robeson structure. On the side next to the village hall was a pharmacy with a gift shop, and a convenient store, both are empty today.

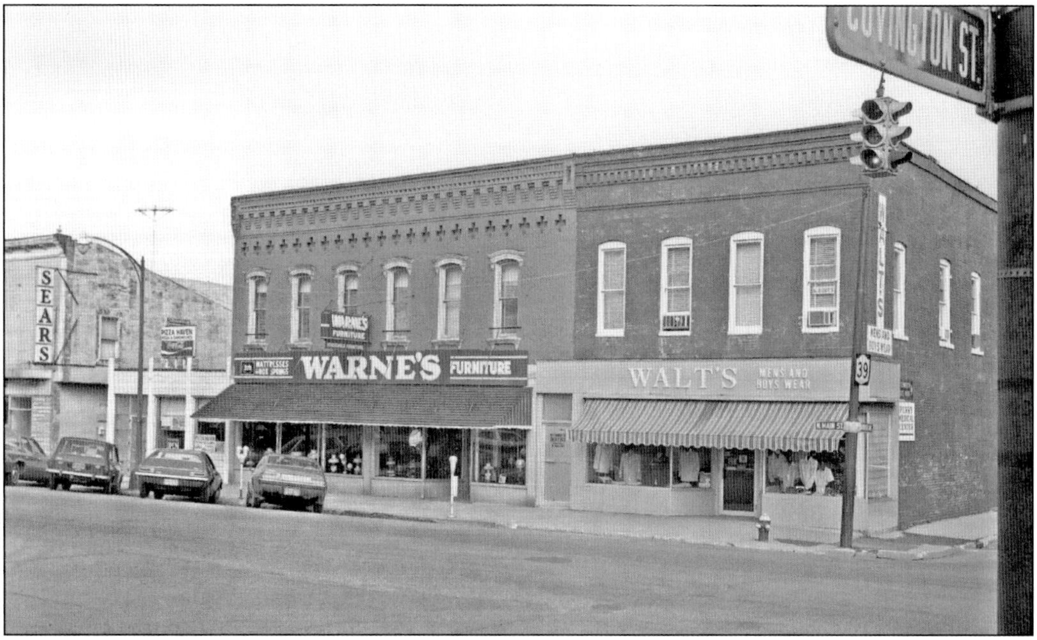

The picture above is of some of the stores on the east side of North Main Street in 1976. Below is the same section in 2009. Bush Hill Florist is in the corner Watson building. To the right is Borden Avenue and the Perry Herald building. To the left in the old Caswell building is the Community Clothes Closet and Thrift Shop run by Caring About Perry, a group from Perry churches. It sells secondhand clothing and is the site of the community food pantry. The Hong Kong Restaurant is to the left. (Above, Henry Page Collection; below, photograph by Jennifer Nolan.)

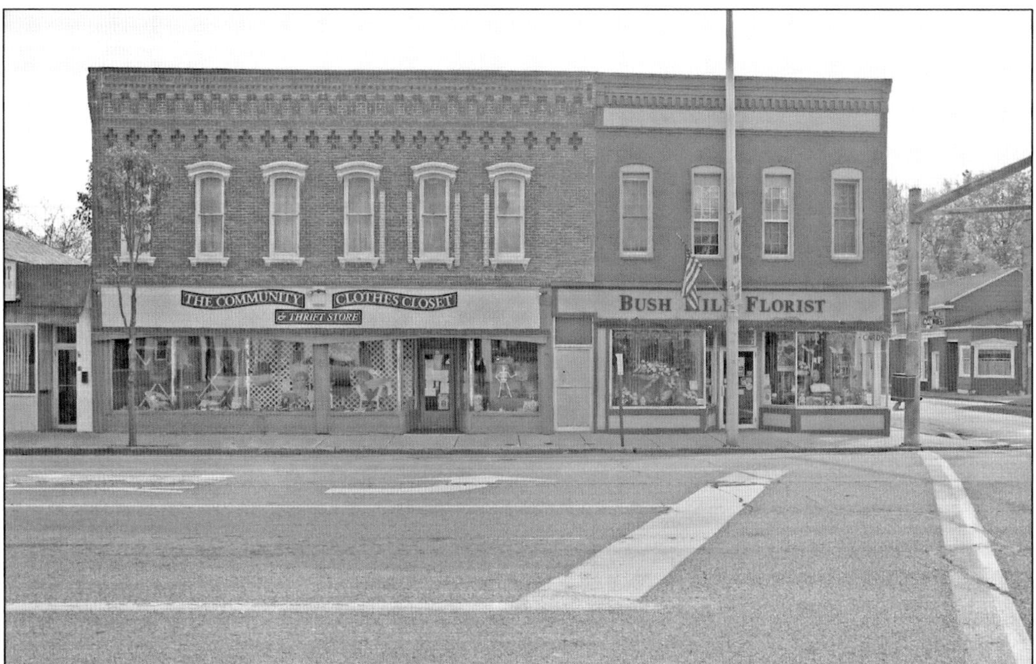

The Borden Avenue iron bridge was built over the outlet in 1894 and replaced in 1916. The Perry Herald building on the right was constructed in 1900. It included public bath facilities because when the water system began (1896) not everyone had facilities at home. This structure burned in 1961. Toward Main Street is Masten's livery, then the brick Bussey structure.

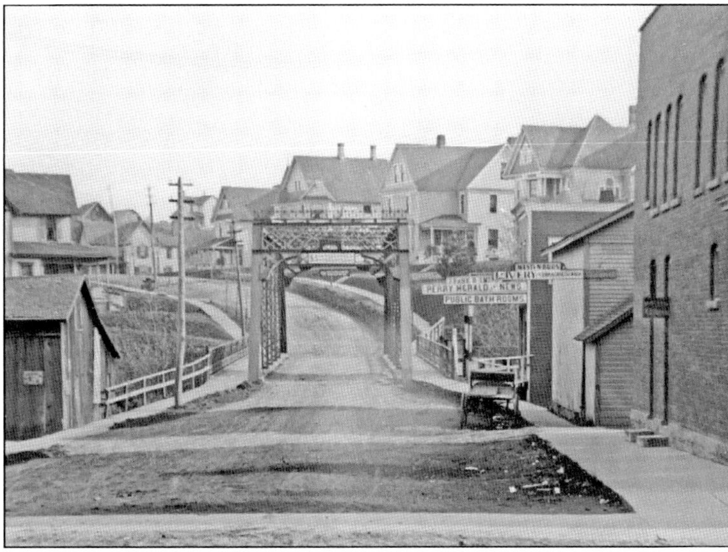

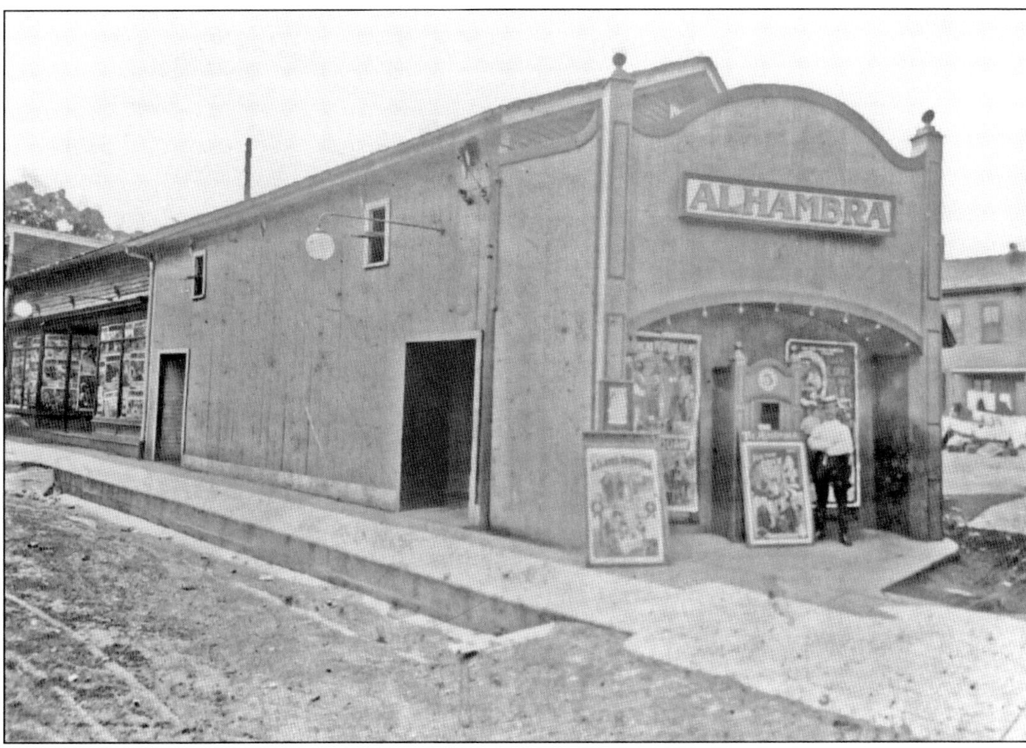

The Alhambra Theater, known as the "horseatorium," was originally the horse barn for the Hotel Perry, and later Masten's livery stable. It was bought in 1916 for the *Perry Herald* newspaper and is still in use as the Perry Shopper office. Borden Avenue divides North and South Main Street. We will now look at the east side of South Main Street.

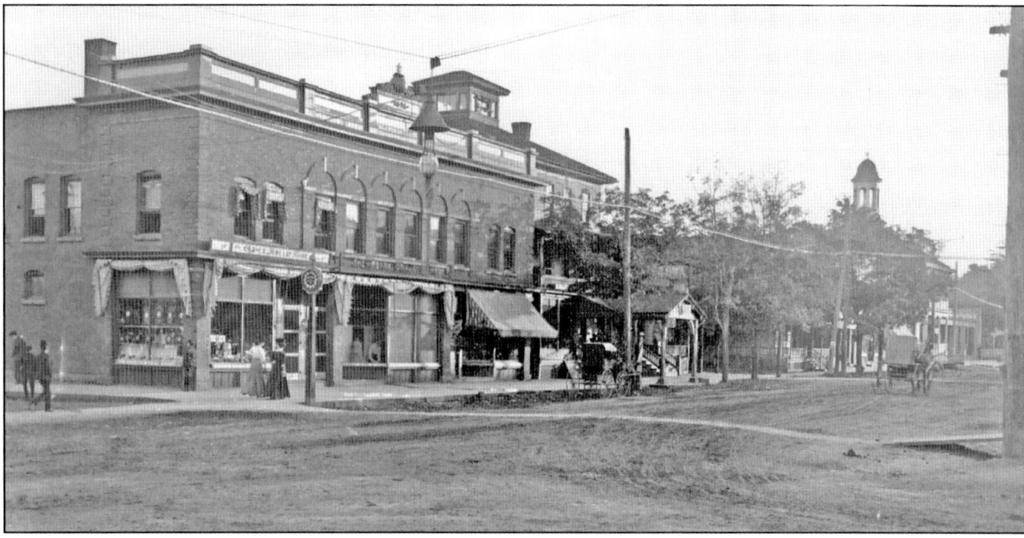

The Bussey building on the corner of Main Street and Borden Avenue was constructed in 1898. In this picture, the Corner Jewelry Store occupies the first section. Next is the Perry Dry Goods Company, and the last section is unknown. The Hotel Perry, earlier the Walker House, with the cupola is next. The tower of the first Perry Town Hall, also built in 1898, is in the background.

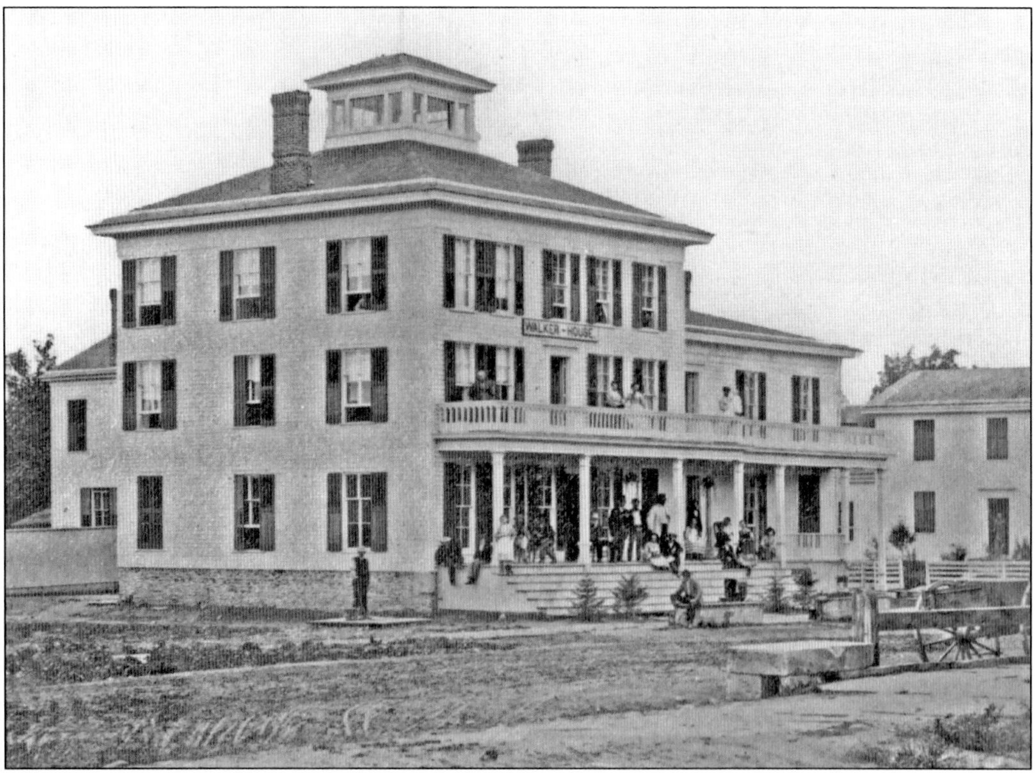

This second Walker House on Main Street opened in 1869 on the site of the first Walker House that burned in 1857. Today this is a parking lot and the site of the M&T's drive-through bank. The building to the right is probably the Lynd home, later the site of the Citizens Bank. A. B. Walker sold this hotel in 1880, and it became the Harford House, then Hotel Perry.

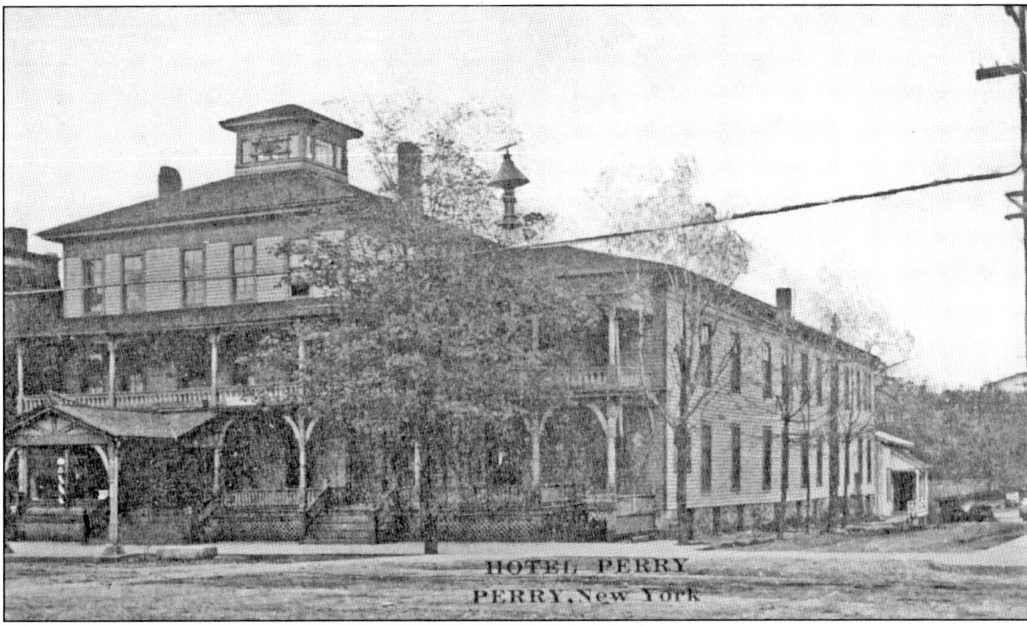

T. H. Bussey bought the Harford House in about 1884 and renamed it Hotel Perry. In 1898, the Bussey building was constructed between this hotel and the corner of Borden Avenue and Main Street. In this picture there is a barbershop in the left front and to the right is the alley to the Andrus sawmill. The Hotel Perry was remodeled in 1914 and became the Tavern. (Henry Page Collection.)

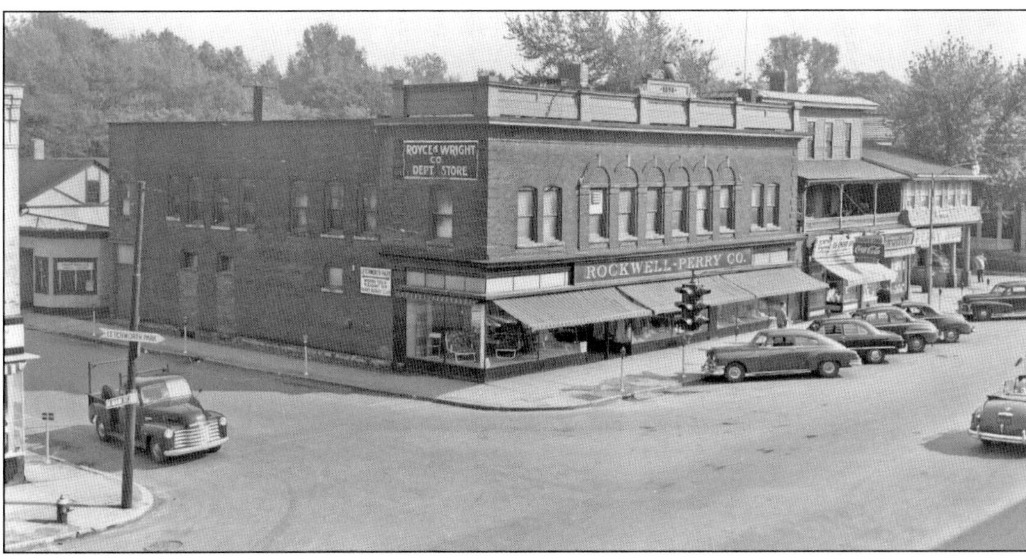

In this picture the Rockwell-Perry Company is now on the corner where the Royce and Wright department store was for many years. The Perry Herald building is behind this on Borden Avenue. To the right on Main Street, with the cupola gone, is the old Hotel Perry-Tavern building. It was divided and here has an ice cream parlor, a grocery store, and the Perry Inn.

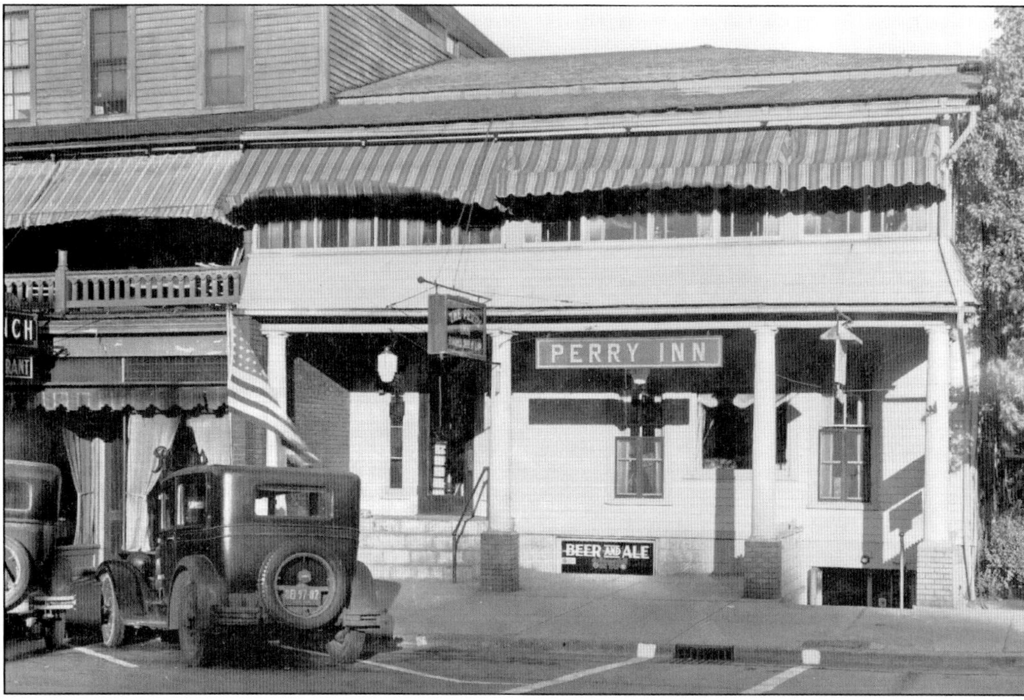

The Perry Inn had once been the Walker House, the Harford House, the Hotel Perry, and the Tavern. At the time of this picture, Mr. Bennett's bar was located downstairs. There was a restaurant to the left. When the Perry Inn was destroyed by fire in 1965, the second J and C Luncheonette was located here. It was demolished in 1967. (Henry Page Collection.)

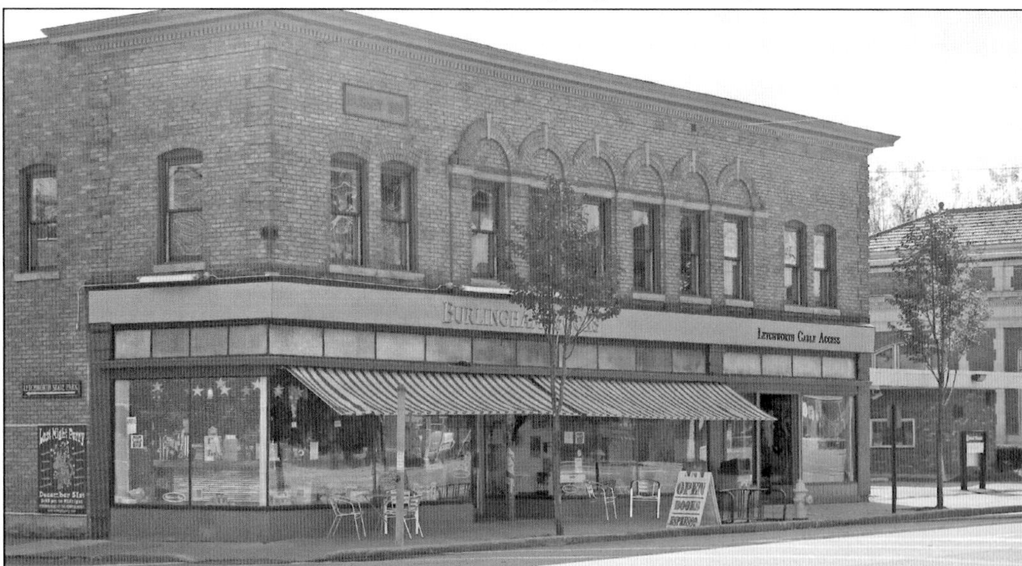

Jayson's department store was at this location starting in 1965 and into the 1990s. Today the Bussey building has been renovated and contains Burlingham Books and Letchworth Cable Access. Upstairs are offices including the owner's InSite: Architecture business. On the right, the new town hall in the old bank building can be seen behind the M&T drive-through. (Photograph by Jennifer Nolan.)

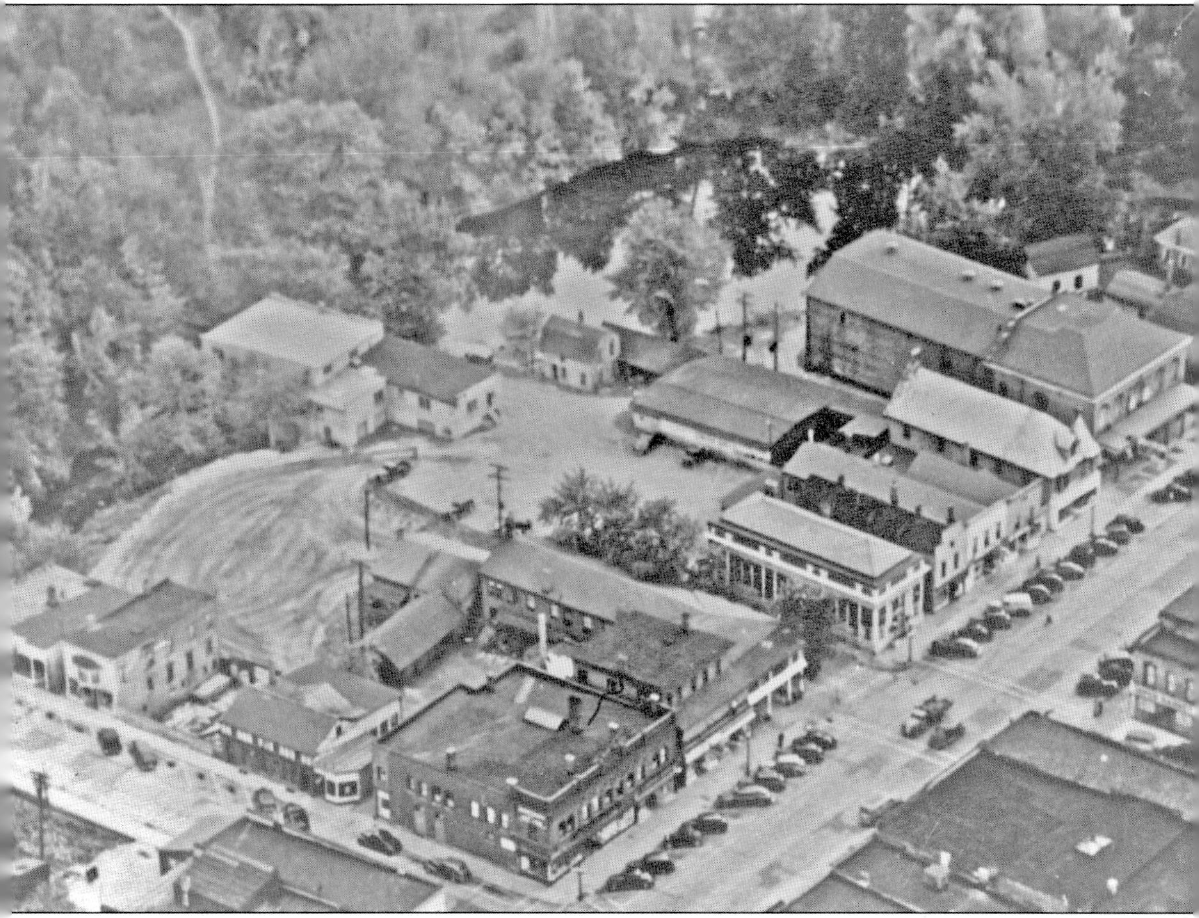

This aerial view is from about 1940. The Bussey building is in the middle foreground, with the Perry Inn next, then the alley to the Andrus sawmill. The Andrus millpond in the outlet is in the background, now a parking lot. The buildings left of the pond belong to the sawmill, rebuilt after a 1924 fire. The gambrel-roofed building is the office, and the lumber sheds to the right are behind Main Street structures. The large building on Main Street at the right is the town hall and auditorium. On Borden Avenue, lower left, there is a gap between buildings due to a fire at the Silver Grill in 1939.

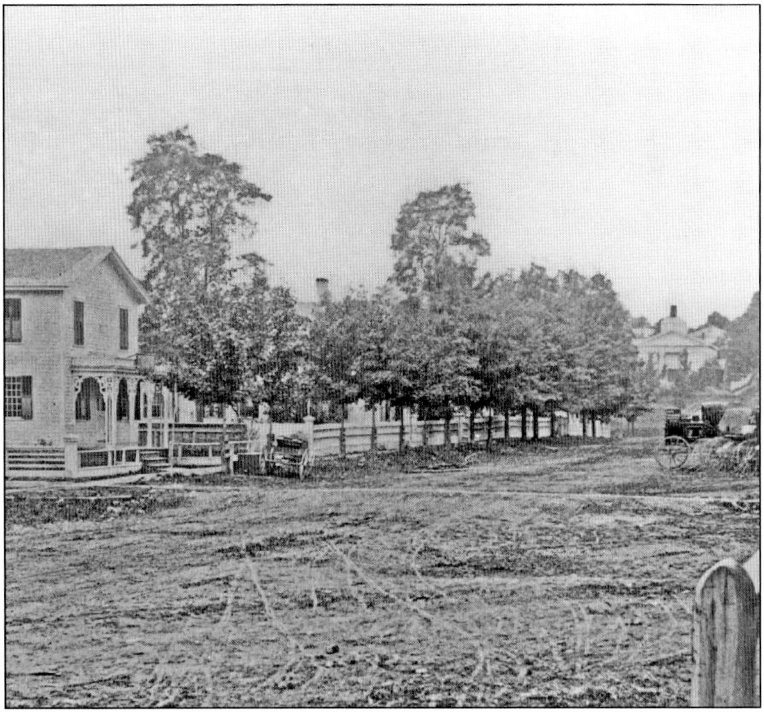

This is the east side of South Main Street looking south. The residence of Andrew Lynd, photographer, was south of the Andrus sawmill alley and became the site of the Citizens Bank and later the second Perry Town Hall. The Universalist church is to the far right at the corner of St. Helena Street. Dr. Goodwin's home and others were in between.

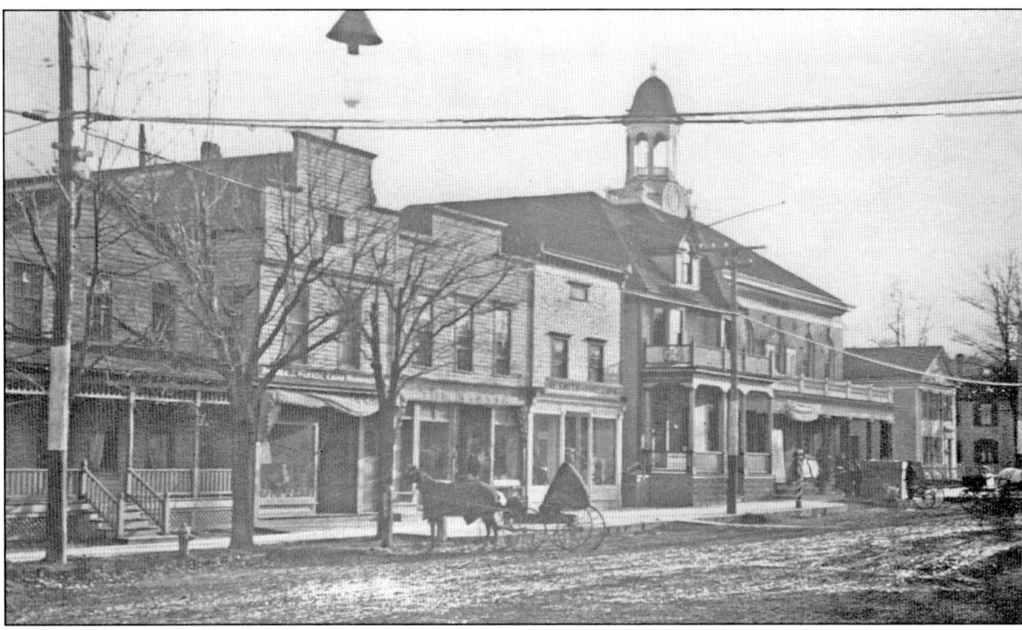

The Lynd-Rollah house is first in this picture taken prior to 1908. O'Leary's Cigar Store, today Commodore Liquor Store, is next with the Bazaar, now the Changing Image, to the south. Nesmith and Phillips Clothing Store is next to the Perry Club. The town hall with its tower is next, then Dr. Goodwin's home. The last is the Fred Sage Garage, later White's Variety, then Bailey's Sewing Center. (Henry Page Collection.)

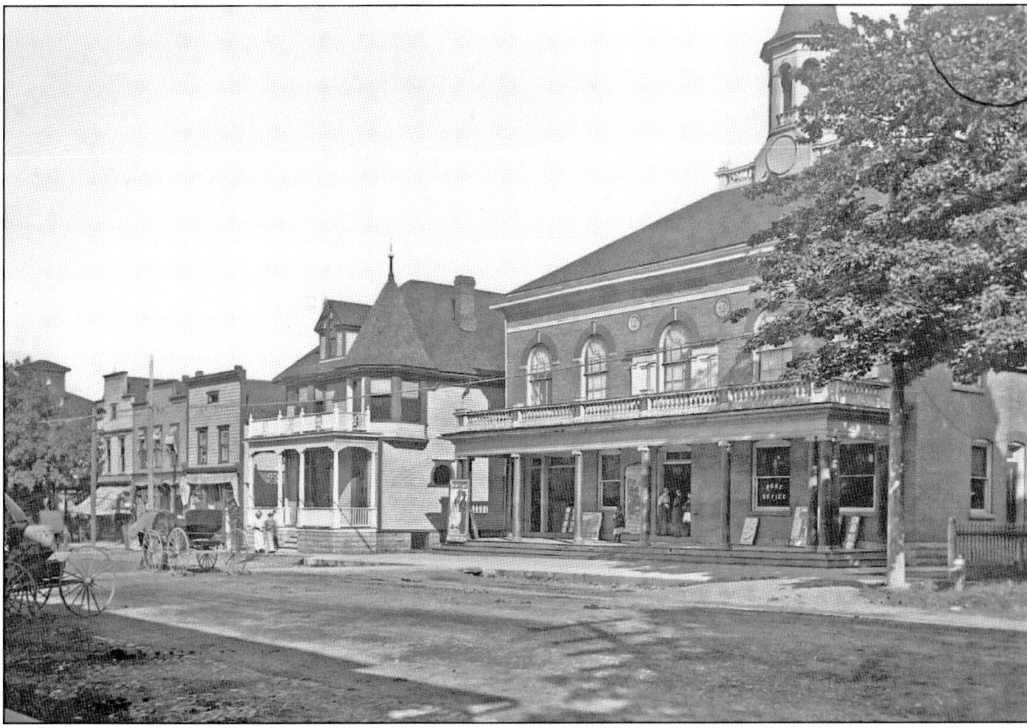

This is looking north with the Perry Town Hall on the right. This was built in 1898 and included the Auditorium Theater, a second-floor ballroom, the town offices, and the post office. In 1908, it was voted to remove the tower. The auditorium was being restored by the Arts Council for Wyoming County when this building was destroyed by fire in 1983. This space is now a parking lot.

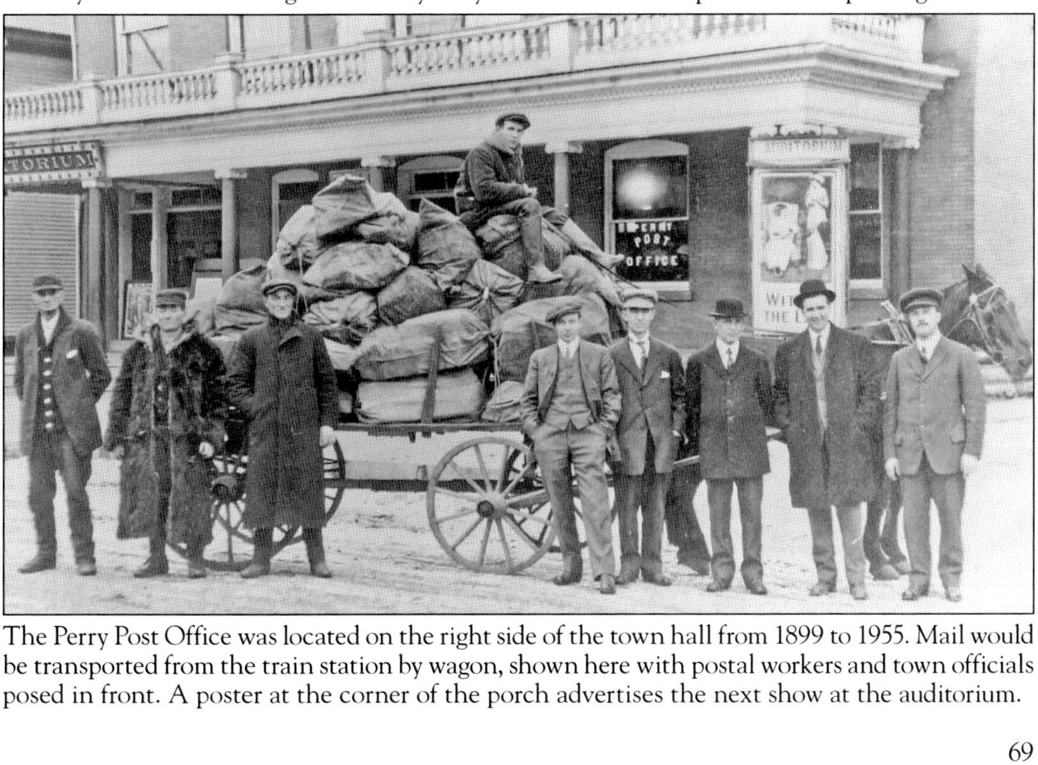

The Perry Post Office was located on the right side of the town hall from 1899 to 1955. Mail would be transported from the train station by wagon, shown here with postal workers and town officials posed in front. A poster at the corner of the porch advertises the next show at the auditorium.

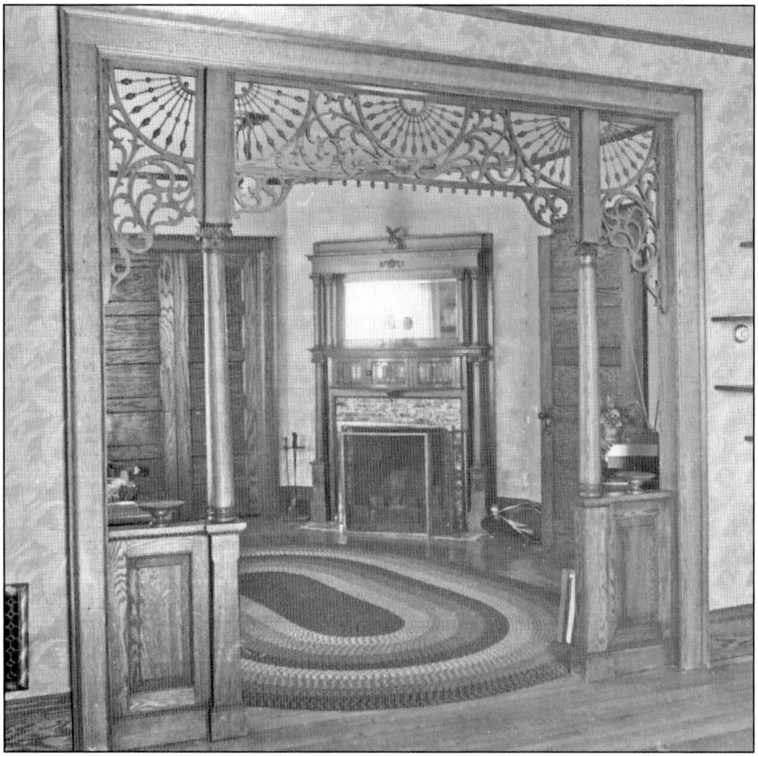

This is the second-floor living room of the Perry Club, located north of the town hall. This was a men's social organization that had a reading room, card rooms, pool tables, and in the basement a bowling alley. A barbershop was located downstairs on the left. This would become Bonadonna's grocery, then Silver Lake Restaurant, and is now Country Kitchen Restaurant.

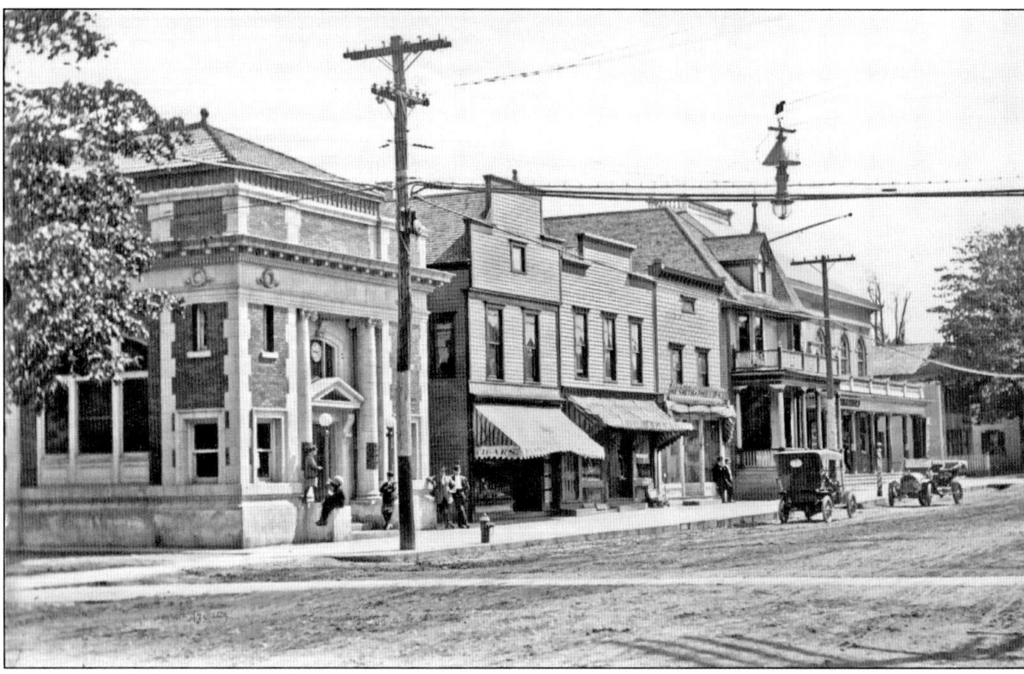

The Citizens Bank, left in this picture, was built 1909. The bank formed in 1888, with the first location at the corner of Main and Lake Streets in the Olin (Smith) building. This merged with the First National Bank in 1962 to form the Bank of Perry using the National Bank building across the street. At the town hall and auditorium, the tower is now gone.

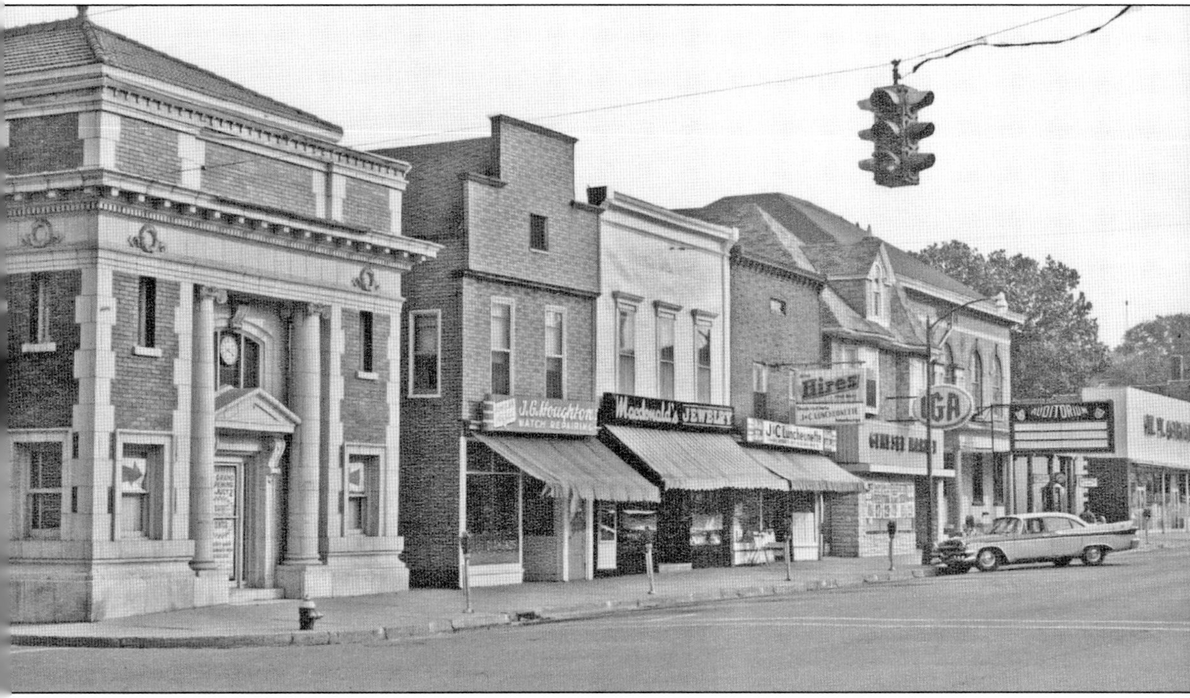

In 1964, the Citizens Bank building on the left was probably an information center. Ferris TV was here later, changing the front to a large window with a door on each side. The next store is Houghton's Jewelry, which used to be Kershaw's Jewelry, earlier a cigar store. MacDonald's Jewelry succeeded Lippman's and the Bazaar. The original J and C Luncheonette is in a building that had been Nesmith and Phillips clothing store. This building was torn down in 1965 to enlarge the Bonadonna's Genesee Market in the old Perry Club next door. The old town hall with the auditorium sign is next. The W. T. Grant store was built on the site of Dr. Goodwin's house. White's Variety Store is last. (Henry Page Collection.)

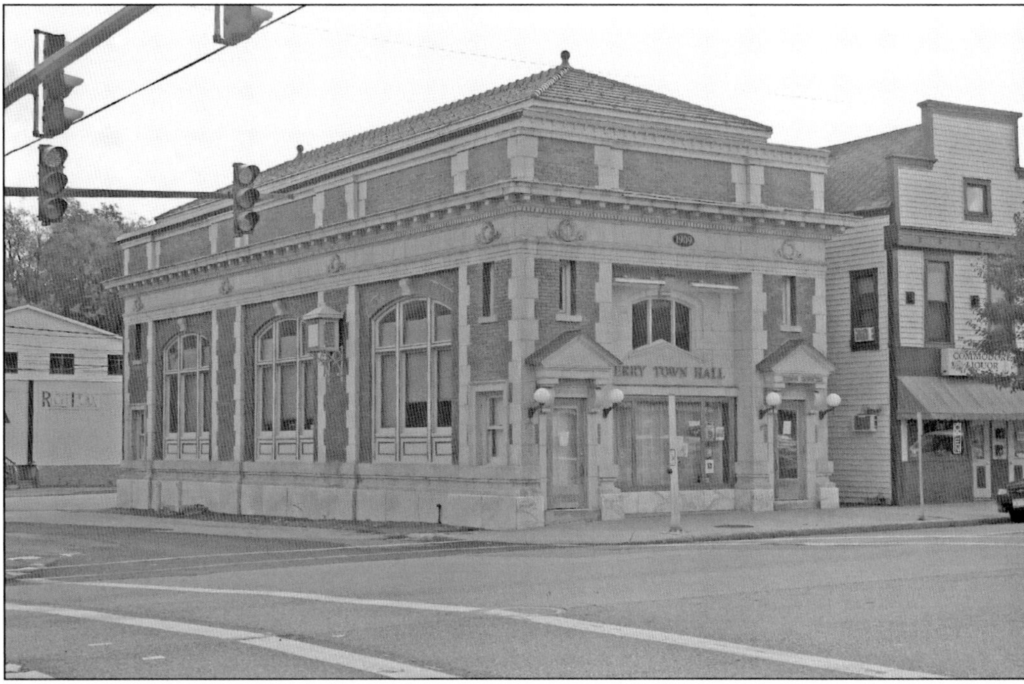

Today the Citizens Bank building is the new Perry Town Hall. The Commodore Liquor Store is to the right in the old cigar store. On the left and behind is the unoccupied Rich Plan building on the site of the old Andrus sawmill. The alley north of the town hall provides access to this, the M&T drive-through, and parking lots. (Photograph by Jennifer Nolan.)

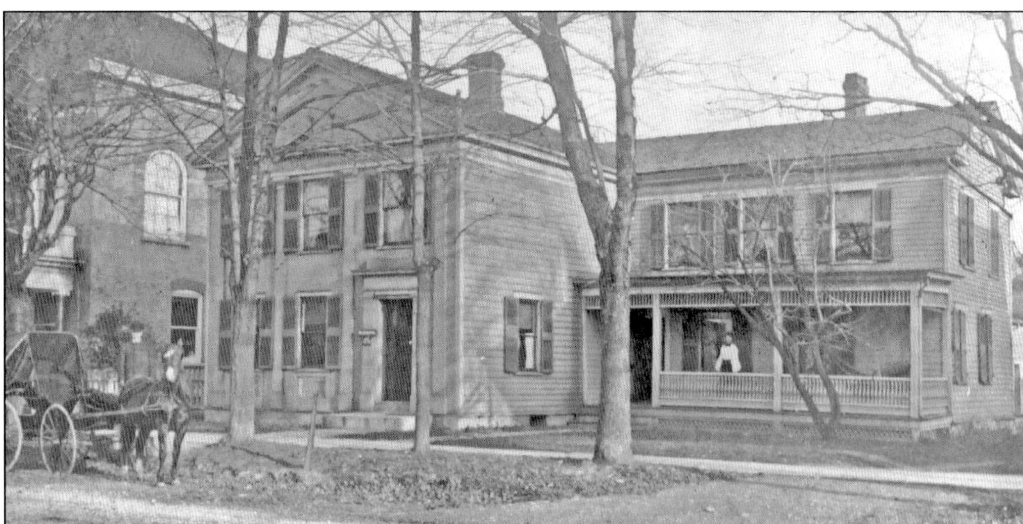

Dr. Goodwin's home and office were south of the original town hall and auditorium. The barn for the horse and carriage was in back of the house by the Andrus millpond. This residence burned in the late 1950s. A W. T. Grant store was built here, later occupied by a Ben Franklin store. Today the building is shared by the NAPA auto parts store and South Main Redemption Center.

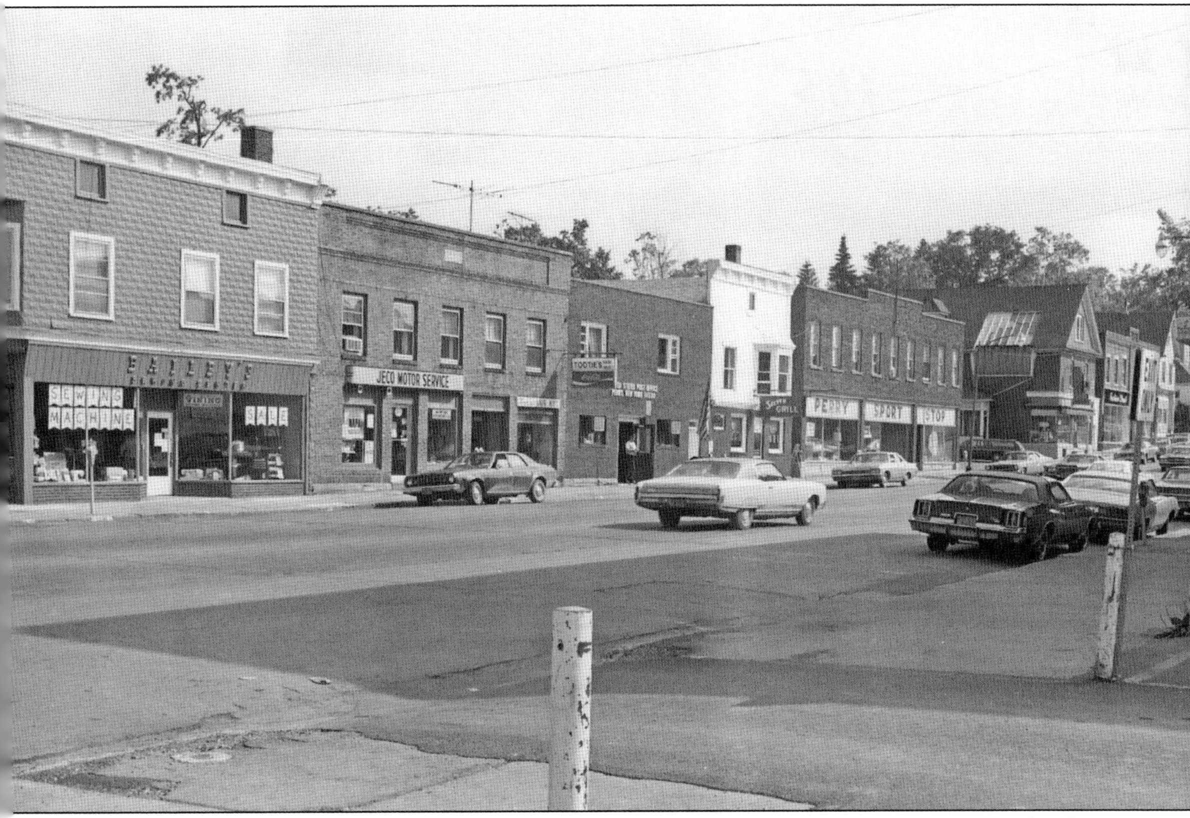

This is the rest of South Main Street on the east side in 1976. Bailey's Sewing Center is the first store on the left, which had been White's Variety Store and is now an empty lot. Jeco Motor Service and Tootie's Hair Hut share the next building. This is empty today, but at the top is written, "Perry Record 1894–1925, Established by Carl G. Clarke." The next three buildings were damaged in a 1980 fire. The post office remains empty. The Silver Grill, the remodeled fire hall, was razed and rebuilt. The Perry Sport Stop in the Dolbeer building was torn down and is a park today. Across Dolbeer Street are the Bassett Art Shop and the S. D. Wainman building. The two-story frame house is now Tuff Toys.

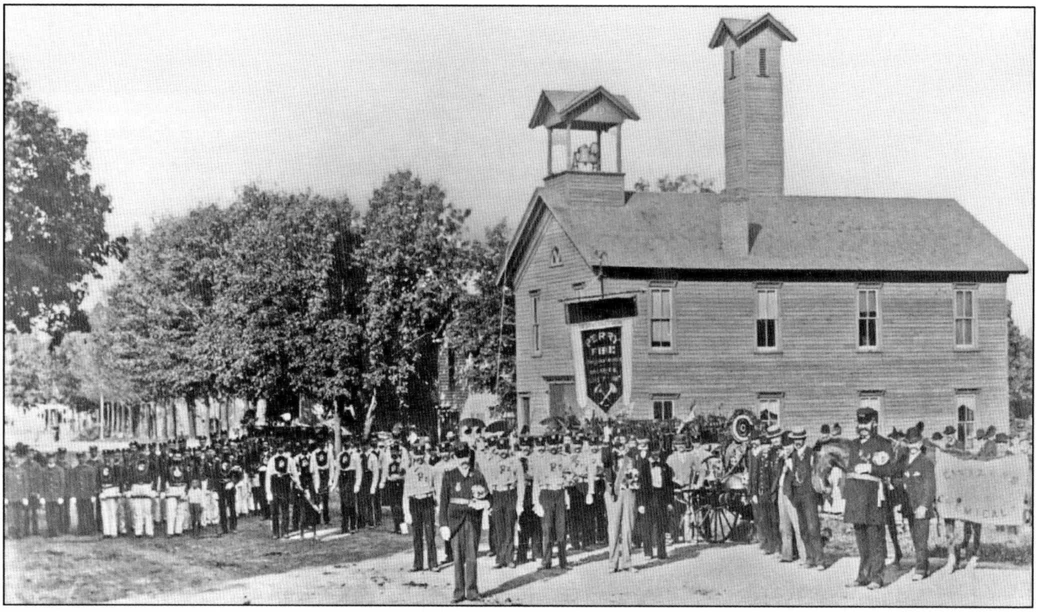

The Perry Fire Department was formed in 1887 and first met in the basement of White's Hall. In 1893, the Perry firemen posed for this picture at the fire hall built on the east side of South Main Street and on the north side of Silver Lake Outlet. The tall hose tower in the center of the roof was used to hang hoses to dry. The jail was in the basement. Both moved to the new village hall in 1913. This building was remodeled, had other uses, and later became the Silver Grill.

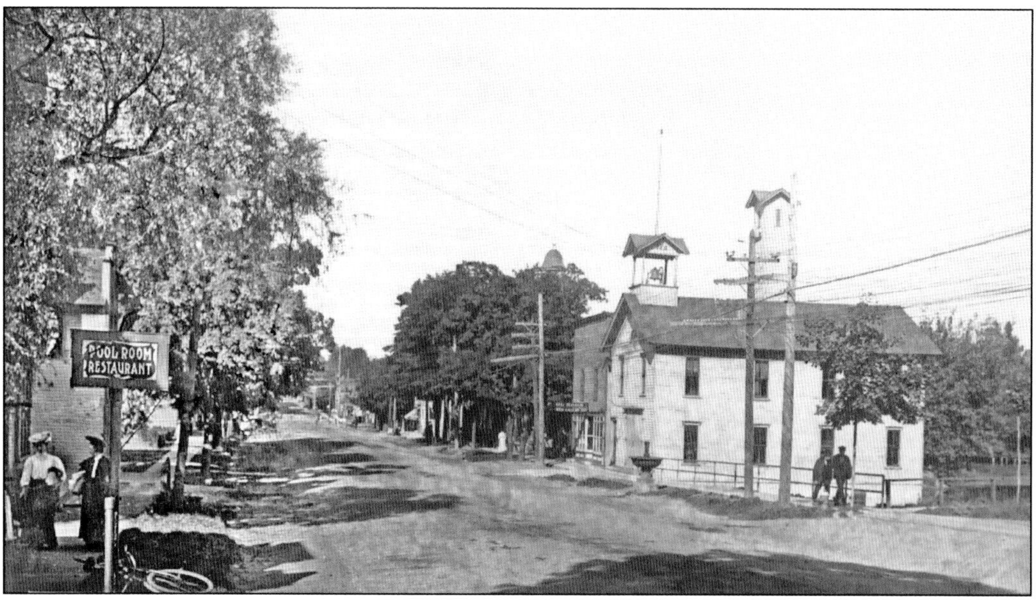

This is looking north on South Main Street, with the Perry fire hall on the east side of the street at the outlet. Andrus millpond shows behind. The water trough has been moved from the middle to the side of the street. The Dolbeer building, with Dolbeer Street to the right, would later be constructed over the outlet. The town hall tower shows above the trees to the left. At the left, across the street, is a poolroom and restaurant.

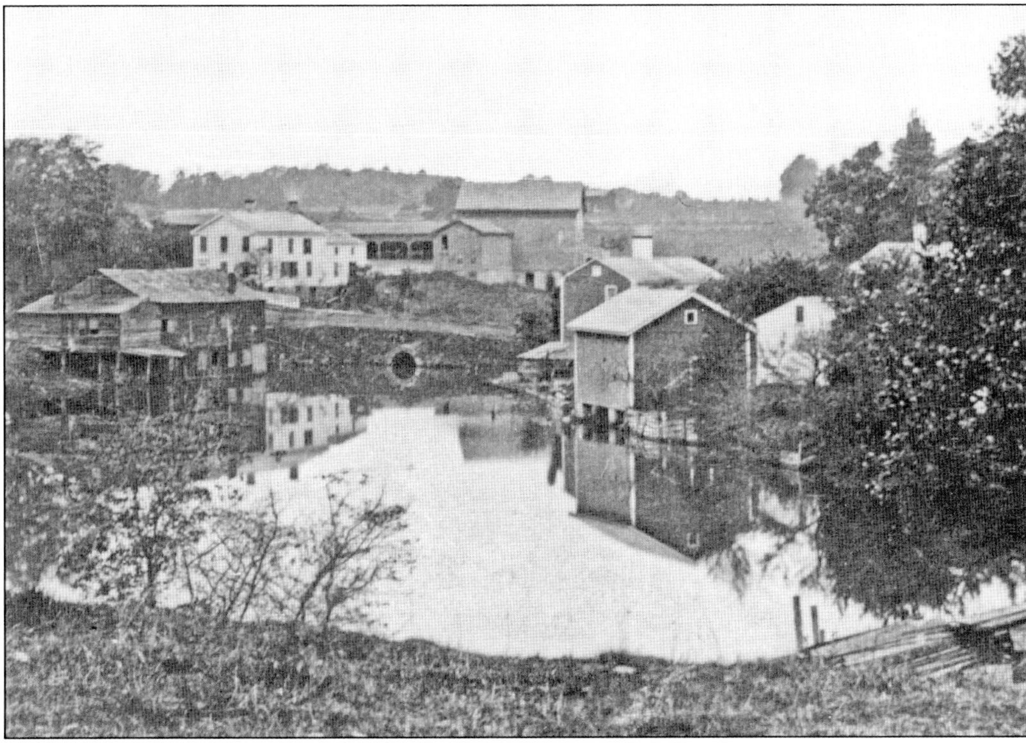

This is an earlier picture of the Andrus millpond looking from the east towards the outlet culvert on the east side of South Main Street. The building on the pond to the left is the blacksmith shop on Dolbeer Street. The white building behind, at the corner of Main and Mill Streets, would become Ireland's hardware store. The mill on the Center Street corner is in the background. On the right is Dr. Goodwin's white house with the barn on the pond.

The Dolbeer building, constructed over the outlet, burned in 1980 and had to be demolished. These culvert sections were put in place between the building abutments to carry the Silver Lake Outlet beyond Main Street. Concrete was poured to seal the culvert, and dirt filled the area to produce a park owned by the village. (Henry Page Collection.)

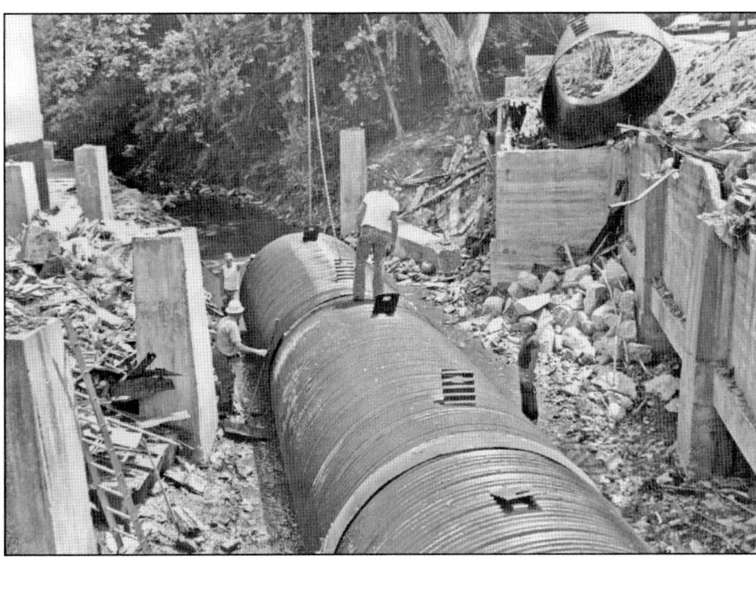

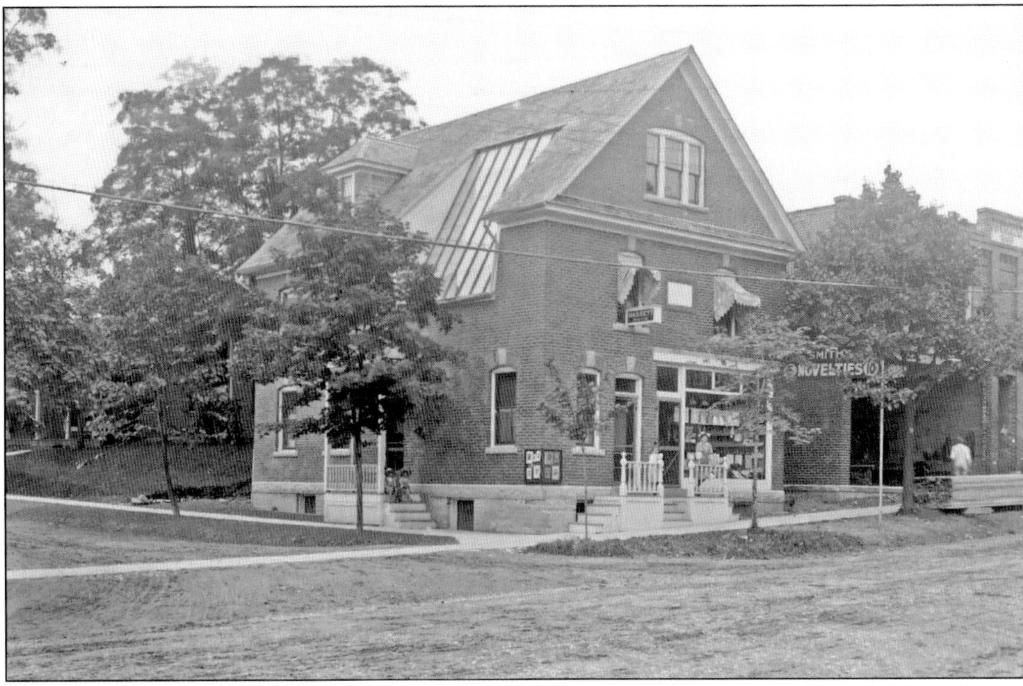

The Bassett building was constructed in 1908 at the corner of Dolbeer and South Main Streets. A skylight on the north side provided light for the photography studio upstairs, with the Bassett Art Shop downstairs. Today it is Dr. Ralph's dental office. The Wainman building to the right, also constructed in 1908, at one time held the Fashion Shack and the Big Z Shoe Store. It was later a jewelry store, and today is empty.

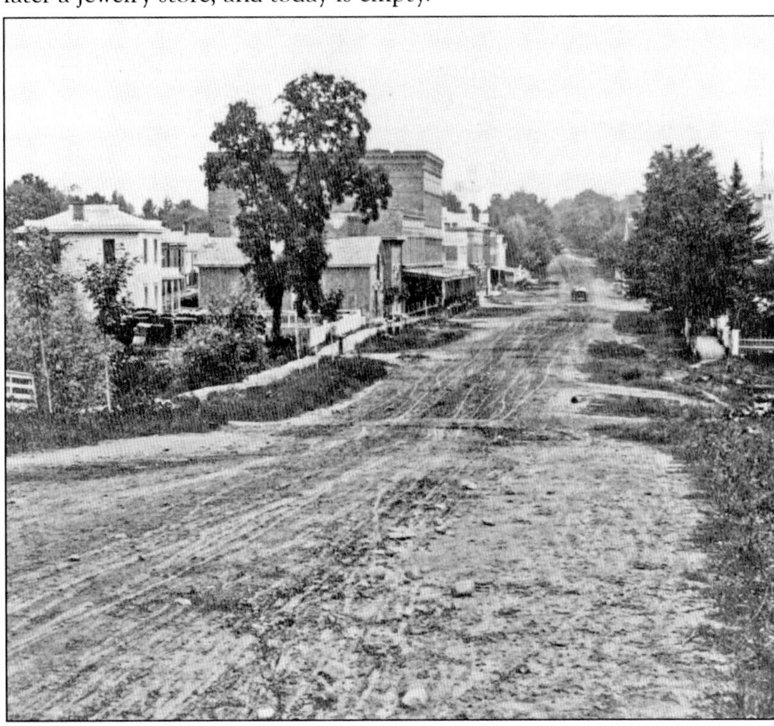

This early picture looks north at the west side of South Main Street. White's Hall would be built at the left in 1886. The white residence, probably Dr. Traver's, would be moved to build the Hotel Commodore. This picture is before the 1891 fire in the Smith (Montesano) building at the corner of Lake and Main Streets.

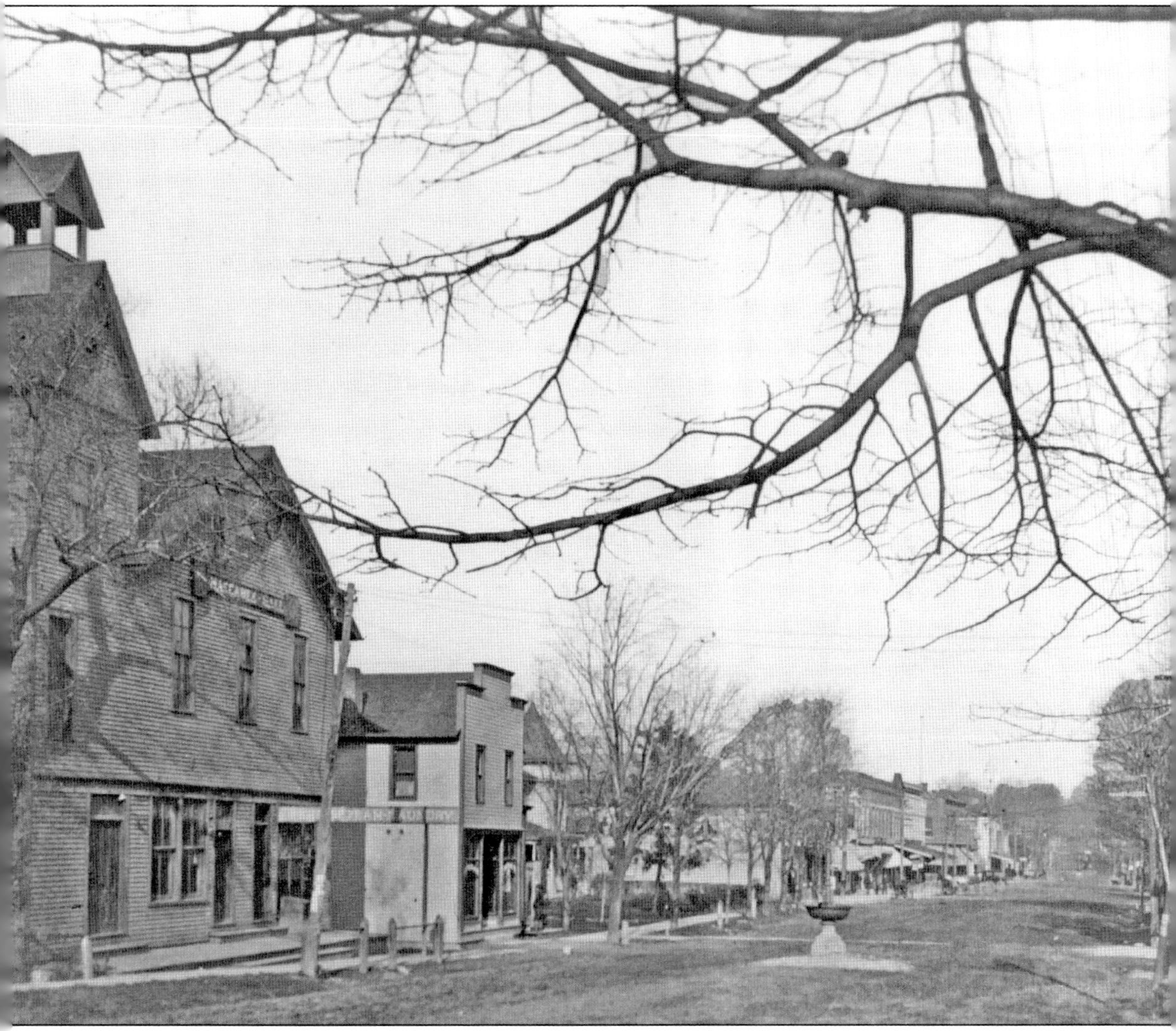

White's Hall, also known as White's Opera House, was a place for social gatherings and public meetings until the larger town hall was built. The fire department met in the basement before the fire hall across the street was built. In this picture, a sign for Maccabee Hall is on the second floor, and Perry Steam laundry is on the ground floor. This building later became Bucknam's livery stable, and then Davis's garage, and was torn down in 1947. It was replaced with a brick building that was Pavilion Natural Gas Office, now H&R Block. The next building contains Sutherland Granite Works and the Perry Record's first office on the second floor. The water trough was installed in 1896.

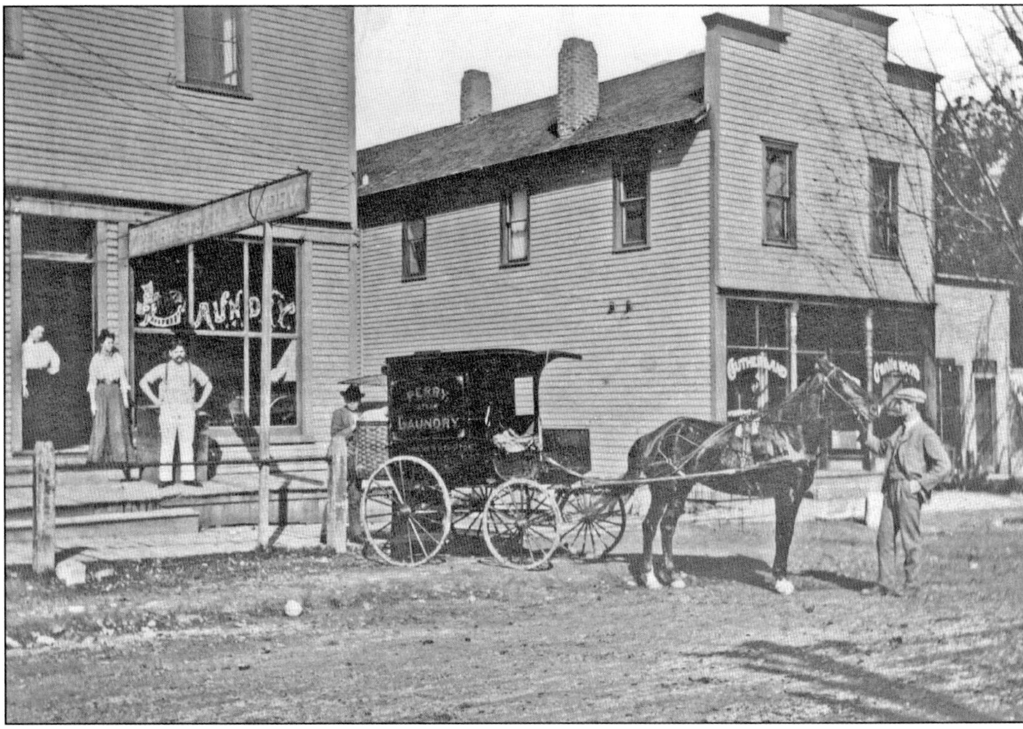

Perry Steam Laundry in White's Hall on the left, moved to Borden Avenue, and later to Covington Street. On the right, Sutherland Granite Works would stay in the family and become Gibney Monument Works on North Center Street. The building would become the Good News Book Shop, now Grover and Bates.

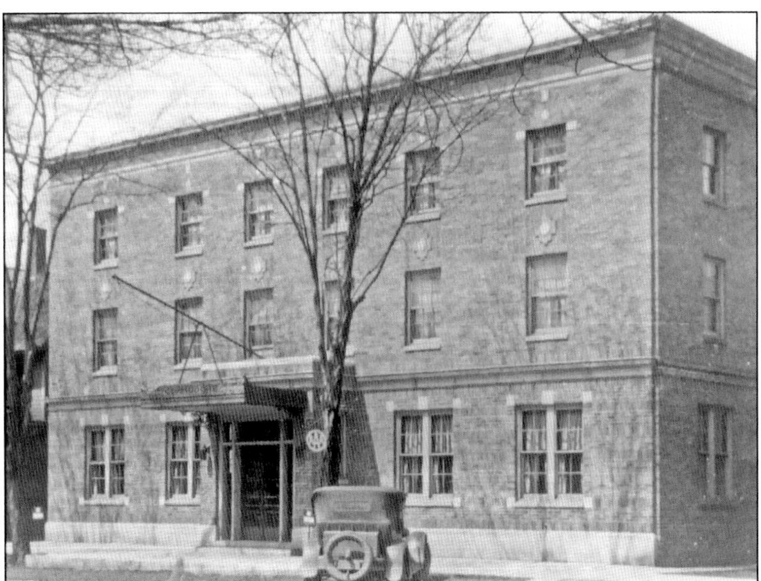

Hotel Commodore, complete with lobby, dining room, and ballroom, was built in 1924 on the site of Dr. Traver's home. This residence was moved back to face Traver Place and burned in 1944. The hotel business was never very profitable, and in 1968, it became Peddle's Hardware Store, later Perry True Value Hardware. Today it is Traver Place apartments.

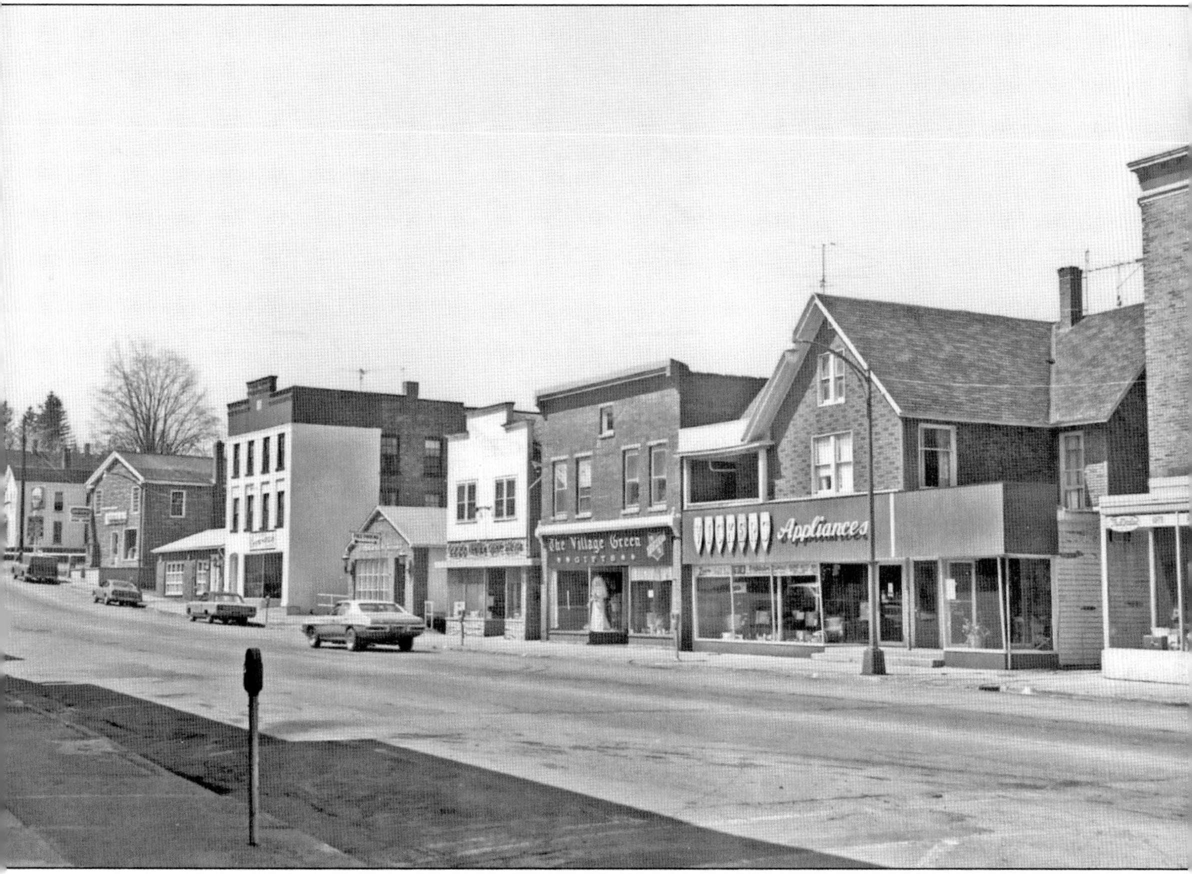

This is the west side of South Main Street in 1976. The Hotel Commodore, on the right, is a hardware store. Vicker's Appliances is in a residence that was moved up to the street for a milliner's shop. The Eggleston building, constructed by the milliners from next door, has the Village Green, today the Episcopal Thrift Shop. Good News Gift Shop is next. The Pavilion Gas office is to the south on the site of White's Hall. The Silver Lake Outlet runs under Main Street at the railing. Next to this is the B. F. Rollah building constructed in 1907 over the outlet, today the Laundromat. The small building is still a lawyer's office. On the corner of Mill and South Main Streets was Ireland's hardware and farm supply store. In this picture it is Karondak hardware, a heating and plumbing business. Today it is an empty lot. (Henry Page Collection.)

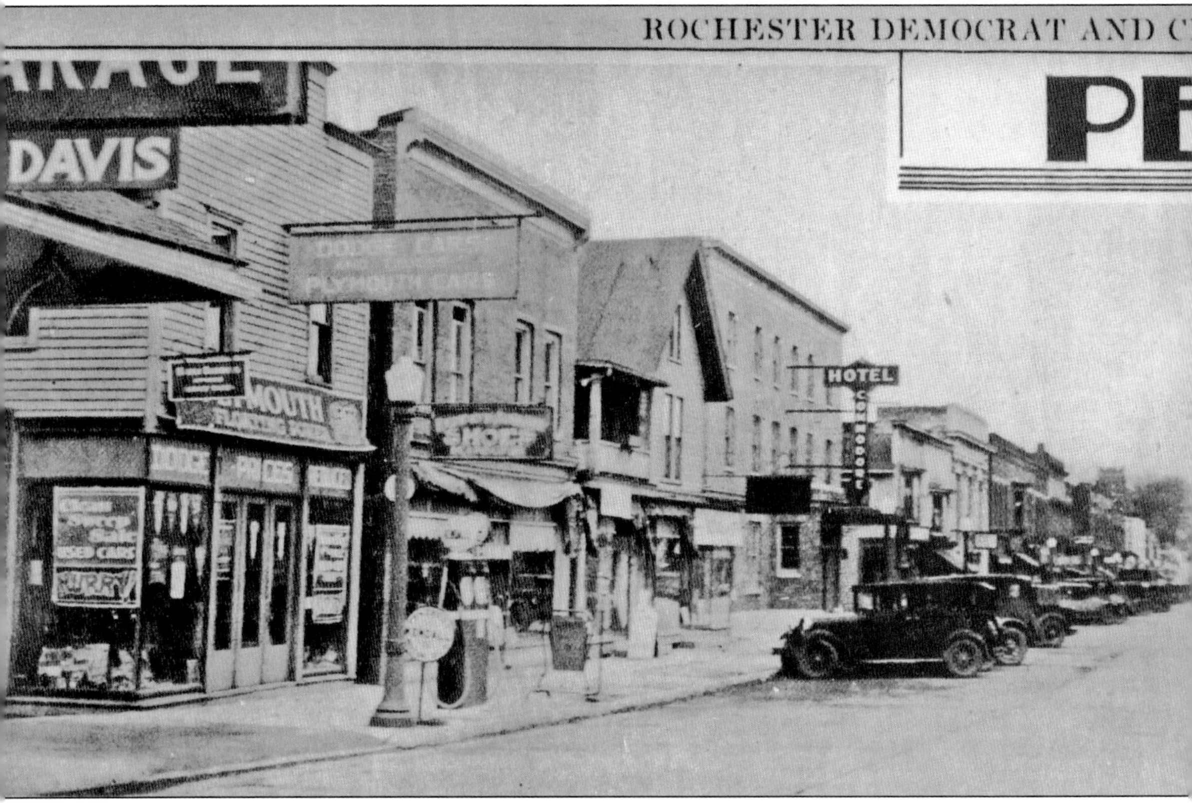

This is looking north on Perry's South Main Street in 1932. On the west side (left), there is a garage in the building once housing Sutherland Granite Works. The Eggleston building has a shoe store. Harry Masten owned the Hotel Commodore at this time. On the east side, right, is the Dolbeer building constructed over the outlet. Kaustine Company offices were in this building

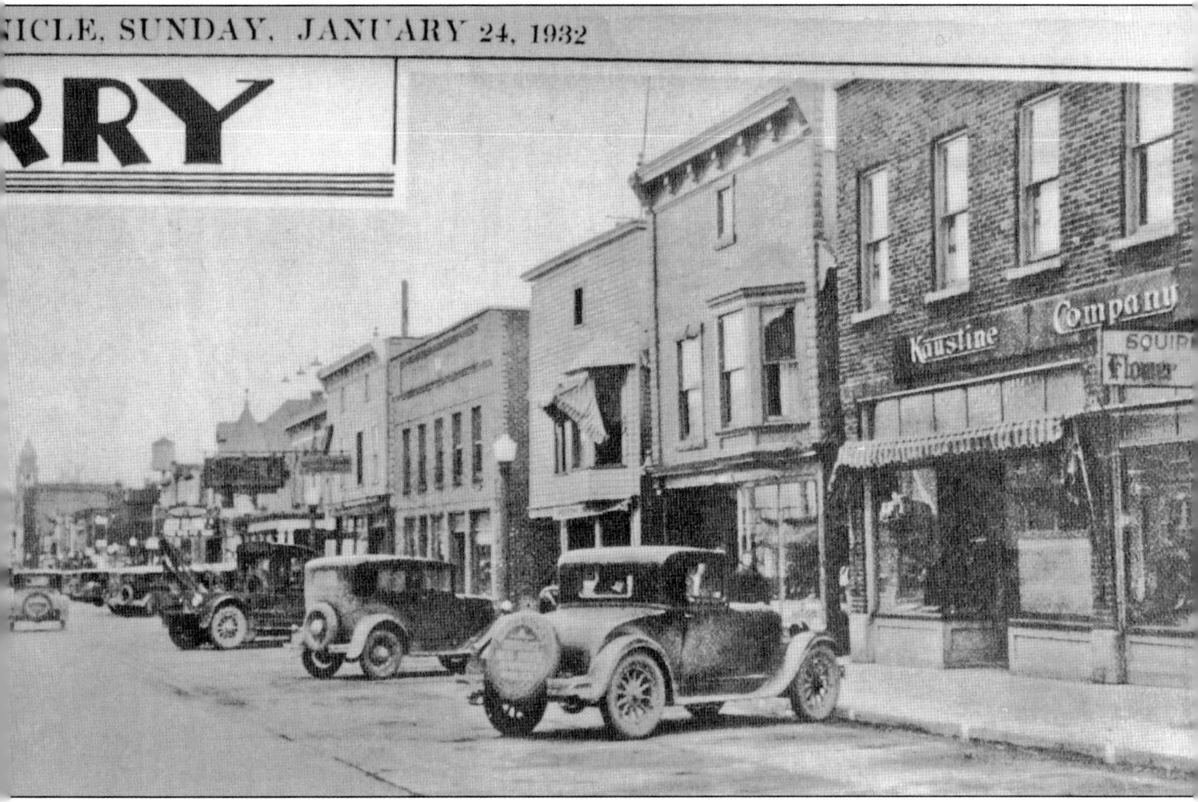

from the late 1920s until moving to the factory site in 1934. Squire's Flower Shop shared this structure. The next building heading north on the right is the old fire hall, later the Silver Grill. The brick post office would replace the next building, and the Perry Record building is to the north. In the distance is the tower of the village hall.

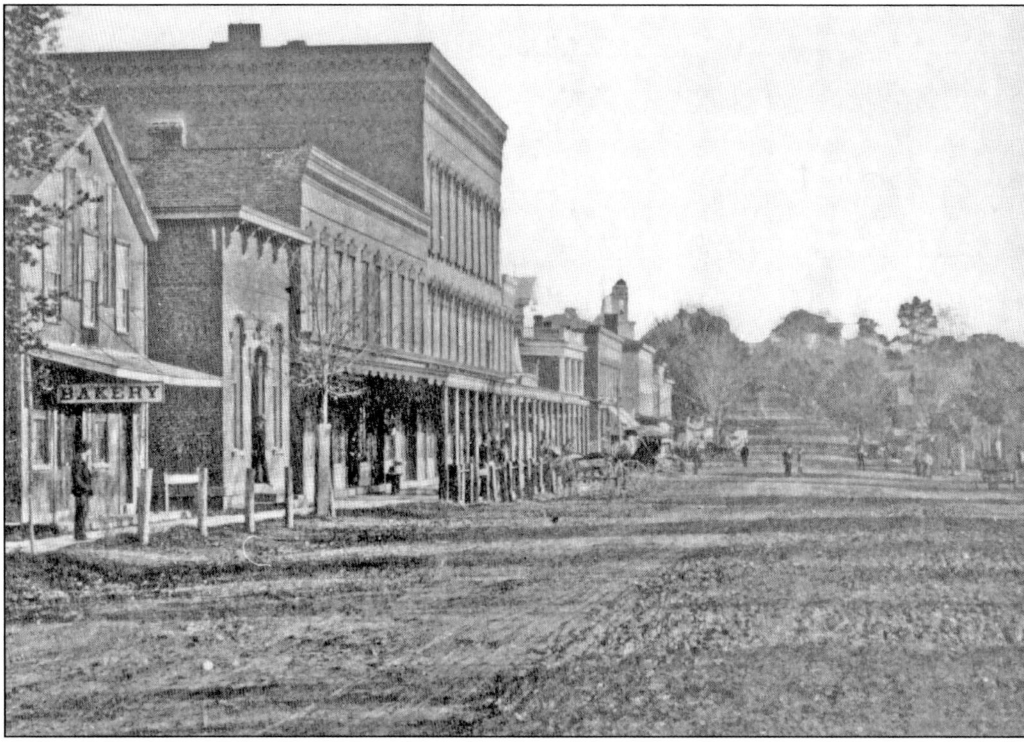

This continues the west side of South Main Street looking north. A bakery is on the left, Smith's Bank founded in 1855 is next, four stores are in the next building, and the three-story Smith-Olin building is at the corner of Lake and Main Streets. The National Hotel is across Lake Street, and the old Presbyterian church steeple is in the background.

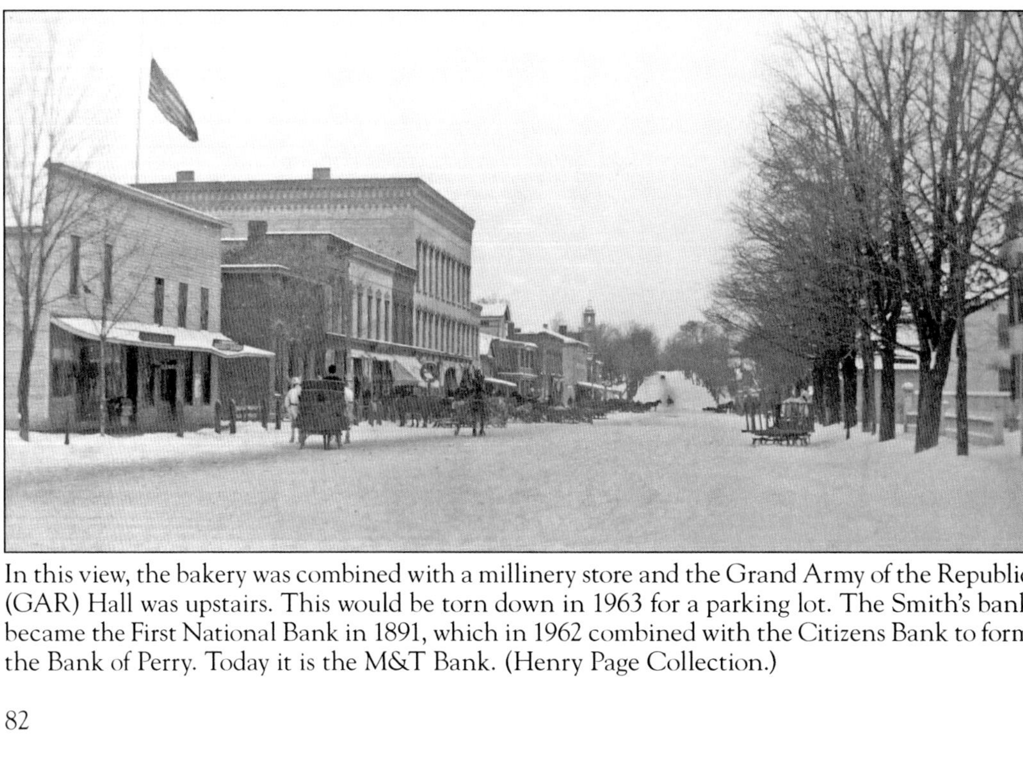

In this view, the bakery was combined with a millinery store and the Grand Army of the Republic (GAR) Hall was upstairs. This would be torn down in 1963 for a parking lot. The Smith's bank became the First National Bank in 1891, which in 1962 combined with the Citizens Bank to form the Bank of Perry. Today it is the M&T Bank. (Henry Page Collection.)

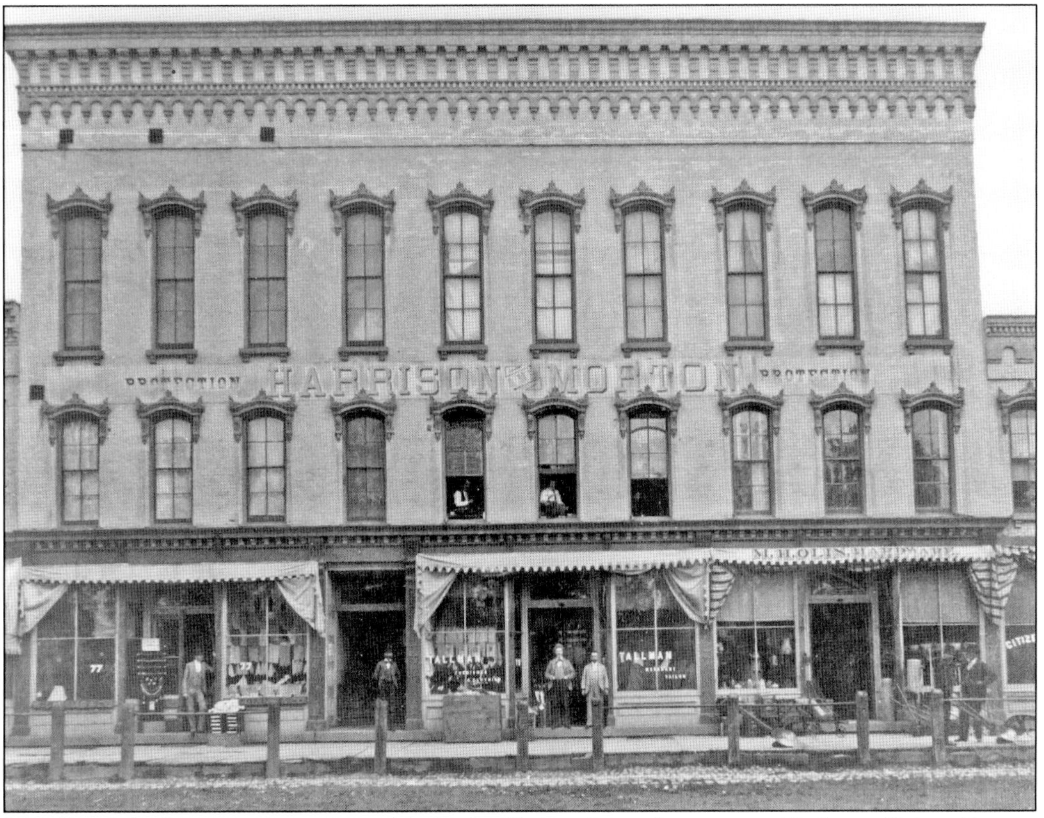

The Smith building was constructed by Rufus H. Smith on the corner of Lake and Main Streets after fire destroyed earlier buildings in 1865. The third floor was known as Smith's Hall, and later remodeled by M. H. Olin into the Olin Opera House. The second store is the Tallman's store, then M. H. Olin's Hardware, and the Citizens Bank founded in 1888 on the right.

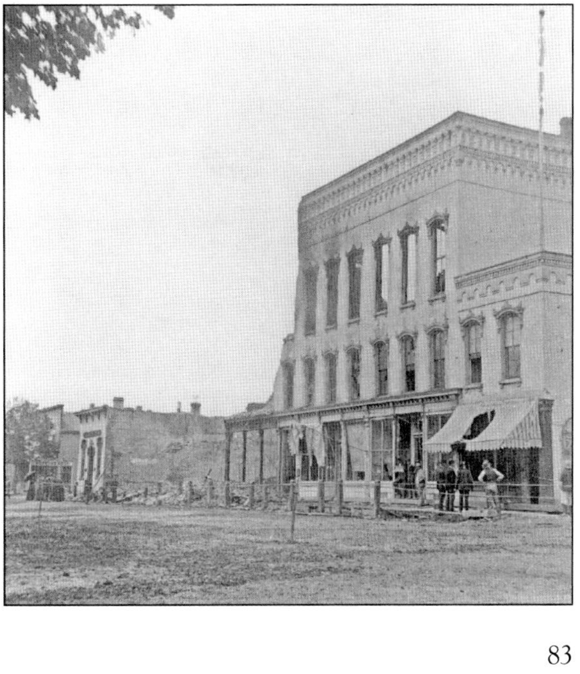

This is the structure after the fire of 1891, looking from the corner of Lake and Main Streets. The Smith's Bank to the left survived with just a burned cornice. The building with four stores—Goldwater clothing, Herron's grocery, and two others—was destroyed. The Smith-Olin building was badly damaged, and the third floor was never rebuilt.

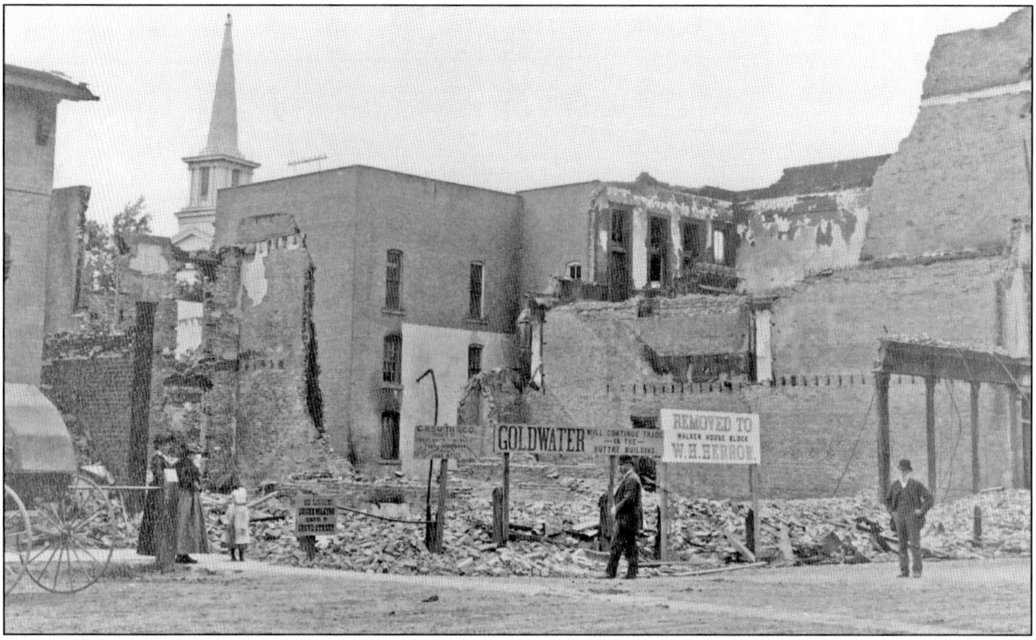

This view is looking north with the Smith's bank on the left. The spire of the Methodist church on the north side of Lake Street shows behind. The lower sign says "Kate Gates, Dressmaking removed to Grove Street." The next says, "C. S. Smith removed to the Crocker building, the Public Telephone to Smith's Shoe Store." The next business is Goldwater, then "Herron removed to Walker House" (the National Hotel building).

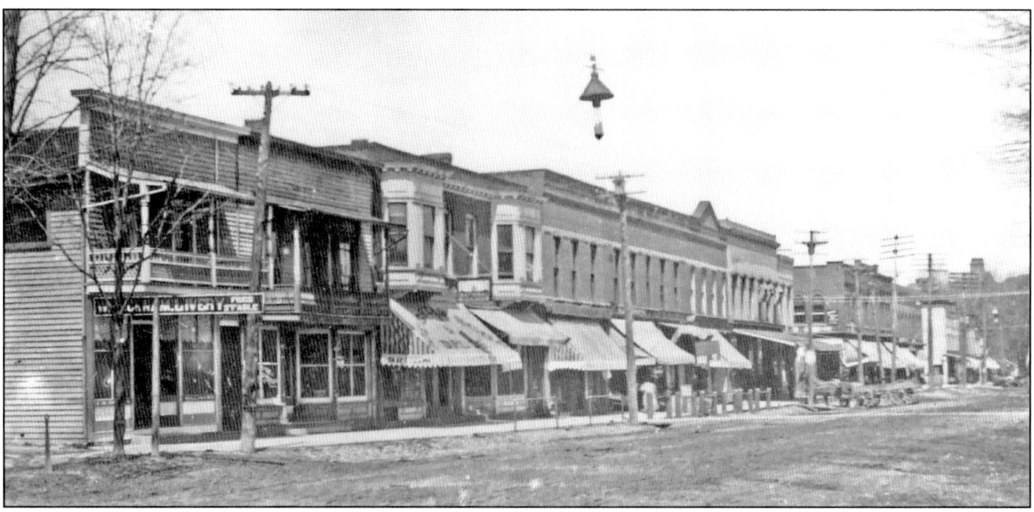

This is a view of the west side after the fire. A livery stable is now in the frame building on the left. A new building was constructed and a second story added to the Smith bank to form the next block with awnings and bay windows above. This was the Baker and Roberts Drug Store and the First National Bank. The next destroyed building was replaced and the Smith-Olin building was reduced to two stories.

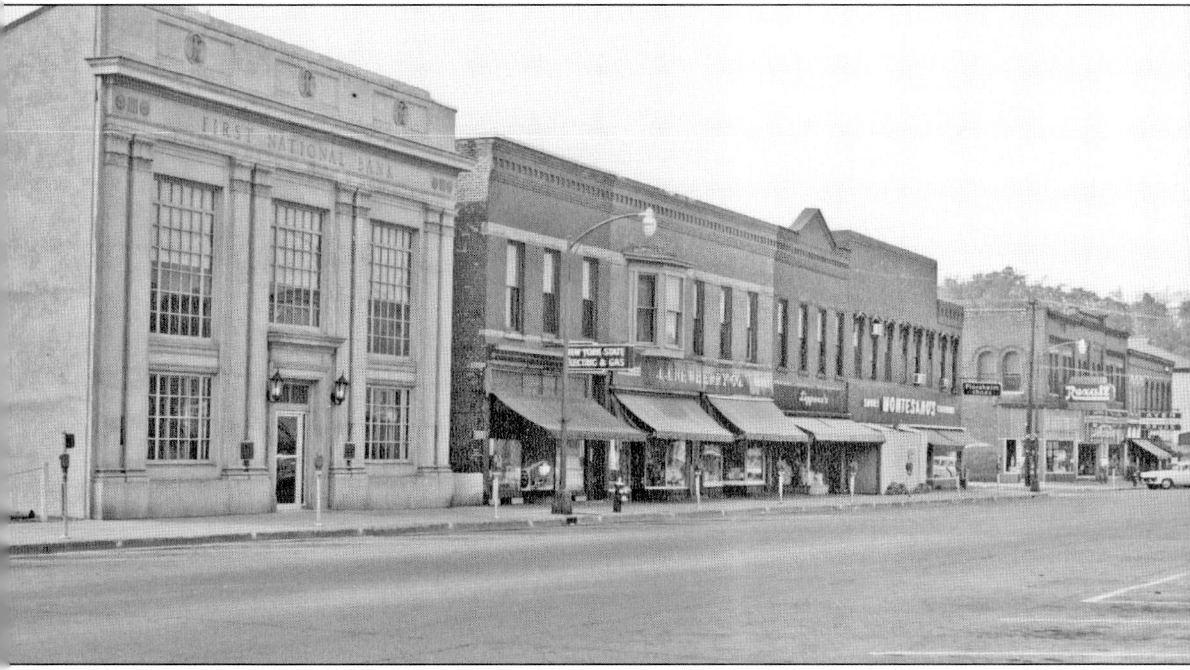

This is a 1964 picture of the same area with a parking lot next to the First National Bank building, later the Bank of Perry, and then the M&T Bank of today. Part of the north wall of this structure was the north wall of the original Smith bank. The New York State Electric and Gas office had been the C. A. King menswear store, earlier the Goldwater's store. Today it is the Ultimate Salon and Fitness. A bay window was added to the next section that contained Ellsworth's grocery and another store. This became the J. J. Newberry store, later an antiques store, and is now empty. Lippman's is next, today the Arts Council for Wyoming County with 1895 on the peak. Montesano's is in the old Smith-Olin building. (Henry Page Collection.)

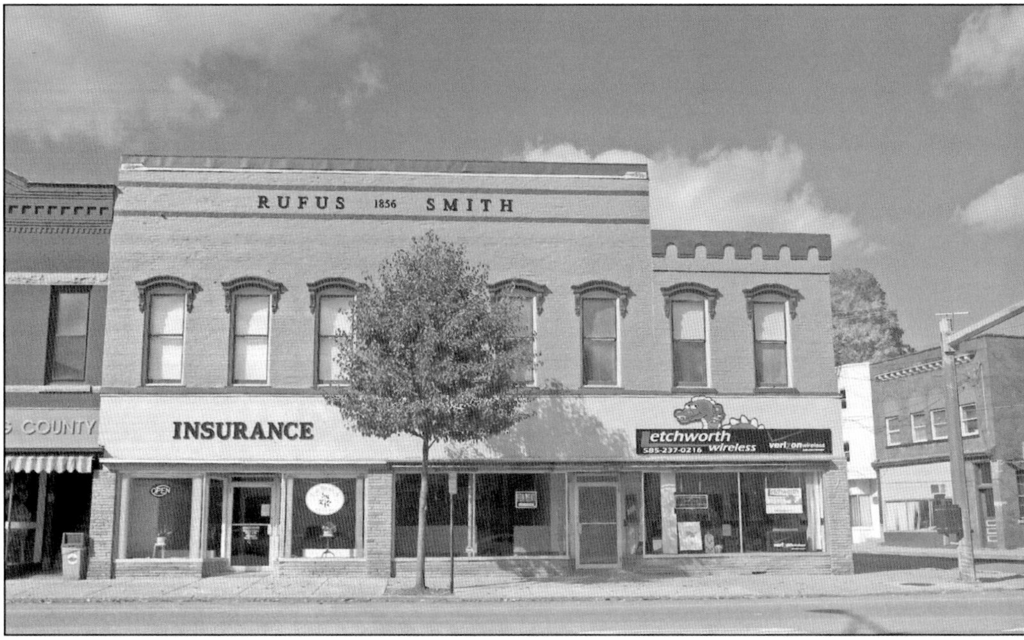

The building on the south corner of Lake and Main Streets was originally constructed by Rufus H. Smith. It became the W. T. Olin building, later the Mary Martin block, and was the Montesano building when purchased by a group of Perry investors. Today known again as the Rufus H. Smith building, it is beautifully restored and almost full of businesses. The arts council is on the left, and Lake Street is to the right. (Photograph by Jennifer Nolan.)

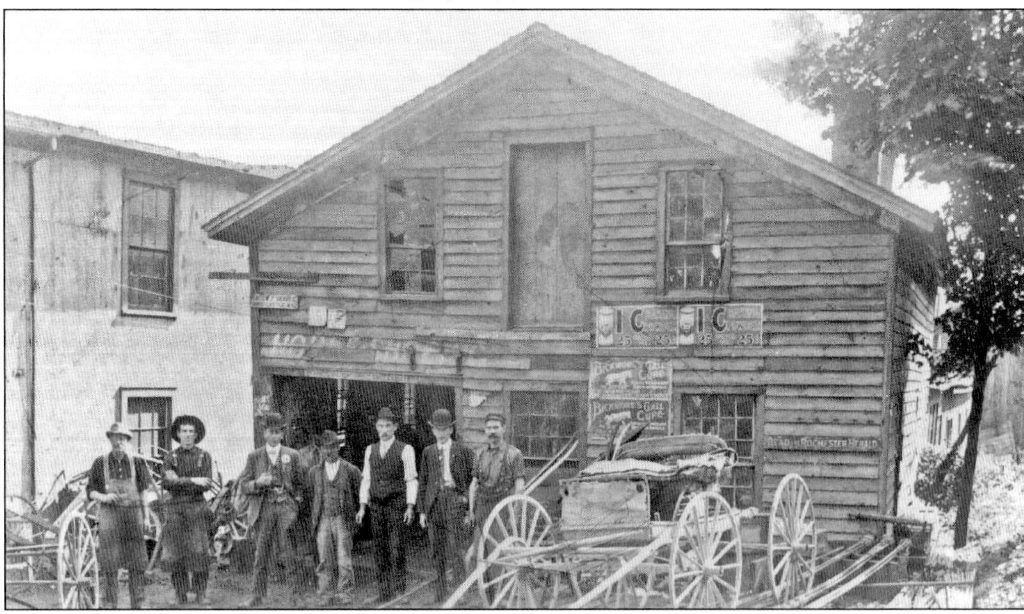

Joseph Ireland's blacksmith's shop was on the south side of Lake Street, behind the Smith-Olin building. This is the site of the telephone company structure today. In 1911, Mr. Ireland, on the right, started Ireland's hardware and farm supply store on the corner of Mill and Main Streets. The shed on the left in this picture was west of the alley behind Main Street businesses. (Henry Page Collection.)

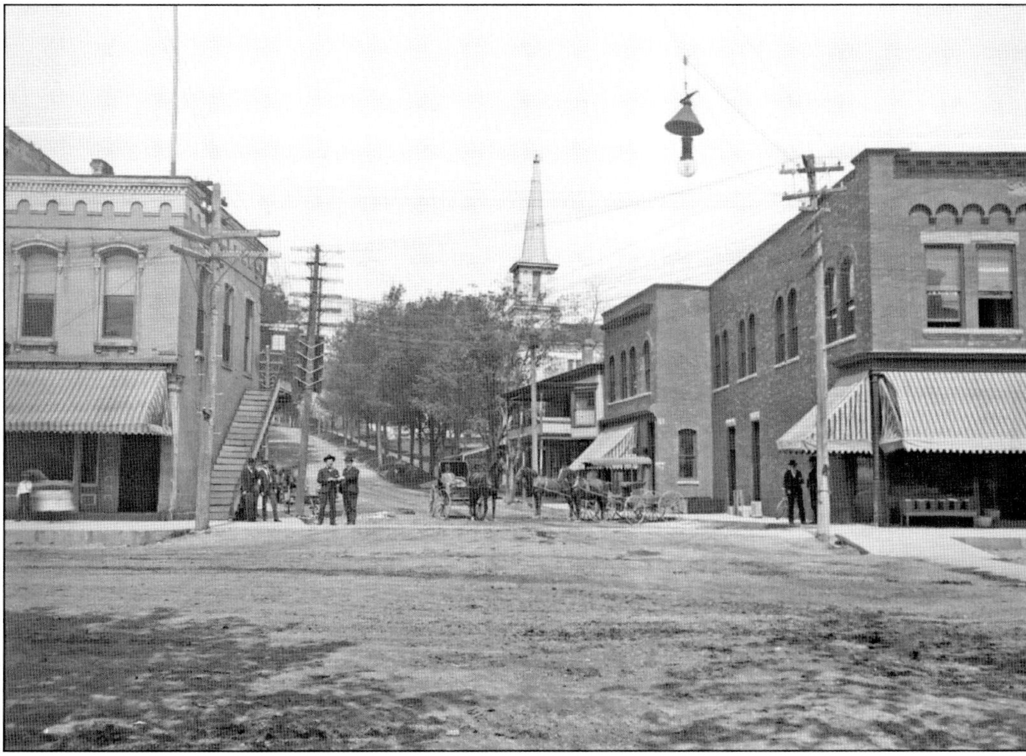

This is the Lake and Main Streets intersection before 1907. The Telephone Company and the Perry Electric Light Company are in the Smith-Olin building, up the stairs on the left, where all the wires converge. The building on the right, constructed by Garrison in 1901, holds a grocery store. The Wise buildings behind this on Lake Street were constructed in 1903.

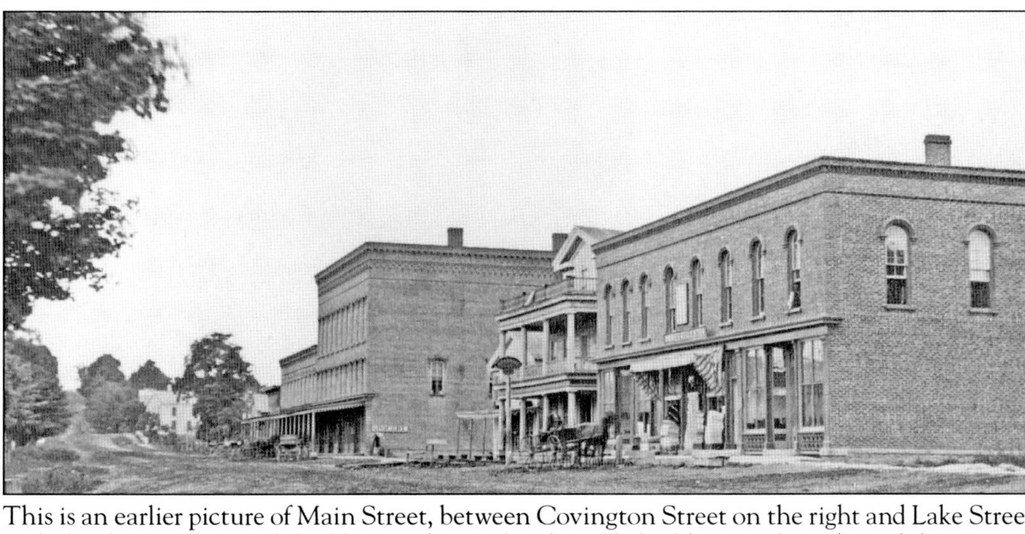

This is an earlier picture of Main Street, between Covington Street on the right and Lake Street with the three-story Smith building to the south. The Cole building on the right and the Wygant building, both constructed in 1867, appear as one brick structure. The National Hotel is next to the south, then the frame Garrison building.

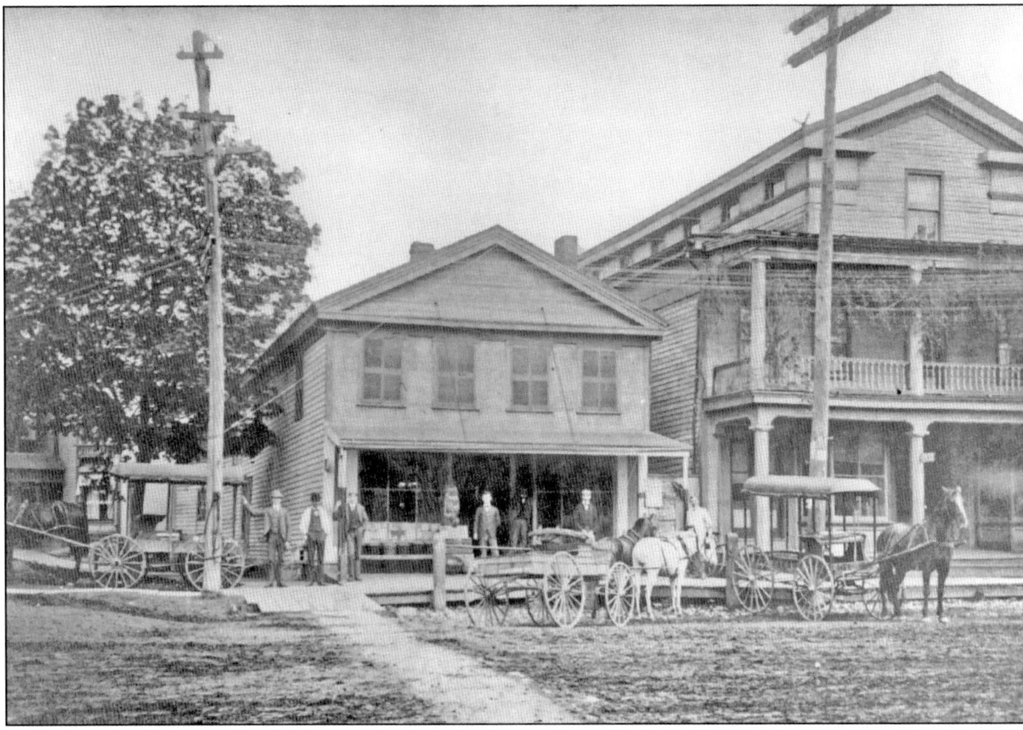

These two frame buildings were on the northwest corner of Lake and Main Streets. The left structure occupied by Garrison was moved to the east side of Main Street and south to become the Perry Record building. It was altered with a stone facade and became Jeco Motor Service in 1976. The brick Garrison building replaced this in 1901. The National Hotel is on the right.

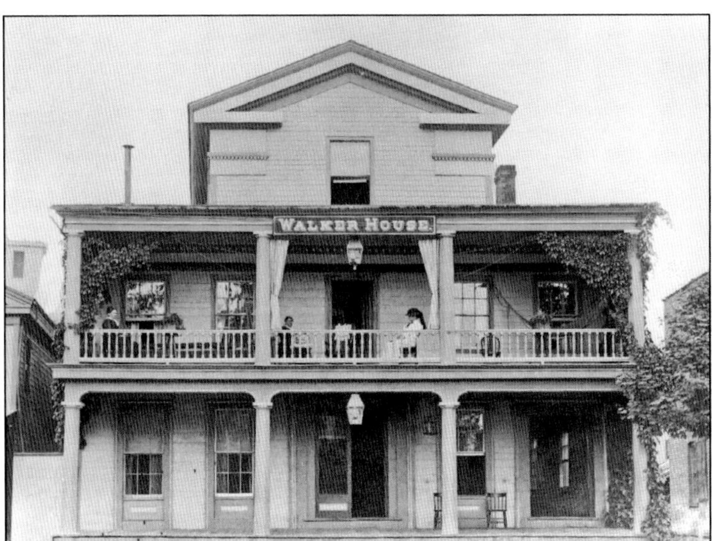

This was the fourth Walker House, and the former National Hotel, owned by A. B. Walker from 1880 until his death in 1889. Charles Wise bought the building and moved it to the south side of Covington Street where it became Hotel Covington with a gambrel roof; later it became the Covington Apartments. Wise constructed a brick building on the Main Street site in 1901.

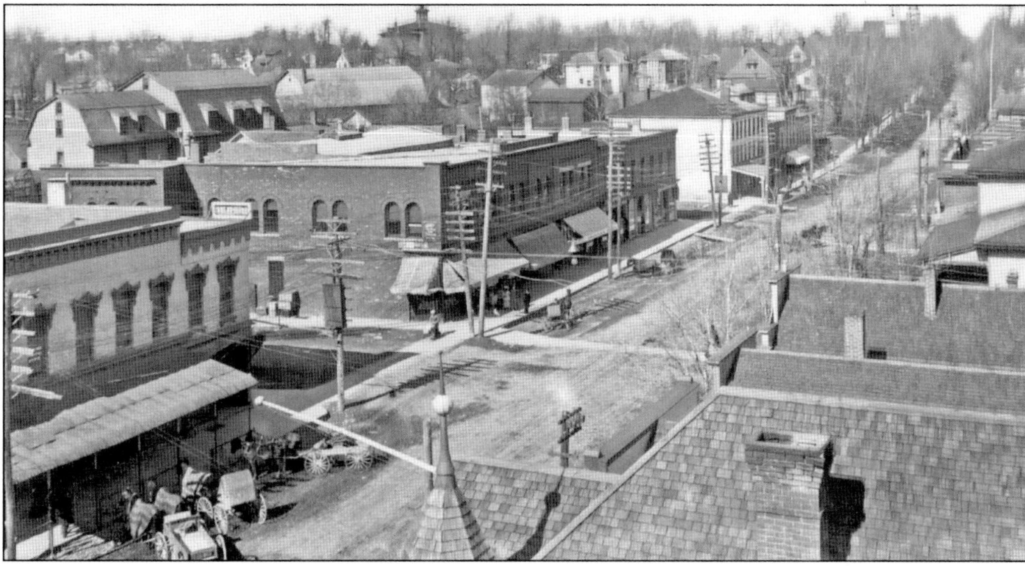

This rooftop view was taken from the town hall tower; the Perry Club turret is in the front center. The section of Main Street between Lake and Covington Streets contains all brick buildings, therefore it is after 1901. The double gambrel roof building at the upper left is Hotel Covington, moved from Main Street. In the upper middle of the picture is the Perry Academy building. The Presbyterian church steeple is seen upper right.

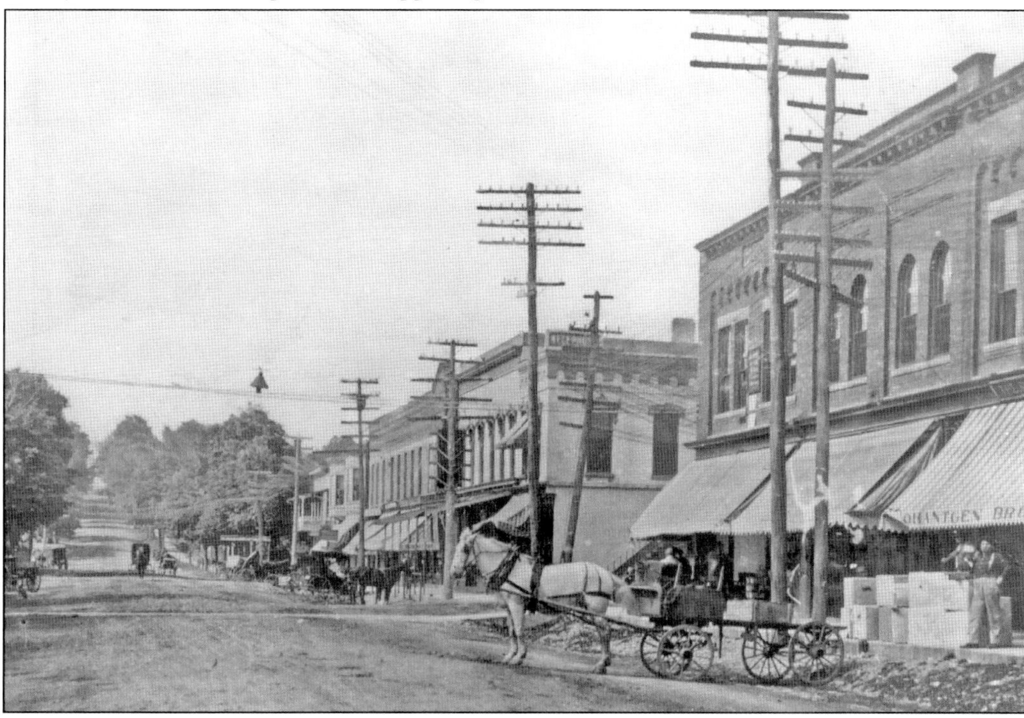

This view is looking south at the west side of Main Street at Lake Street. The first brick structure on the right is the Wise building with F. W. Johantgen menswear store and the Charles Wise dry goods store within. The Garrison building, on the corner, has a grocery store. Today these have all become the Family Furniture Store.

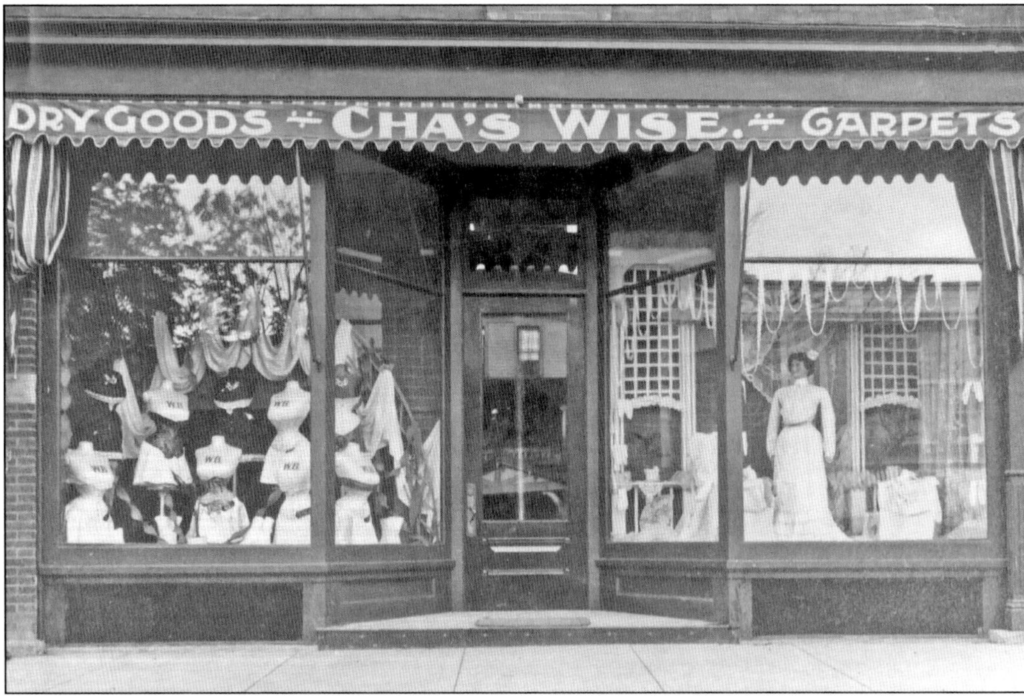

Charles Wise opened his department store in two-thirds of the Wise building. In the top image, a display of corsets in the left store window reflects the style of the time, about 1901. Carpets are also advertised. The bottom picture shows the inside of the left-hand side of the store with attractively displayed merchandise. The staircase leading to the second floor, in the back center, can still be seen today in the Family Furniture Store. Today the furniture store includes all of the Wise building, plus the Garrison and the Wygant buildings.

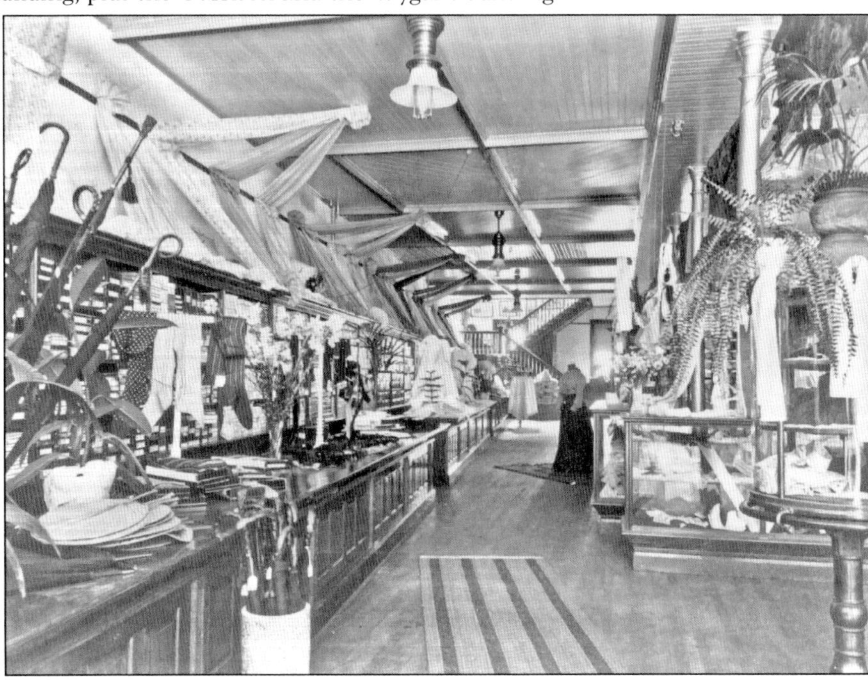

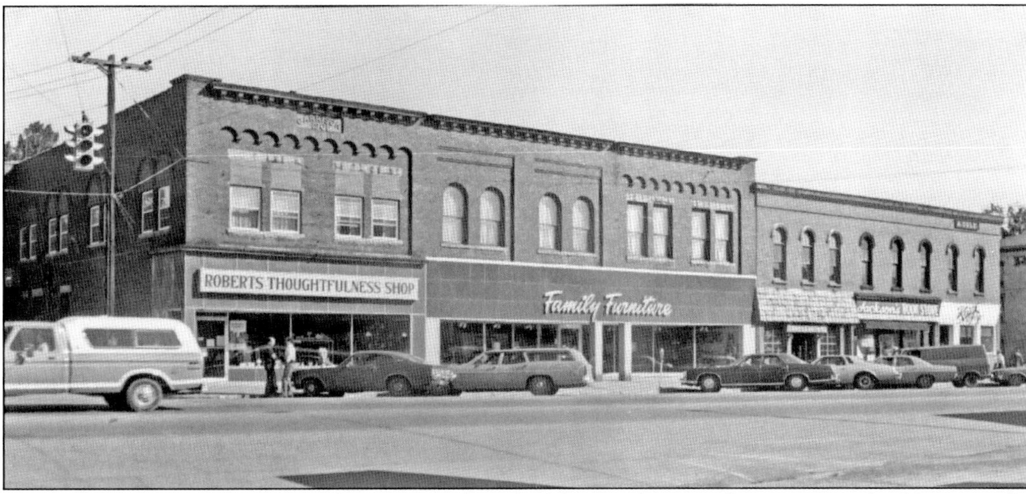

In 1976, this section contained Roberts Thoughtfulness Shop in the Garrison building on the left; earlier it had been Roberts Rexall Drugs. The Family Furniture Store is to the north with its carpet section next. Jackson's Book Store had been Rich's Book Store, formerly Jenckes' bookstore, and today is Hart's Insurance. Keif's Restaurant is on the corner. Today it is empty. (Henry Page Collection.)

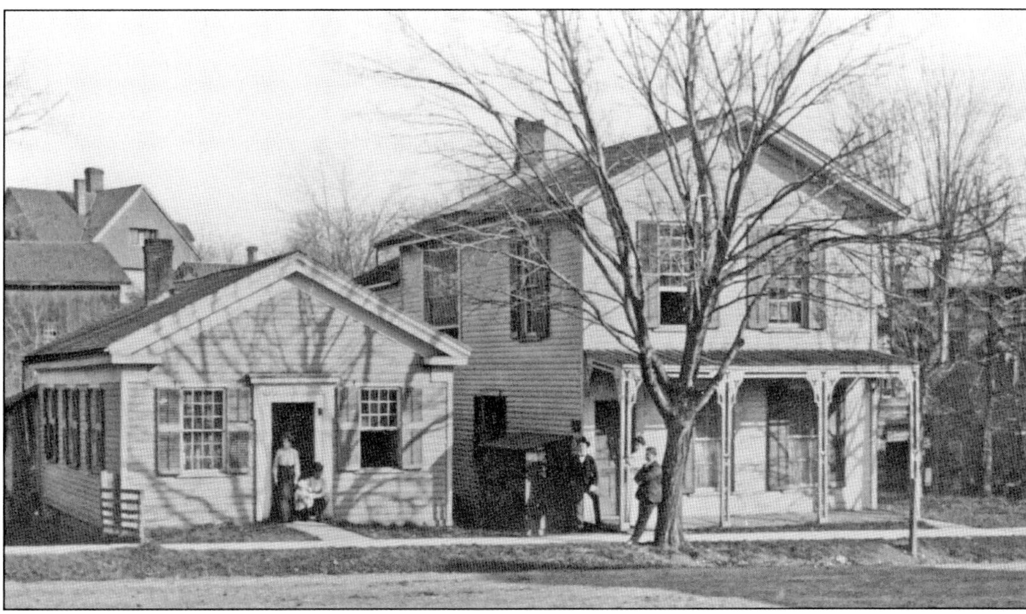

On the right is Crocker's photography studio (inside front cover) on Covington Street about 1910, when his son Frank Crocker, D.D.S., had his office upstairs, and a medical doctor's office was downstairs. This later became the Little Studio; today it is looking for a new photographer. The building on the left was once the Presbyterian church, and later the Catholic church. At the time of this photograph, it was probably a residence.

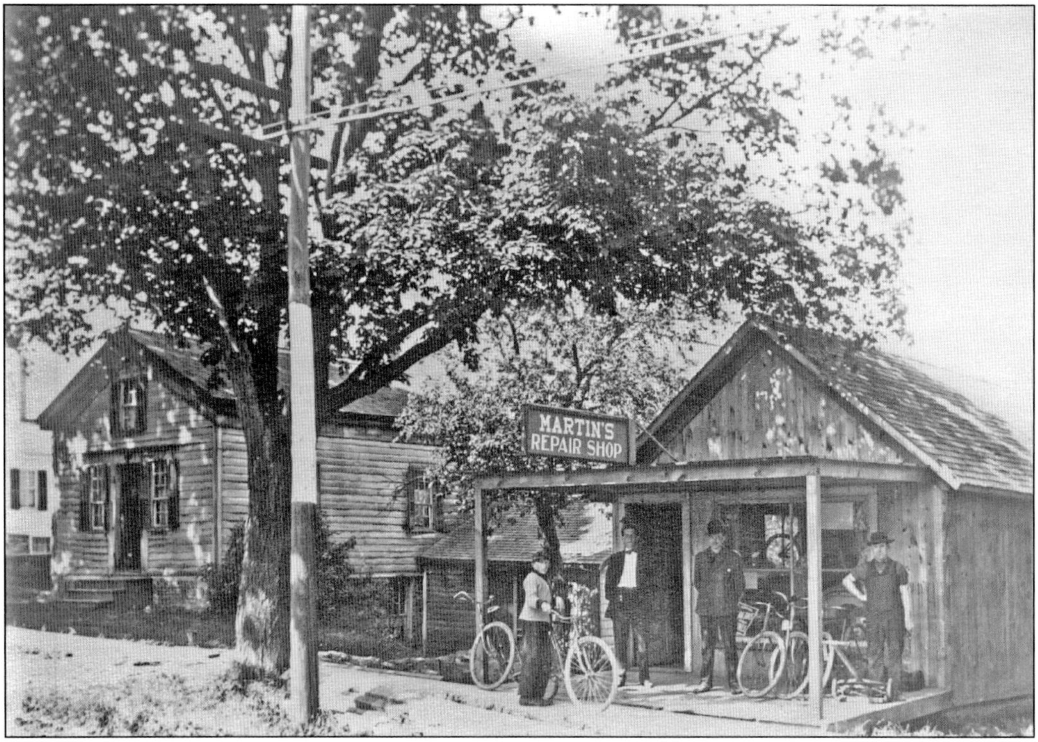

Martin's Repair Shop was on the north side of Covington Street, next to the little church. It is labeled as Martin's third and last bicycle shop. This was replaced later with the garage (below), built in 1917 by Watkins and McKurth for their Ford agency. Today it is Perry Bowling Center, with the Henry Hill school bus garage to the left. Across Covington Street, at the east corner of Short Street, the J. Olin building was constructed in 1908, and later became the Perry Baking Company. Today it is Rocker's restaurant. The Tarplee building to the east—later Zanghi's Market—and the Sweet building—later G and L Laundry—were both constructed in 1908.

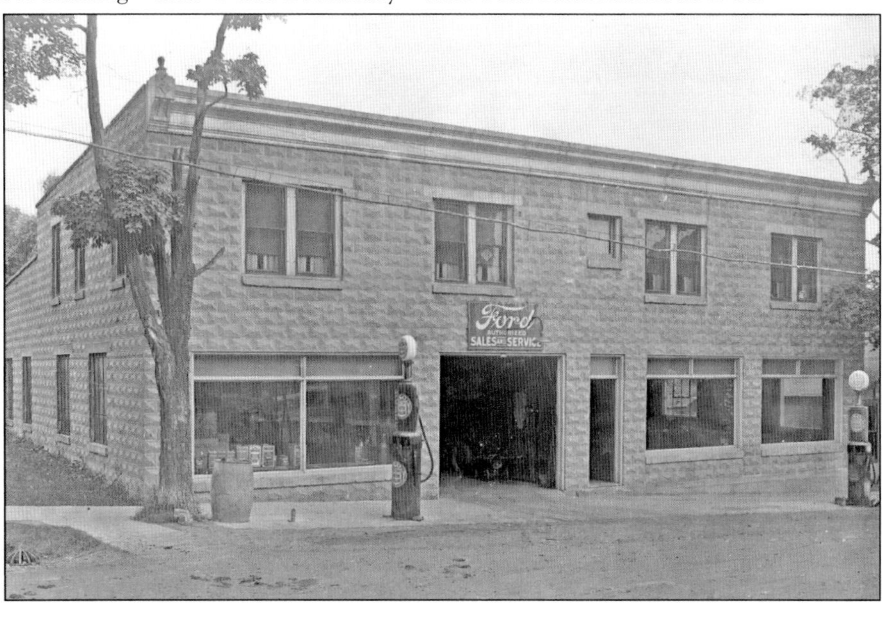

Six

Industry and Business

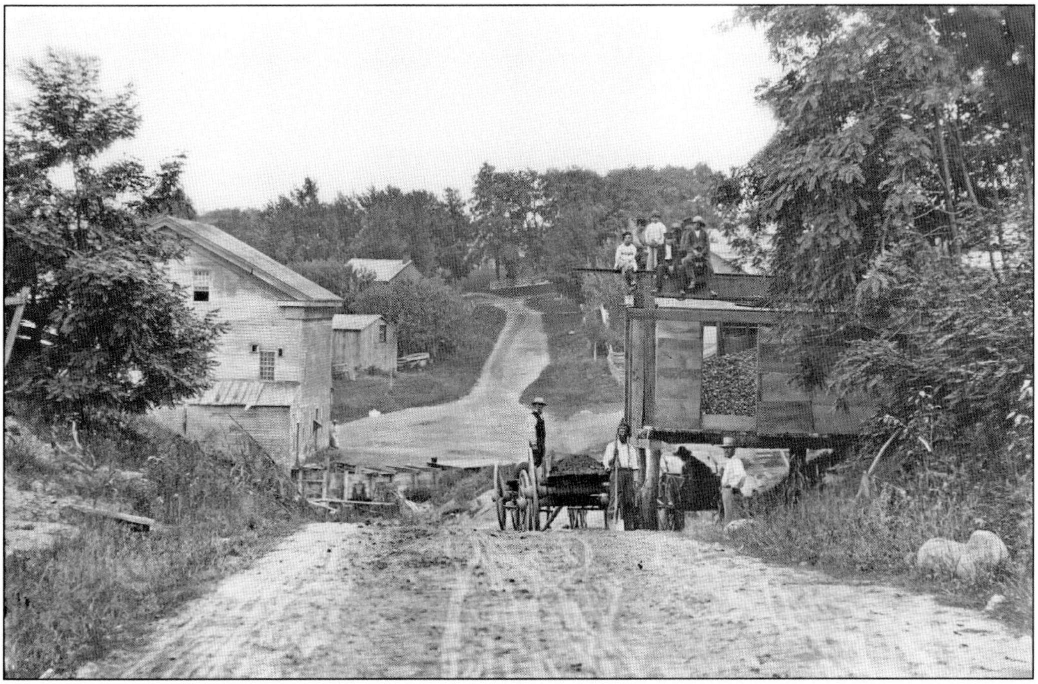

This is looking south on South Center Street at an early industrial site. The building on the left is a gristmill originally constructed by Benjamin Gardner in 1828 between the outlet and Mill Street. The sluiceway is to the right, not completely covered by the road. The dam on the outlet, which created the millpond (now Tomlinson's), was to the right behind the coal bins.

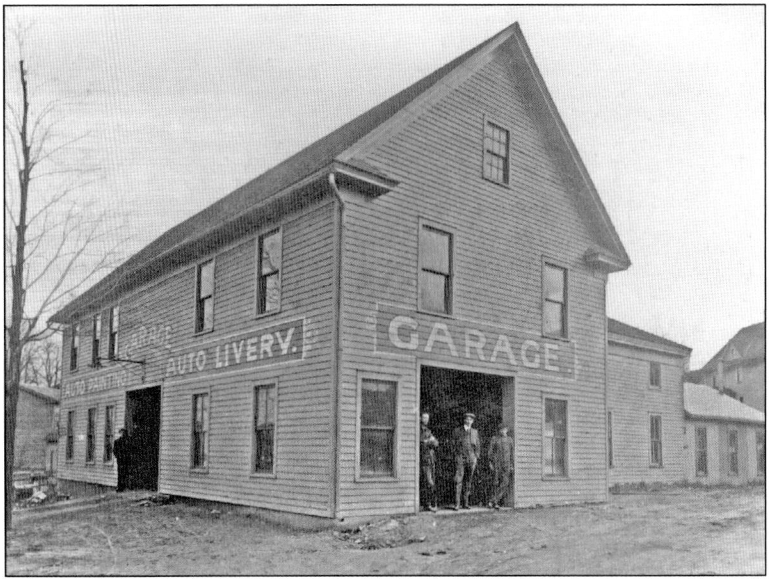

The barn on the corner of South Center and Mill Streets across from the mill would become the first garage. It was used in 1908 by the Kelly family, before they moved their business to Perry Center. It was remodeled to this form, called Link's garage in this picture. Today the ambulance building is on this site, next to Hoy's Home on the site of an old gas station.

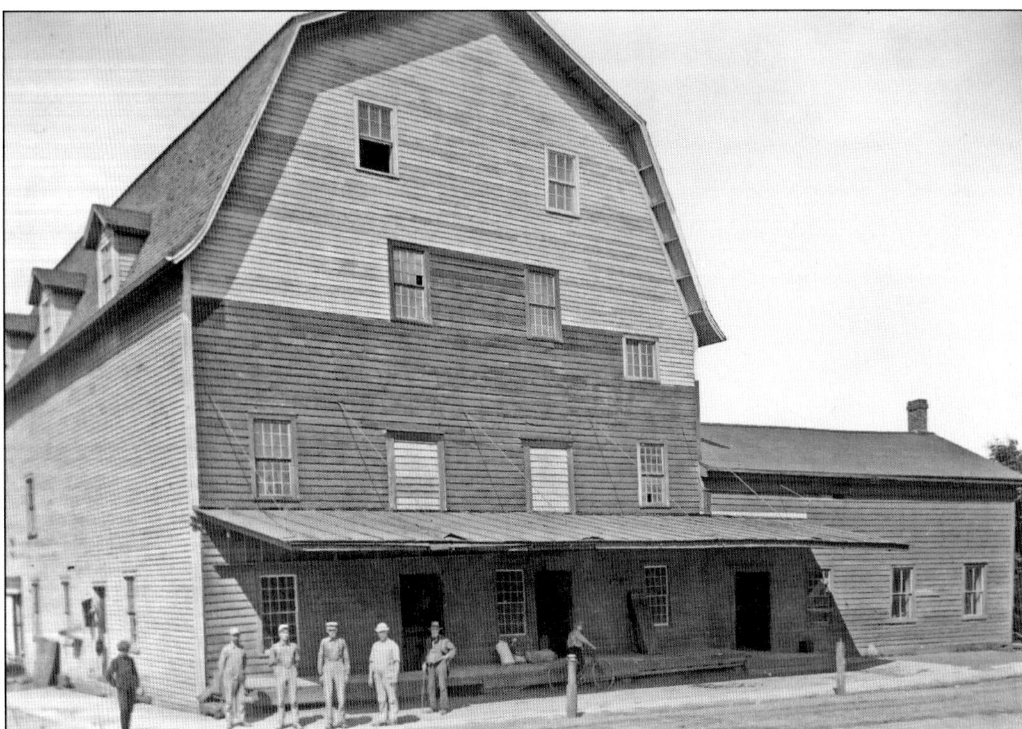

This flour mill faced Mill Street at the corner of South Center Street. The gabled roof in the earlier picture of the mill has been changed to a gambrel roof, and the building has been enlarged. It had many owners, with the last being the Tomlinson family. This building was demolished in 1937. Basil's Auto Repair is here today, and a Rotary rock and plaque marks the mill site.

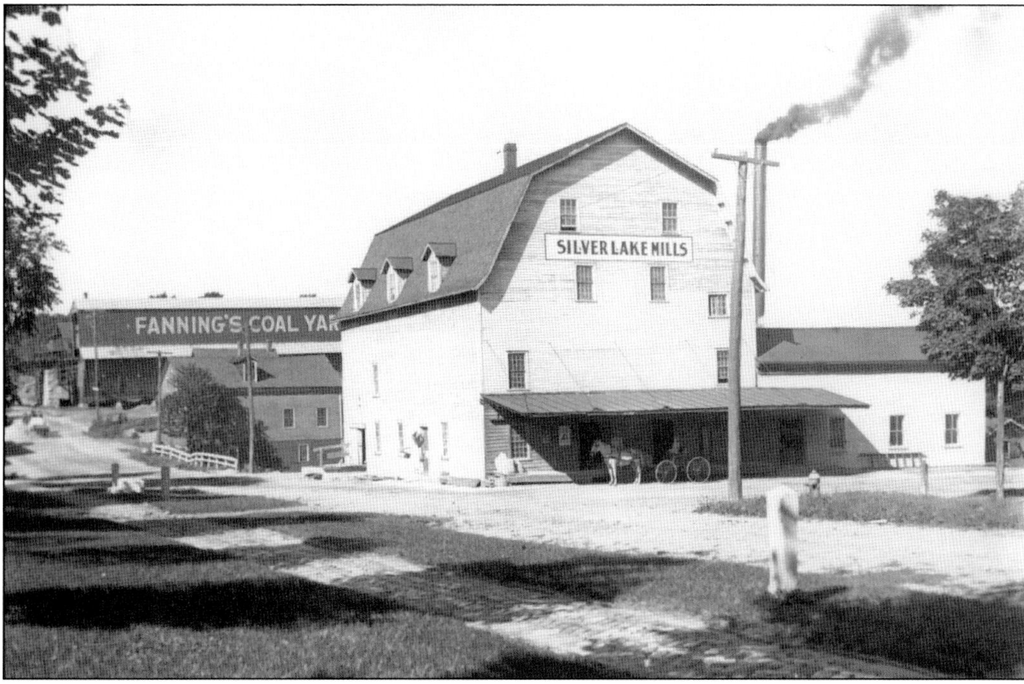

This is looking north on South Center Street at the mill on the corner of Mill Street. The business was known as Silver Lake Mills, or Tomlinson's mill. The Tomlinson residence would be a brick home back from the road in the left foreground, for many years the Rechberger home. Fanning's Coal Yard is on the other side of the outlet, marked by the white railing.

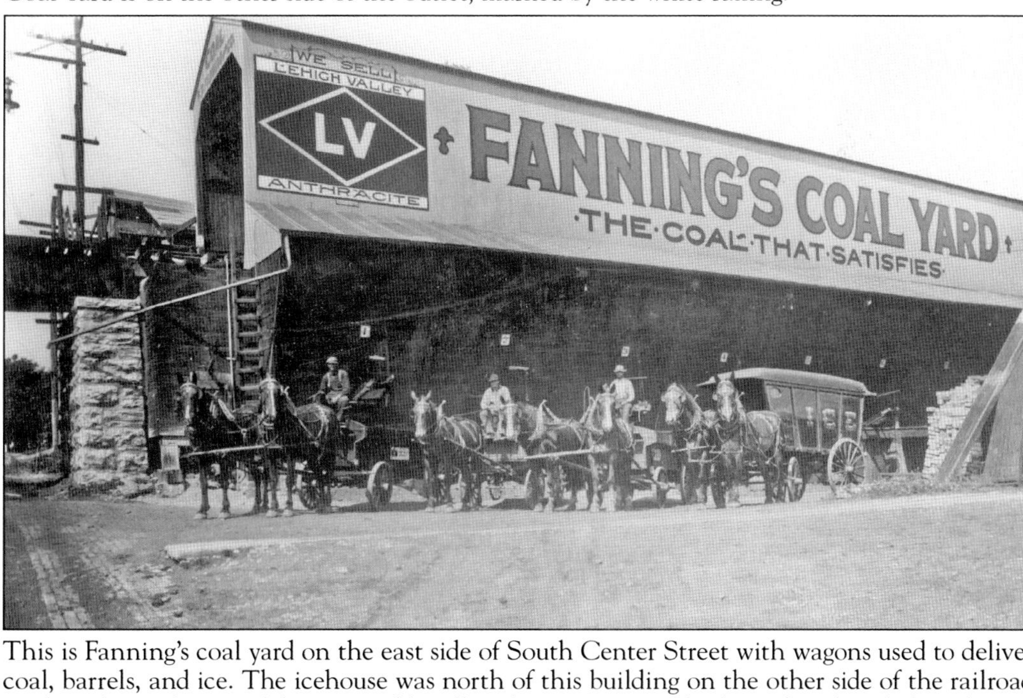

This is Fanning's coal yard on the east side of South Center Street with wagons used to deliver coal, barrels, and ice. The icehouse was north of this building on the other side of the railroad track and stored most of the ice used locally. The cooperage, which produced apple barrels, was north of that building.

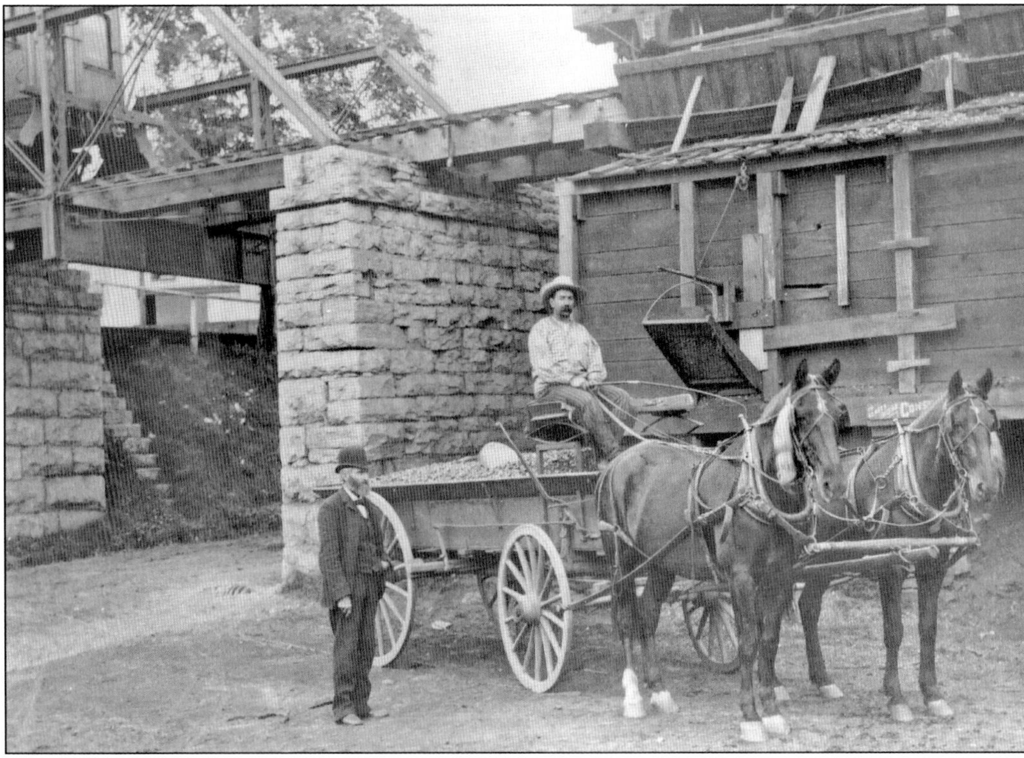

The train station is on the left of the trestle that carried the coal cars over South Center Street to the Fanning Coal Yard, which was the end of the railroad line in Perry. The coal wagon was loaded from the coal bin with the chute for deliveries to customers. Business was conducted here until 1965. Today an office and garage remain on this site.

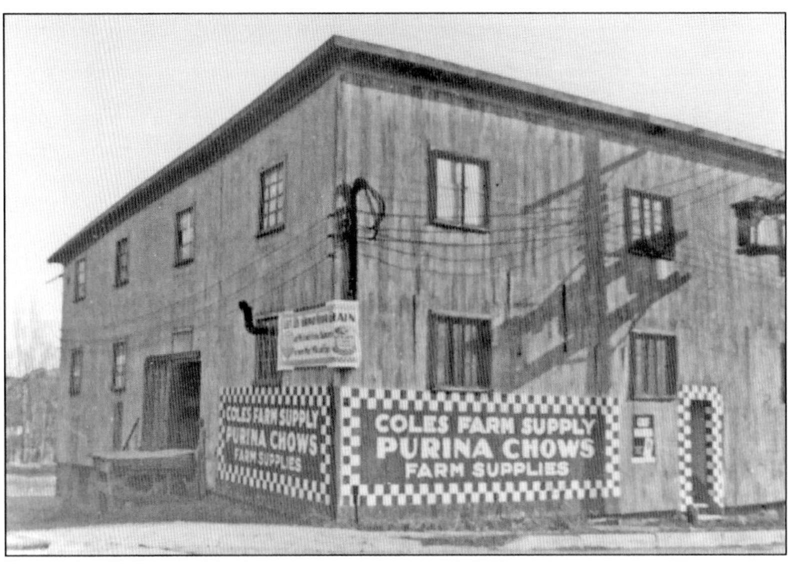

Charles Cole's farm supply business was on the east side of South Center Street in the building that was Fanning's cooperage. This was north of the coal yard, across from the train station. This structure was destroyed by fire, and the foundation of the old cooperage is all that remains.

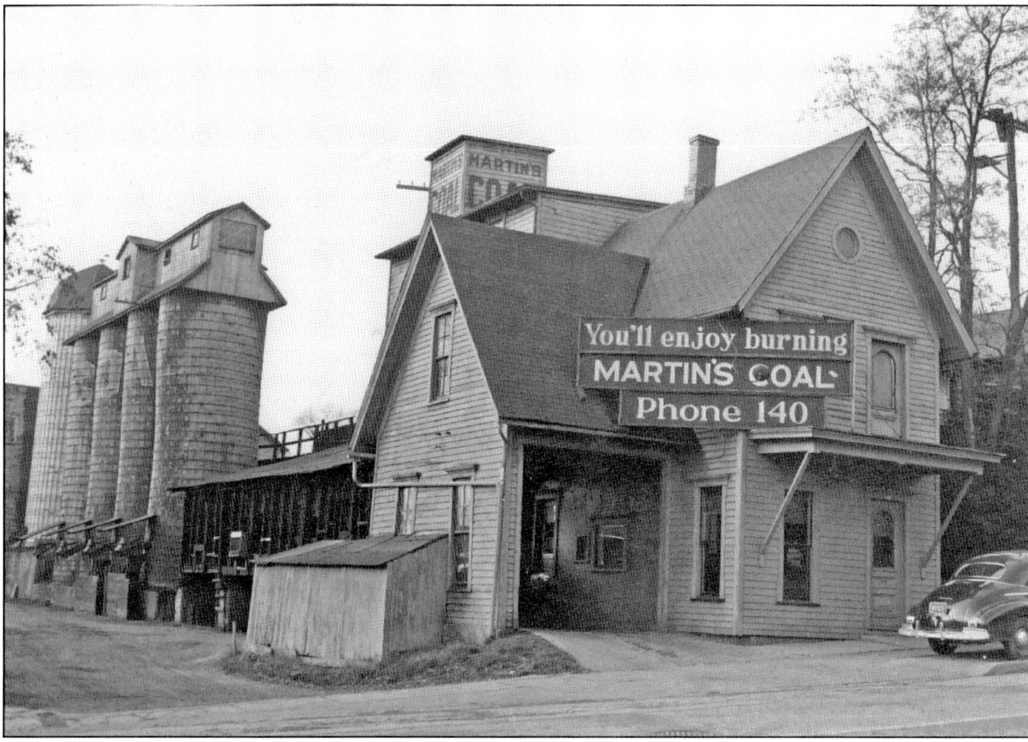

This is Martin's Coal Yard, about 1950, on the west side of South Center Street across from Fanning's. The train station is at the top of the hill on the right. The silos and bins held the coal, while the building held the weigh station and office. After loading coal, a truck would drive through the building to be weighed and to pay. Today this is a private residence.

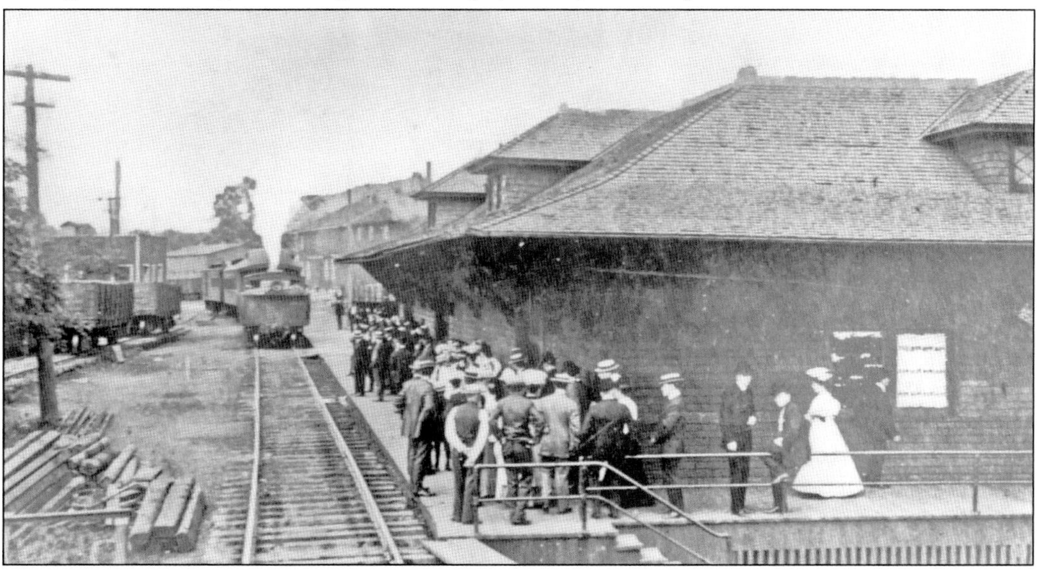

The first train arrived in Perry in 1871, nineteen years after trains had reached Castile. To travel anywhere from Perry, the train went south along the east shore of Silver Lake to Silver Springs where connections were made. This picture shows the new train station on South Center Street built in 1898. The waiting room is facing the tracks.

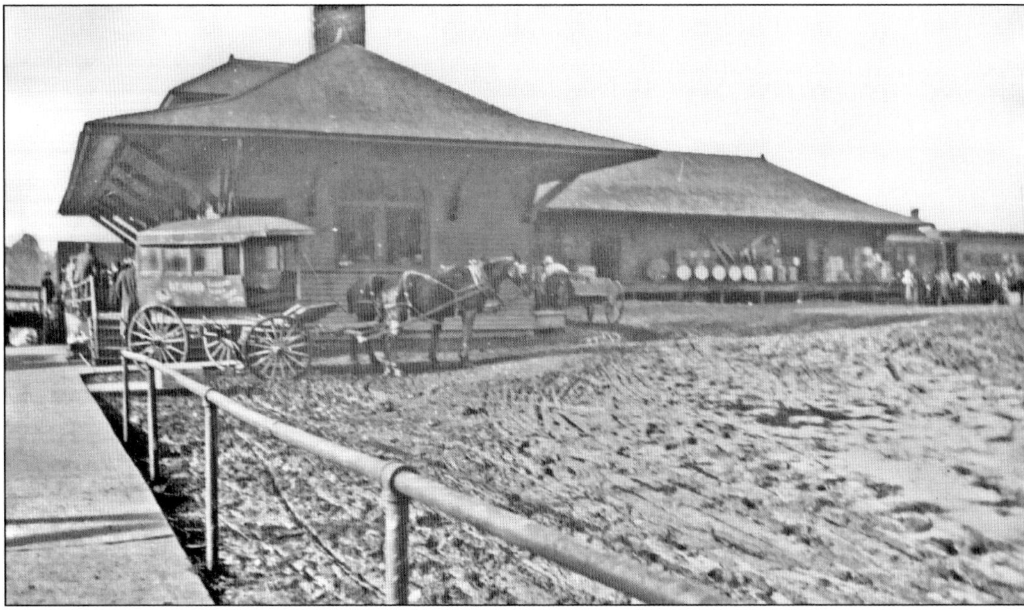

The north side of the train station faced Lake Street with the ticket office to the left at the boardwalk. A horse-drawn bus is waiting to take passengers to town. To the right with the barrels is the freight department. A passenger train can be seen to the right. Perry experienced growth with the arrival of the train, as people and goods could be moved more easily.

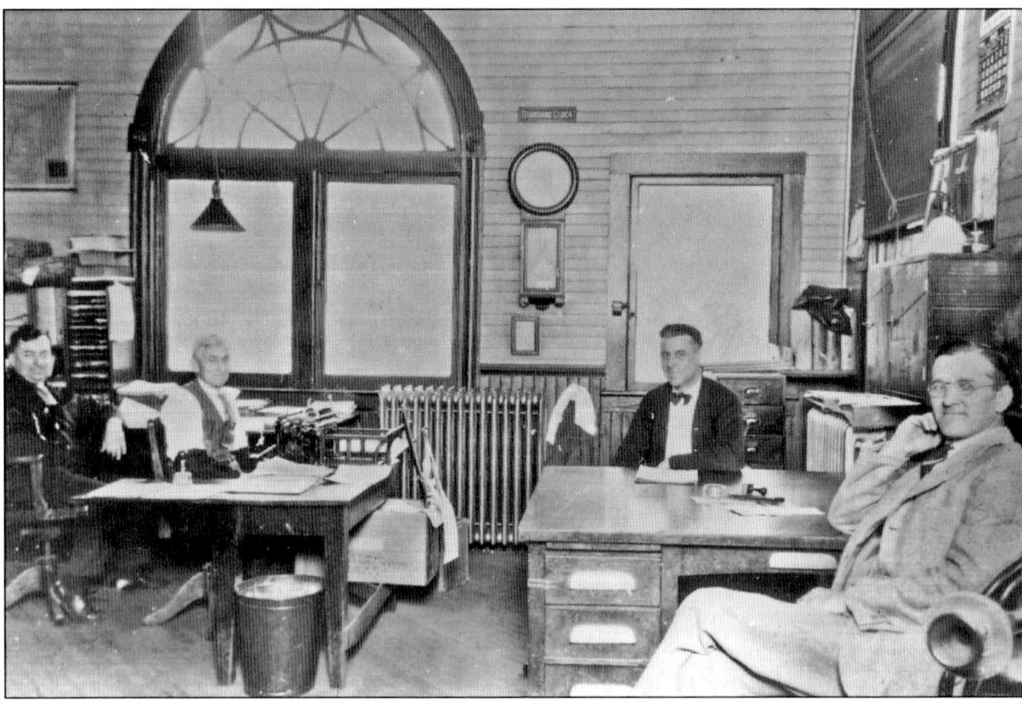

This picture was taken inside the ticket office about 1930. The cashier Walter Nichols is at the left, next is the billing clerk George Gillette, next is the telegrapher Walter Elwell. The fourth man on the right is not identified. The last passenger train from Perry was in 1951; the last freight train was in 1973. The station was used for storage by Sedam's and was later demolished to build a car wash.

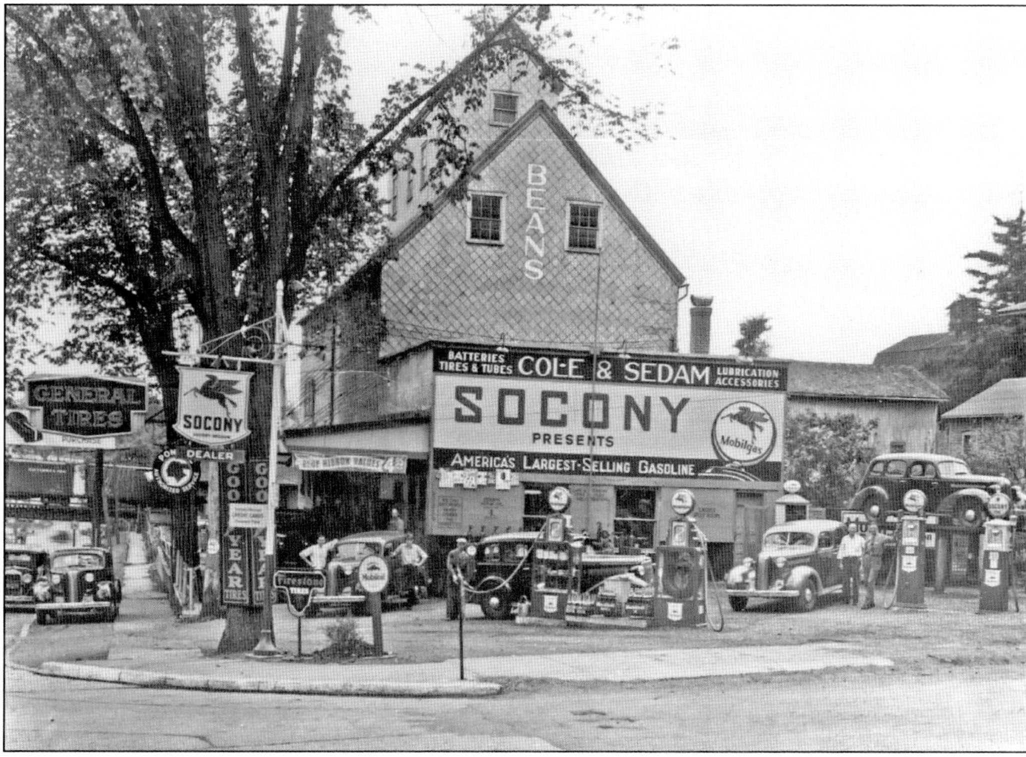

The picture above is the Cole and Sedam business, which operated on the southwest corner of Lake Street and South Center Street from 1926 until 1946. This building was originally constructed in 1908 as a feed mill and grain-processing plant. Gasoline and tires were added in 1926. The lower picture, with a name change to W. Glenn Sedam, was taken in 1976, when the business celebrated 50 years. Today Sedam's is located on Route 246 in the old English Chevrolet dealership. Everything at the old location was demolished, including the train station, to be replaced by an ArrowMart gas station, convenient store, and car wash. (Henry Page Collection.)

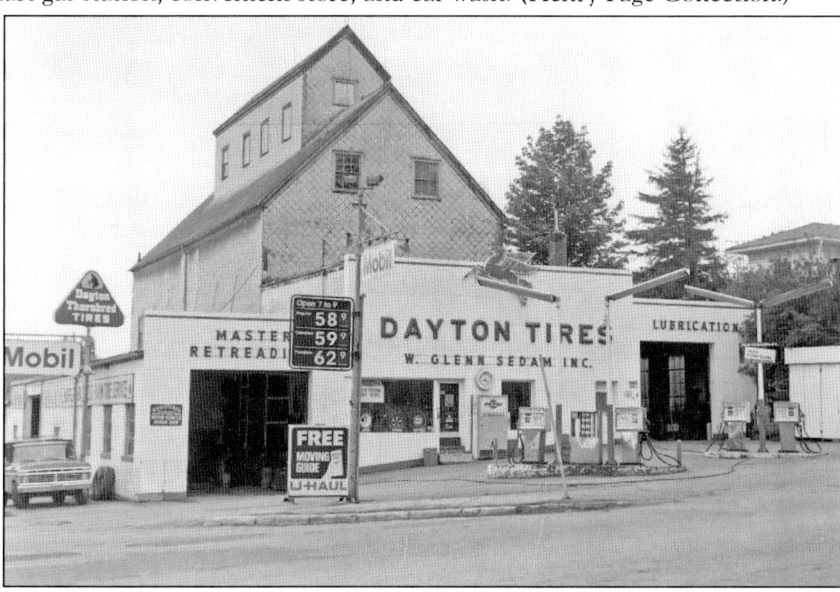

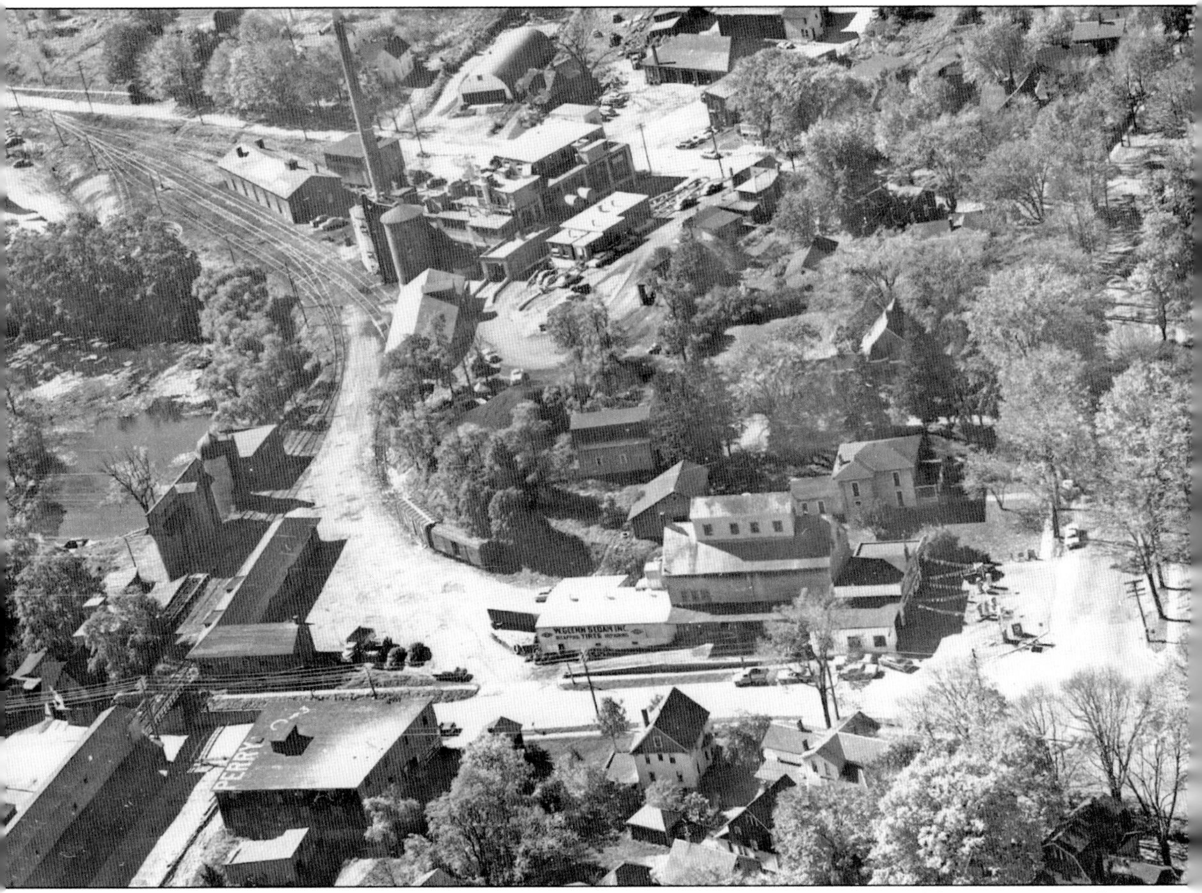

This aerial photograph was taken in 1956 by Henry DeWolf. In the center of the picture, at the corner of Lake and South Center Streets, is W. Glenn Sedam's. The large building at the left with "PERRY" on the roof is Fanning's cooperage and to the left is Fanning's coal yard. Across the street is Henry Martin's coal office, with J. J. Martin's feed mill to the left, now demolished. To the north, or right, is the train station and a rail spur that goes to Sedam's. Following the tracks west from the station, Tomlinson's pond is on the left, and Borden's milk plant with the tall chimney is on the right. (Henry Page Collection.)

The Borden milk plant backed up to Tomlinson's Pond. The Merrell-Soule Company built this plant in 1921 after purchasing land near the railroad and obtaining minor water rights to the outlet. The company turned milk into powder, or KLIM (milk spelled backwards), used mainly for baby food. In 1928, it became part of the Borden Company, which continued with the product and added others.

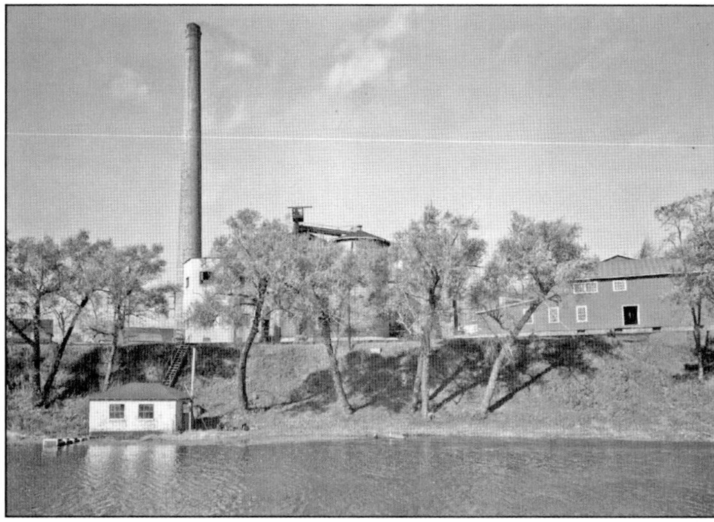

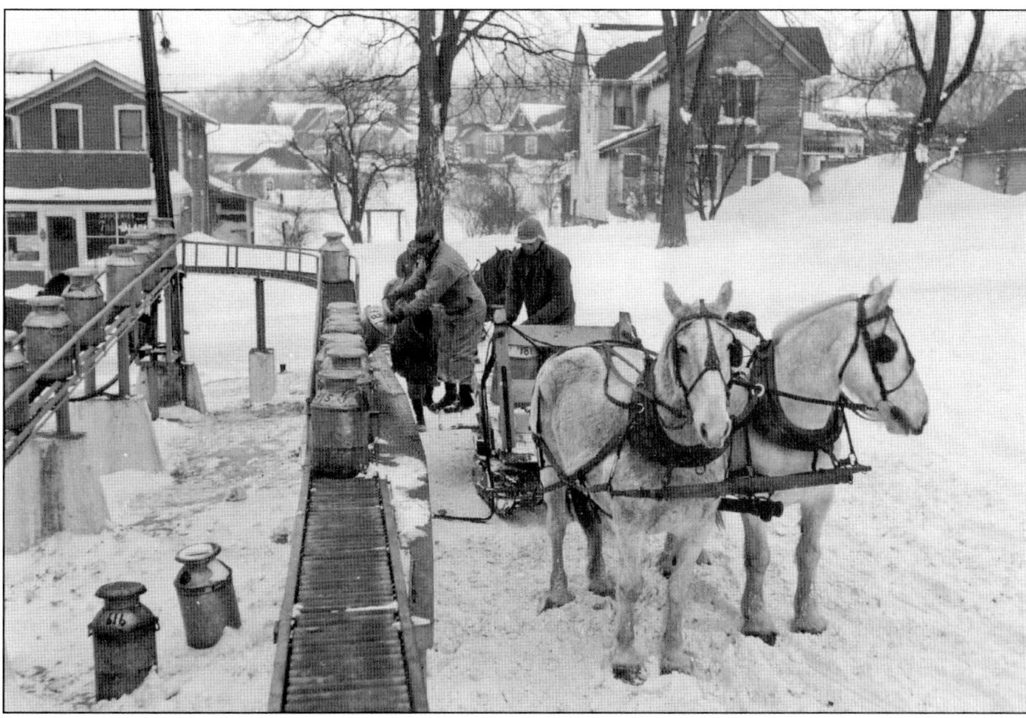

In this picture, milk is being delivered by a horse and sleigh to the Borden milk plant in the winter of 1947. South Federal Street is in the background with a store to the left. After 32 years in Perry, the Borden plant closed in December 1959. In 1964, it became R and S Agricultural Supply, the chimney was torn down in 1972, and today it is Perry Public Storage.

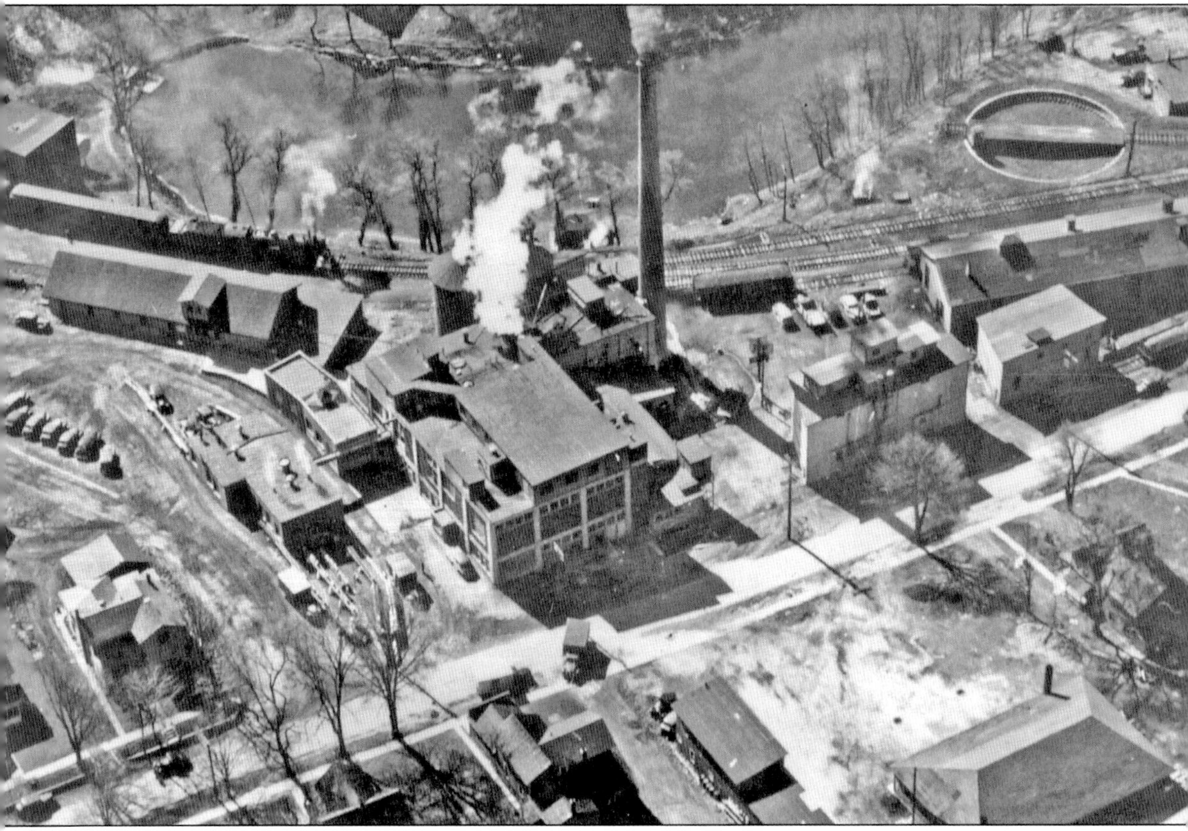

This aerial view was probably taken in 1956, showing the Borden plant in the center of the picture. To the right along South Federal Street are two warehouses of the Hawley Lumber Company. Behind the last one is the rectangular engine house, behind that is the engine turntable. Tomlinson's Pond is in the background, and a train is leaving Perry. At the plant, left of the large building, is the conveyor system that takes the milk cans into the plant. On the west side of South Federal Street, the building with a truck in front is Floyd Smith's store. The Hawley Lumber Company is next, and in the right foreground is the village garage.

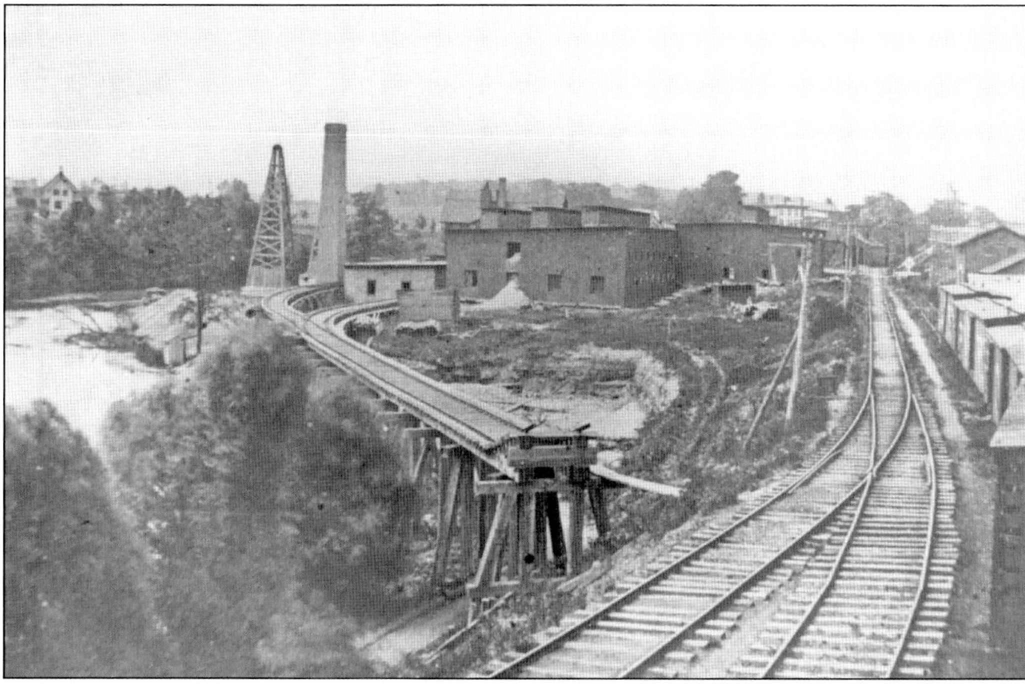

The top picture is looking west towards South Federal Street along the railroad tracks. The Iroquois Salt Company is shown between the railroad tracks and the outlet. This facility was started in 1886 as the Perry Salt Company. The lower picture was taken from across the outlet. The two derricks sit over wells that pump water in and the brine out. Brine vats, used either for storage or evaporating, are to the left of the gambrel roof barn. These vats were on the hill on the west side of South Federal Street with a pipe to carry brine over the street and tracks. The gambrel roof barn is the only building left of this complex, having been used for many purposes over the years.

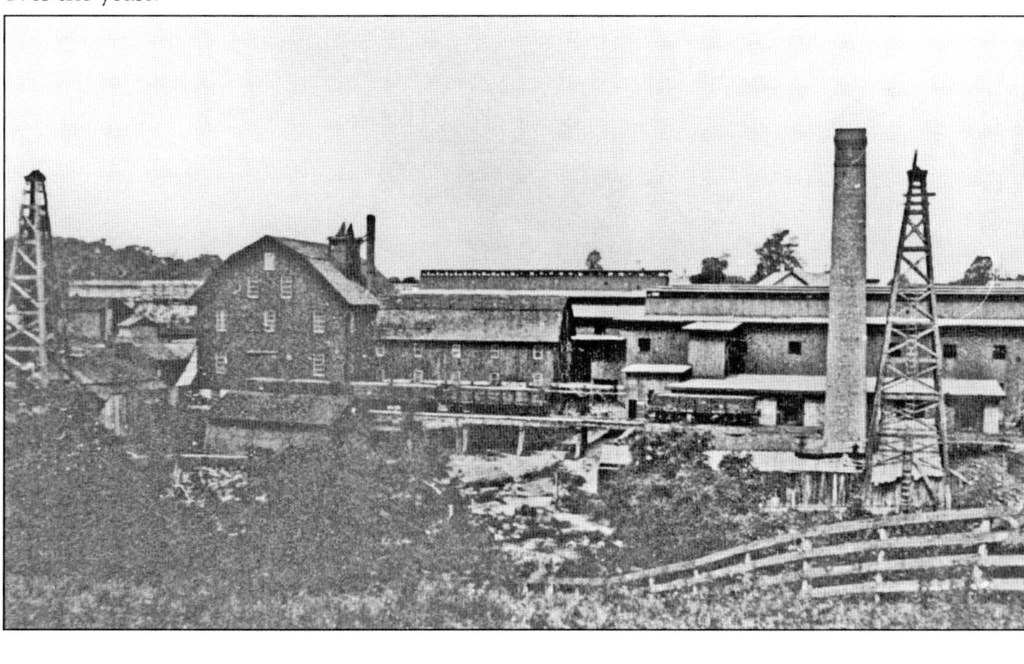

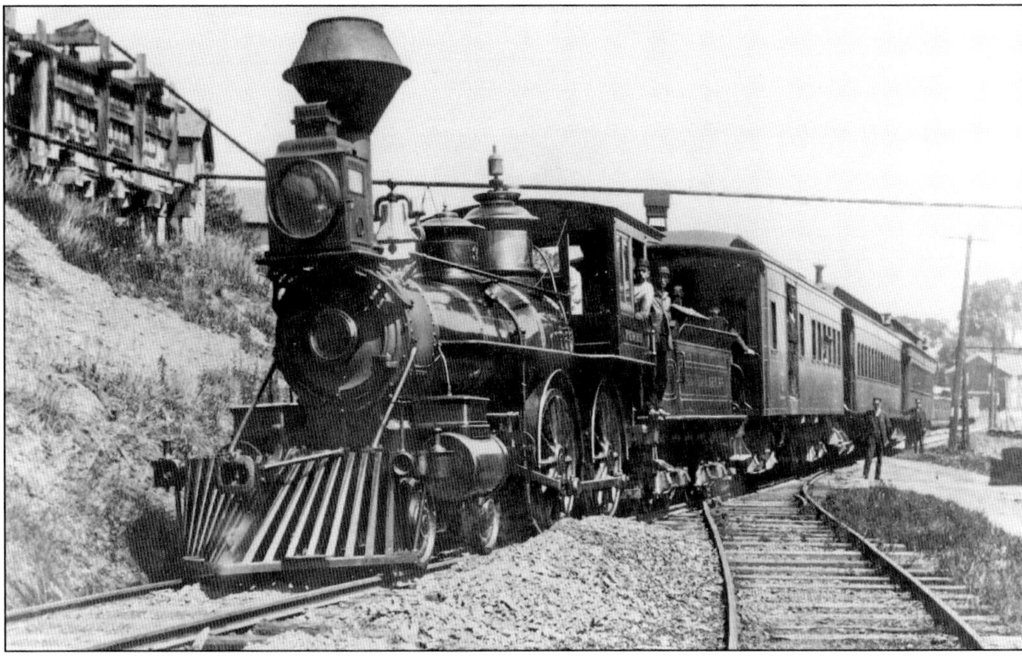

The pipe over the train engine carried brine to the vats, to the left, on the hill west of South Federal Street. This Silver Lake Railway engine is stopped on the Federal Street crossing, facing west, in 1891. The fireman is in the cab, the engineer is in the gangway, the baggage man is in the doorway, then is the conductor, and the trainman. (Henry Page Collection.)

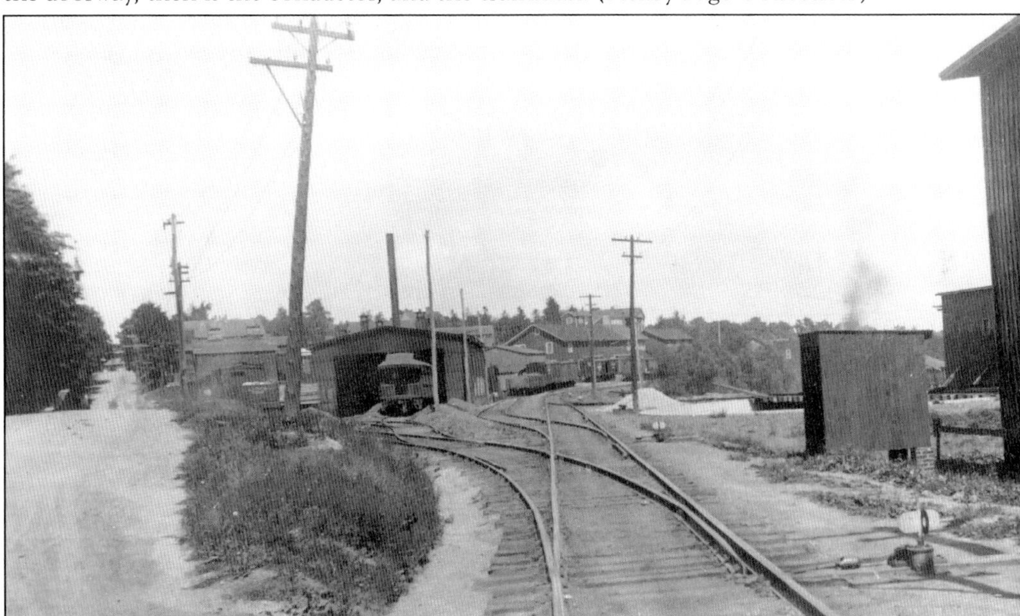

The railroad tracks crossed South Federal Street, left, and continued northwest to the train station. One section of track went left into the train barn and another, behind the small building on the right, led to the turntable. Another siding crossed the street to the south, out of view, and ran between the GLF building and the grain mill, or later the electric company. GLF became Agway, which today is Matson's Farm and Home.

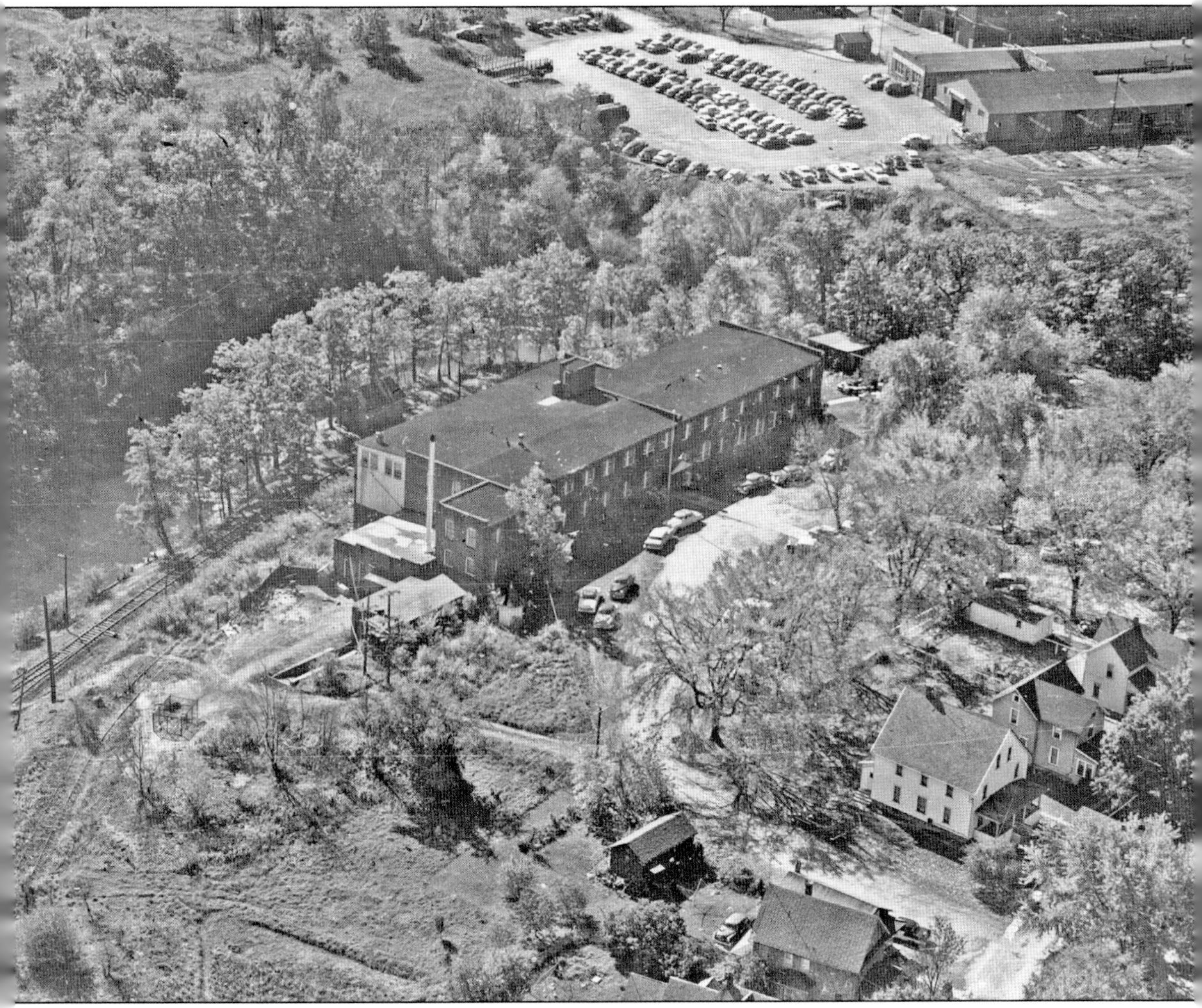

In 1956, Henry DeWolf took this aerial photograph of the area west of South Federal Street. Tempest Street is in the lower right corner. At this time, Duracraft Knitwear was in the Tempest Knitting Company building, the large structure in the center, back from Tempest Street. To the left of the picture is the Silver Lake Outlet with railroad tracks next to it, and an unseen siding to the knitting company. The tracks crossed the outlet and continued on the south side of the outlet past the Kaustine Furnace and Tank Company, in the upper right. A railroad siding, starting near Walker Road, ran to the west side of the Kaustine buildings, out of view. (Henry Page Collection.)

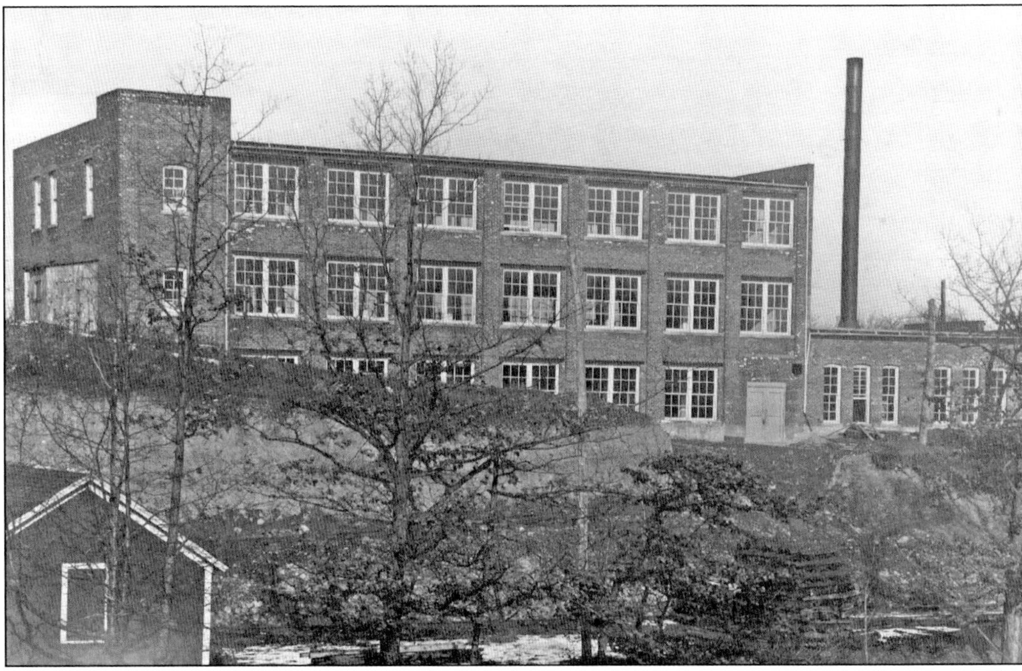

Tempest Knitting Mills Company was founded in 1907 by D. M. Tempest, who had worked at the Perry Knitting Mill. It became Wyckoff Knitting Company in 1916, Rayotex in 1926, and in 1935, Champion moved its division of Duracraft Knitwear here. This is the back of the building facing south on the outlet. (Henry Page Collection.)

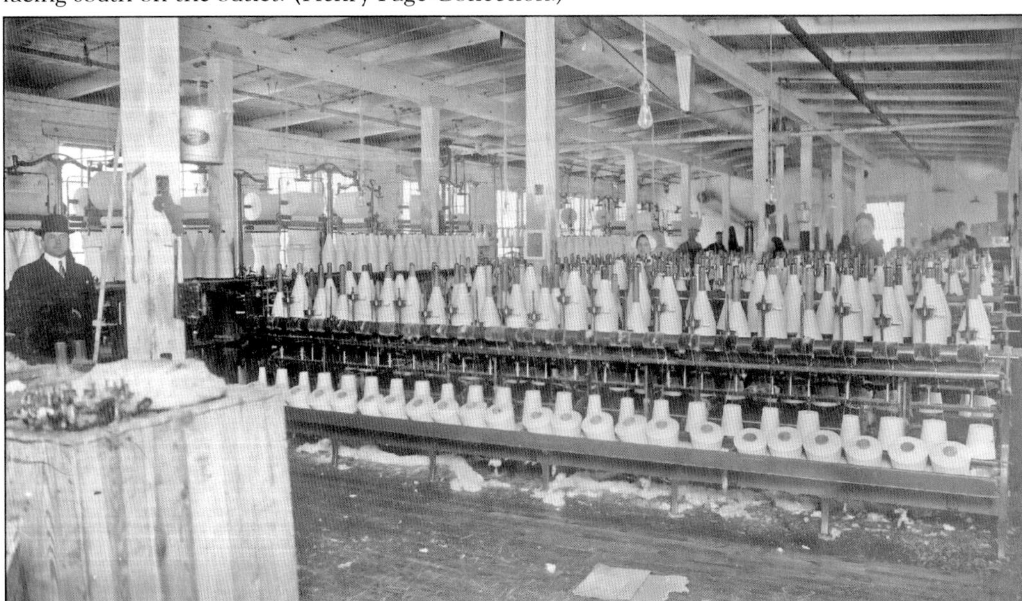

The first product made at the Tempest Knitting Mills was cotton underwear. The company bought the cotton yarn and knitted its own cloth to make the finished product. Wyckoff Knitting continued this, but in 1926, formed Rayotex to produce ladies rayon underwear. In 1934, Perry Knitting Company bought the building, keeping Rayotex as a tenant and using the rest for storage. (Henry Page Collection.)

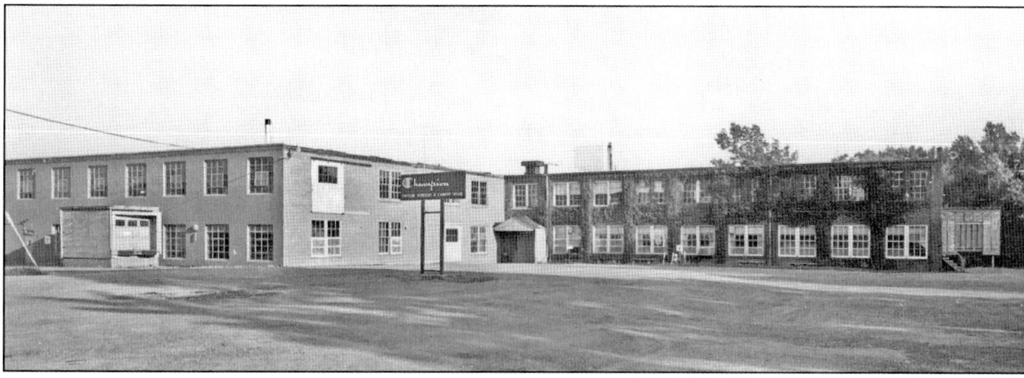

Champion Knitwear of Rochester was a customer of the Perry Knitting Mill, buying sports and leisure wear. In 1935, it was decided to move Duracraft Knitwear, the silk screen-printing division of Champion, to the Tempest Street plant in Perry. In 1962, Champion purchased this property, pictured above. In the lower picture is the Champion factory site on North Main Street, where a warehouse was first constructed in 1958. There were expansions in the 1960s, and at the time of this picture in 1975, the large warehouse on the left had been completed. After downsizing in 1998, Champion closed completely in 2001. Today, part of the plant is used by American Classic Outfitters to make custom sportswear. (Henry Page Collection.)

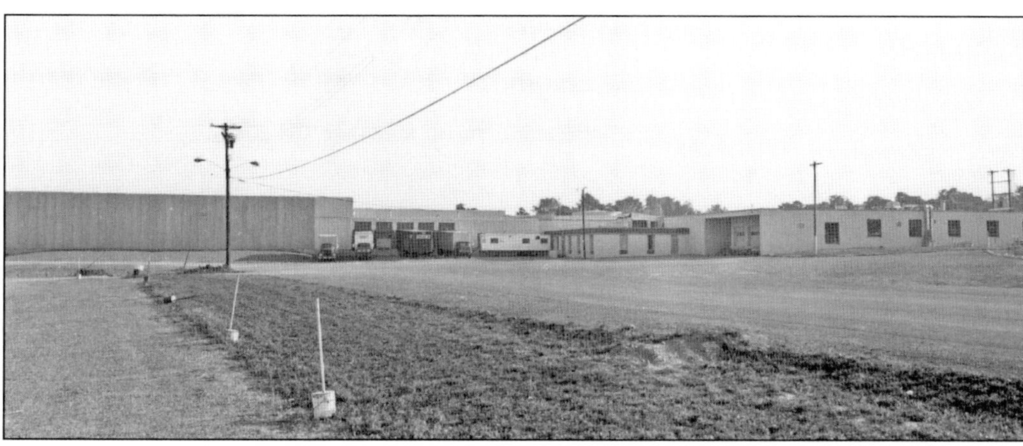

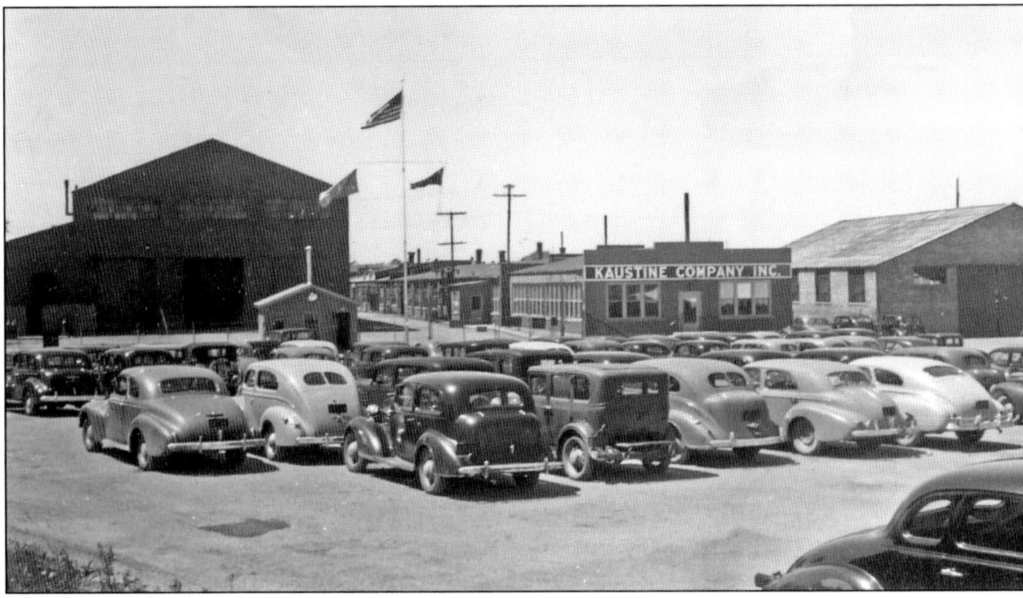

The Kaustine Company, manufacturer of chemical toilet systems, moved to a new building south of the outlet on Washington Boulevard in 1915. It expanded many times, manufacturing all kinds of metal tanks. During World War II, most of the production was for war materials. In June 1945, the company received the Army Navy "E" award for outstanding production. In the top photograph, taken in 1945, the "E" flag is being flown in front of the plant. The bottom picture of the Kaustine Furnace and Tank Corporation is from 1960. The name was changed after the war because of the demand for furnaces in new construction. The company was sold in the late 1970s, and today the buildings are empty.

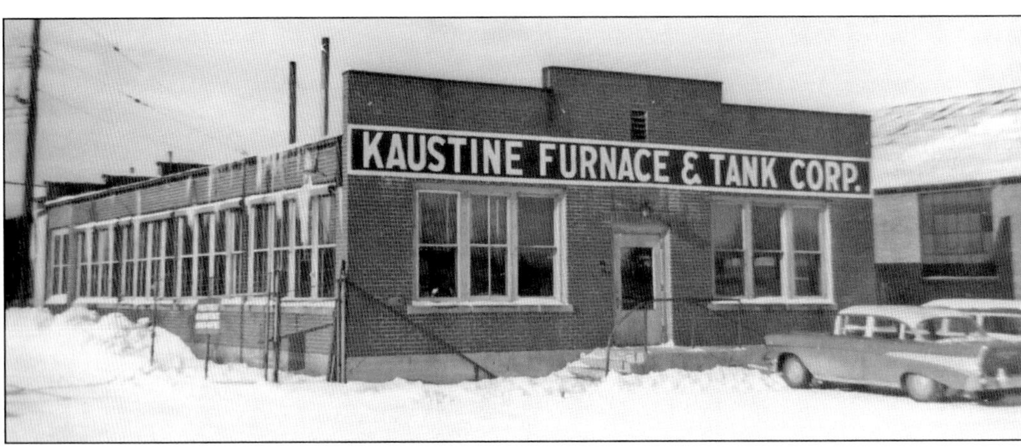

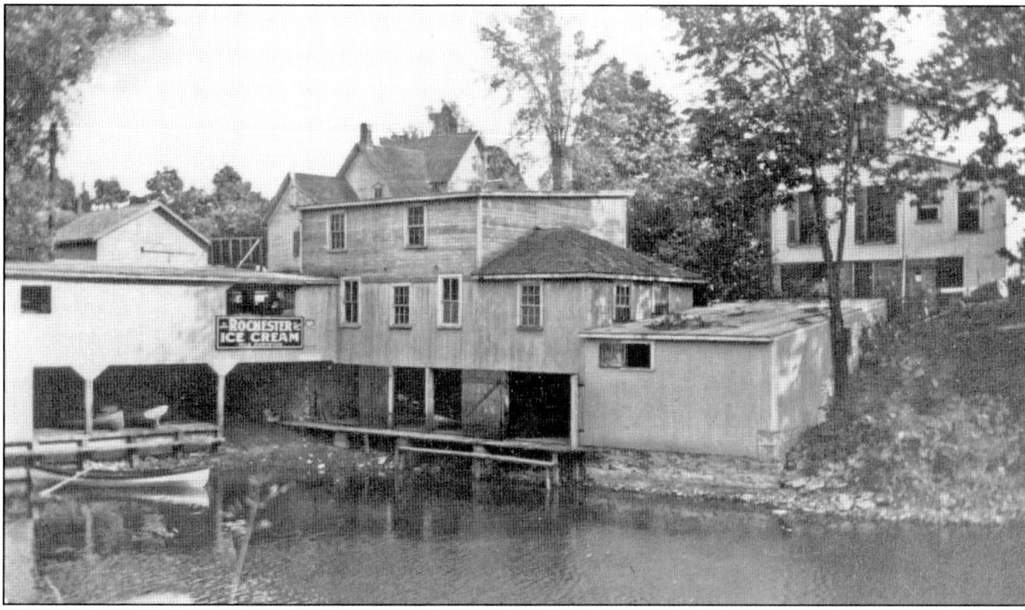

The Whipple boat livery was located on the south side of the Silver Lake Outlet at the South Federal Street dam. Boats, bait, and ice cream were available to purchase. Rental boats could be used for fishing or for a boat ride to the lake. Lake residents boated on the outlet to the livery, docked the boat, and walked downtown. This livery was gone by 1948. (Henry Page Collection.)

The Silver Lake Railway became a division of the Buffalo, Rochester, and Pittsburg Railway in 1910. The Baltimore and Ohio Railroad abandoned the railroad in 1974. These tracks are crossing the outlet from west to east, heading to the village. The outlet runs under the bridge with room for boats to navigate to and from the lake. Today this is a public trail.

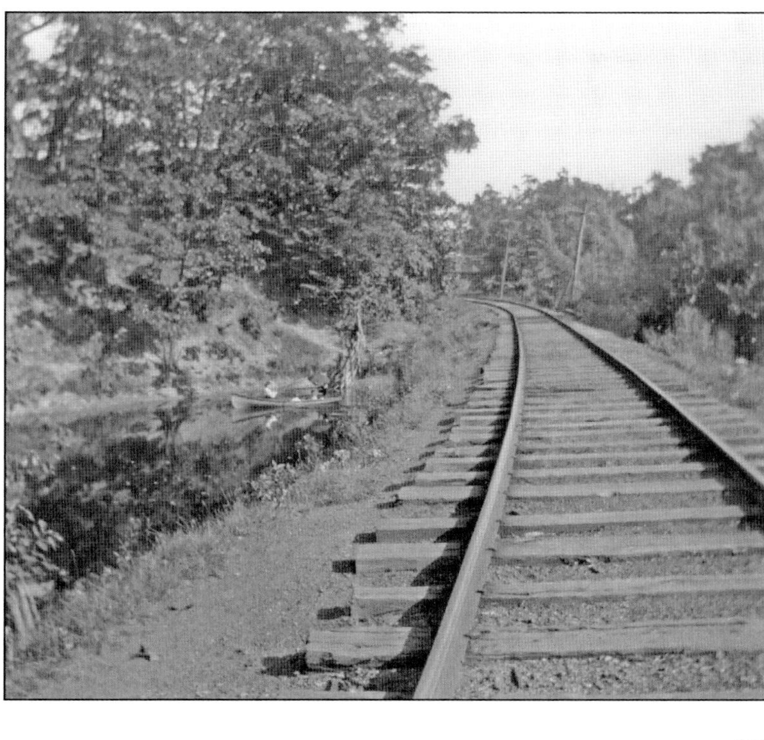

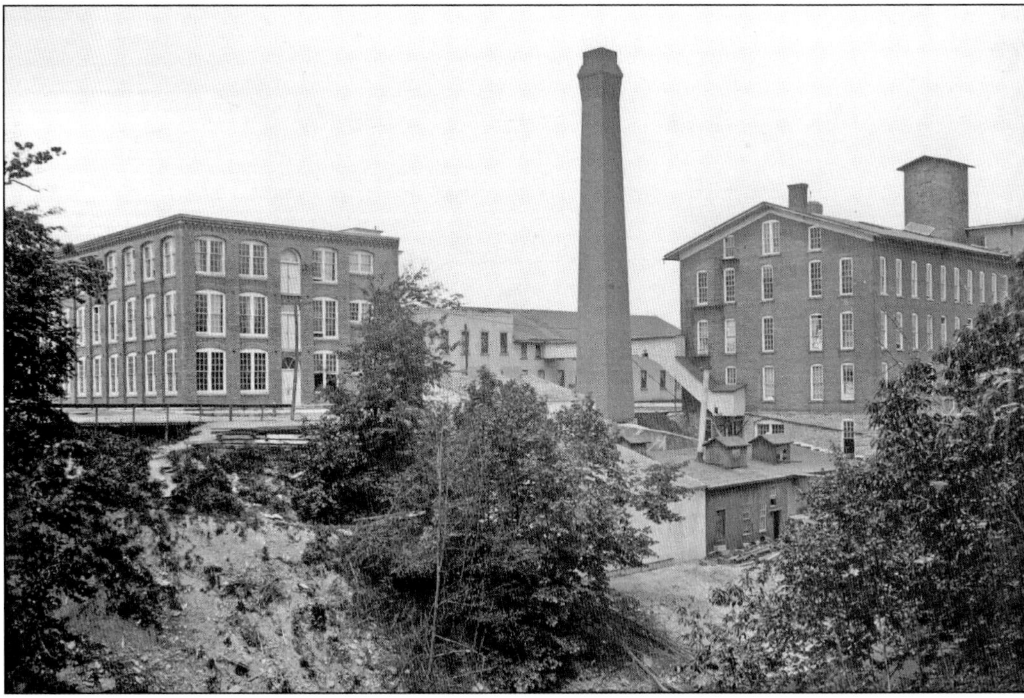

The Perry Knitting Company was organized in 1881 by a group of local residents headed by Milo H. Olin who later became the president. In 1891, when George M. Traber Sr. came to manage the business, there were 60 employees. He became president in 1916, and at the time of his death in 1933, there were 1,110 people employed. Mill No. 1, on the right, was built on the outlet side of Water Street in 1882. In the bottom picture the Walnut Street Bridge, built in 1902, is across the outlet. At the end of the bridge is the box factory, probably enlarged in 1909 to become mill No. 5. To the right is the energy plant with the chimney spewing smoke. (Above, Henry Page Collection.)

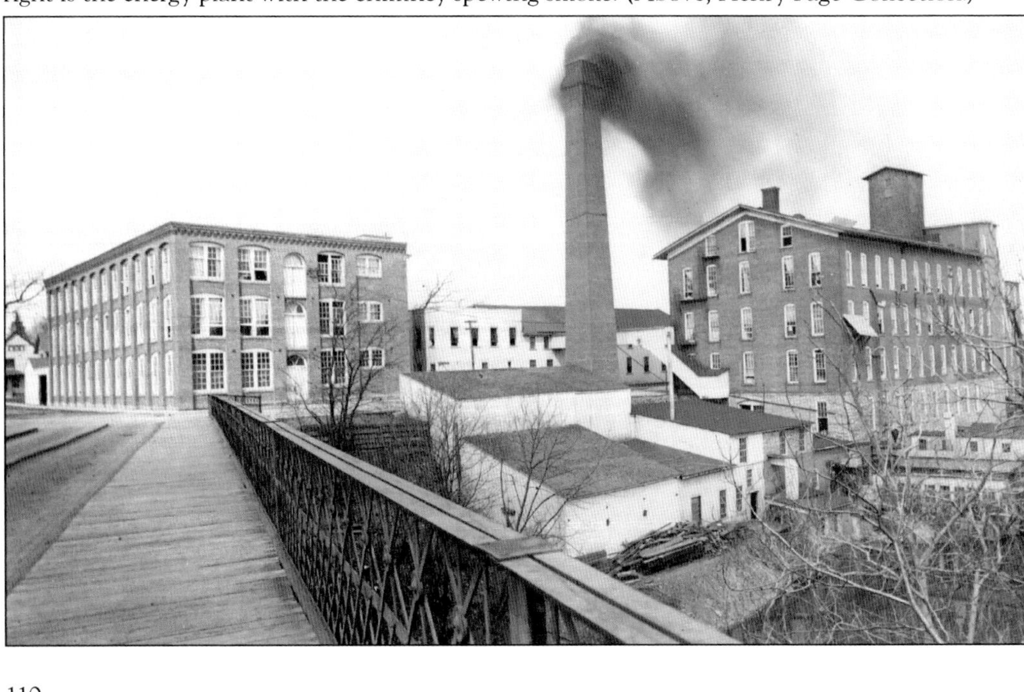

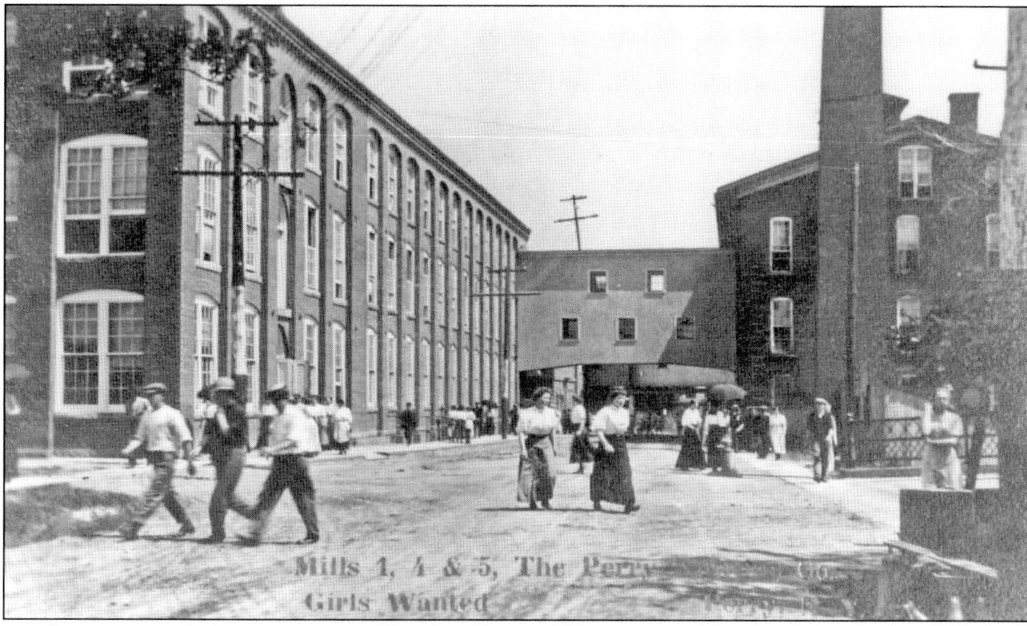

"Mills 1, 4 and 5, The Perry Knitting Mill, Perry, N.Y. Girls Wanted. Photo by Kenney," was the caption of a recruiting postcard or poster for workers. The Walnut Street Bridge is on the right with the chimney next to it and mill No. 1 behind. The covered walkway goes over Water Street to mill No. 5. Mill No. 4 begins at the corner of Water and Elm Streets at the left.

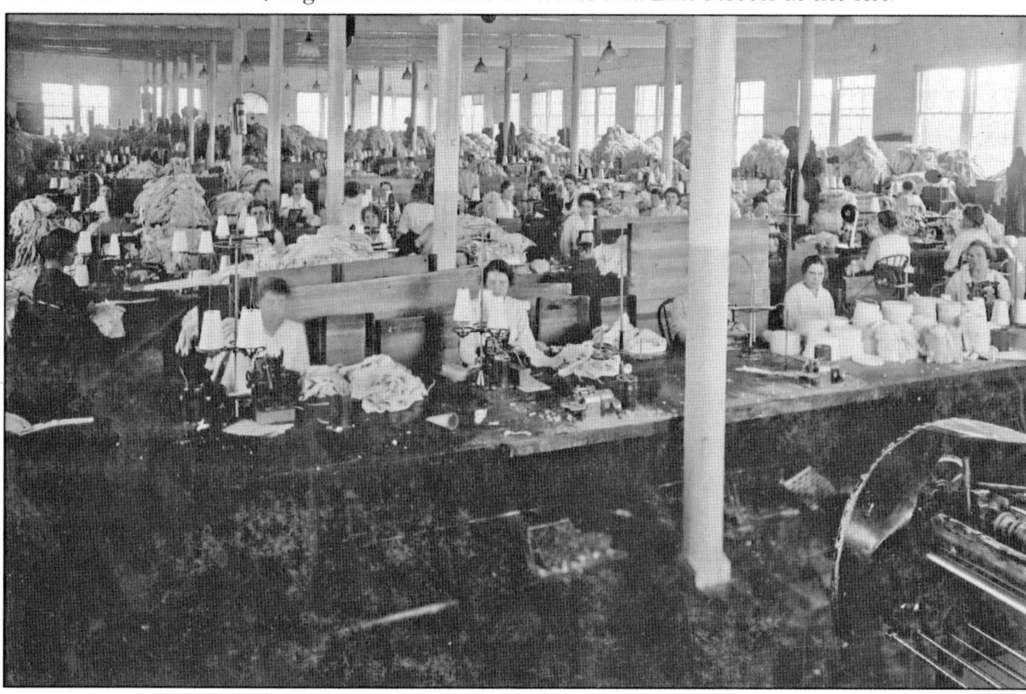

The Perry Knitting Mill used baled cotton to spin into cotton thread to knit into cloth. Pieces were cut from the cloth to be sewn together to make a garment. The plant made a variety of light and heavyweight underwear in two pieces and union suits. The women in this picture appear to be in the sewing factory.

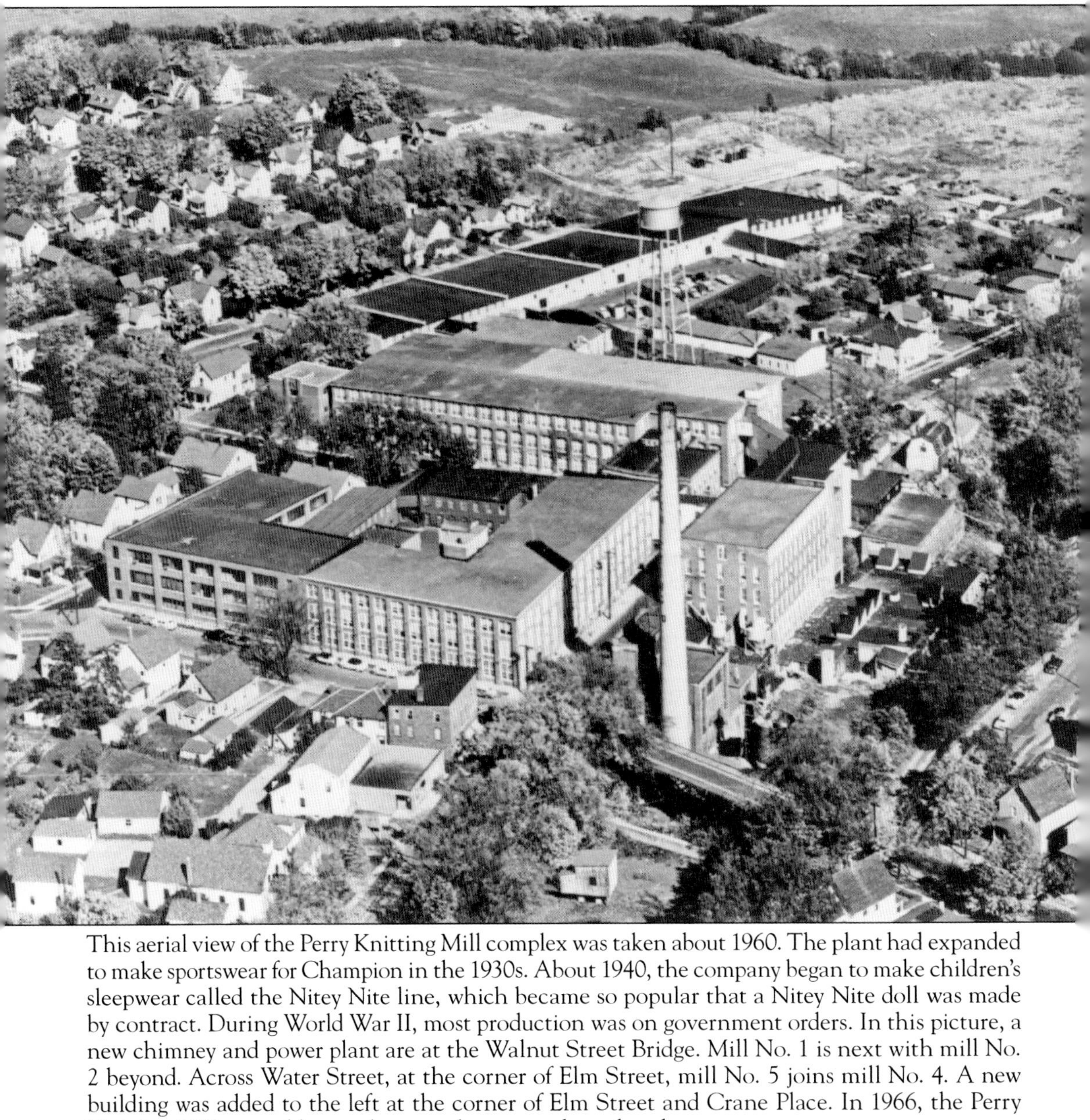

This aerial view of the Perry Knitting Mill complex was taken about 1960. The plant had expanded to make sportswear for Champion in the 1930s. About 1940, the company began to make children's sleepwear called the Nitey Nite line, which became so popular that a Nitey Nite doll was made by contract. During World War II, most production was on government orders. In this picture, a new chimney and power plant are at the Walnut Street Bridge. Mill No. 1 is next with mill No. 2 beyond. Across Water Street, at the corner of Elm Street, mill No. 5 joins mill No. 4. A new building was added to the left at the corner of Elm Street and Crane Place. In 1966, the Perry Knitting Mill was sold, stayed open a few years, then closed.

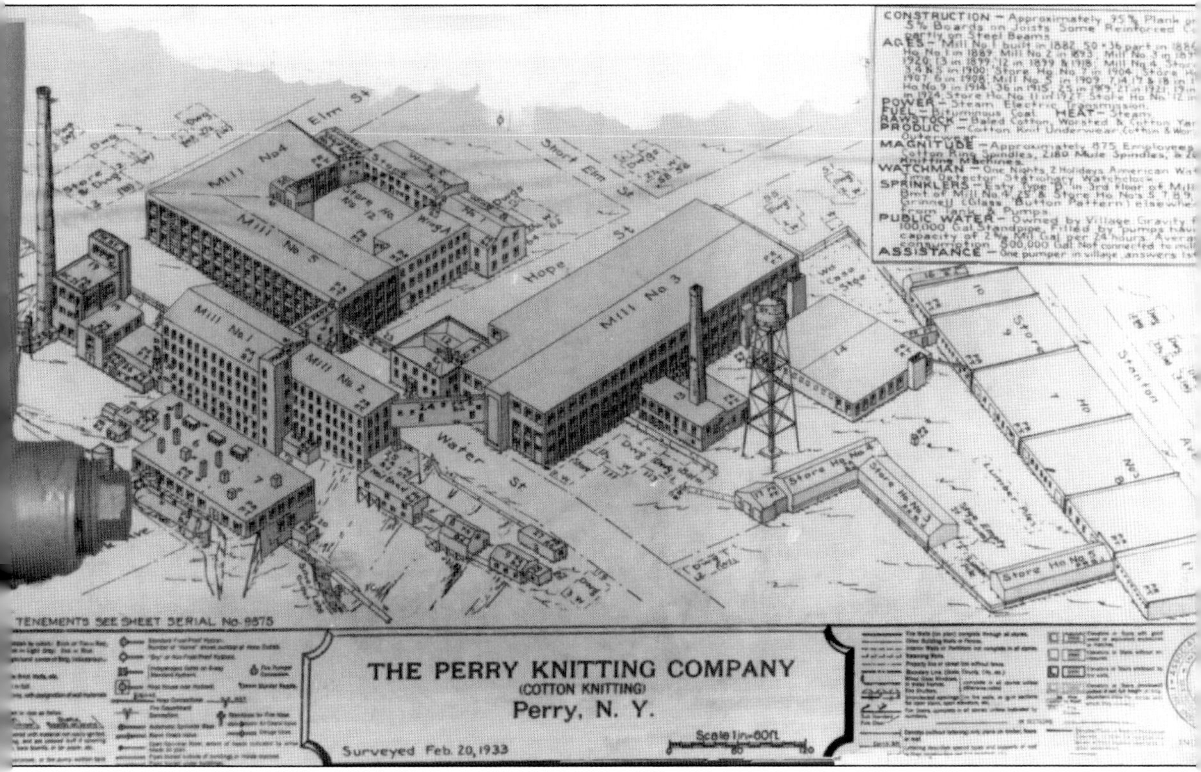

This is a survey drawing made in 1933 of all the mills of the Perry Knitting Company at that time, with labels to help identify the buildings in the previous picture. The Walnut Street Bridge is at the left with the power plant and chimney next to it. Across Water Street at Elm Street are mills four (1900) and five (1909). The new building pictured in the aerial view, at Elm Street and Crane Place (Short Elm) was not built at this time. Mill No. 2 was built in 1893, mill No. 3 in 1899, 1905, and 1920. Next to this mill on Water Street is a store with dwellings and a barn behind. Across Elm Street from mill No. 4 is another store and more dwellings. Today only the newer building at Elm Street and Crane Place is still standing.

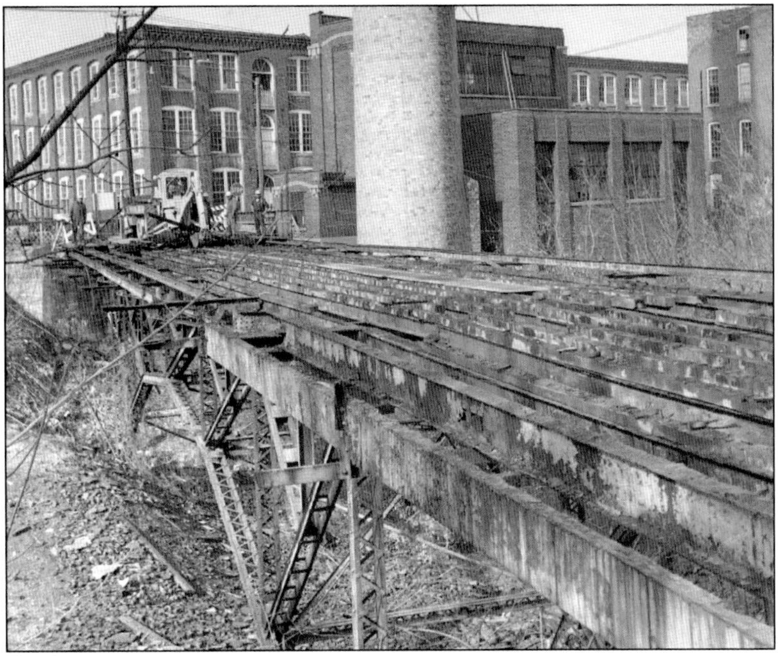

The Walnut Street Bridge built in 1902 is being removed in this picture in 1973, to be replaced with a new bridge. The knitting mill chimney and powerhouse were also demolished that year by the third buyer of the property. All the buildings between Water Street and the outlet were also torn down. Time and fires have destroyed the rest. Only one building is left. (Henry Page Collection.)

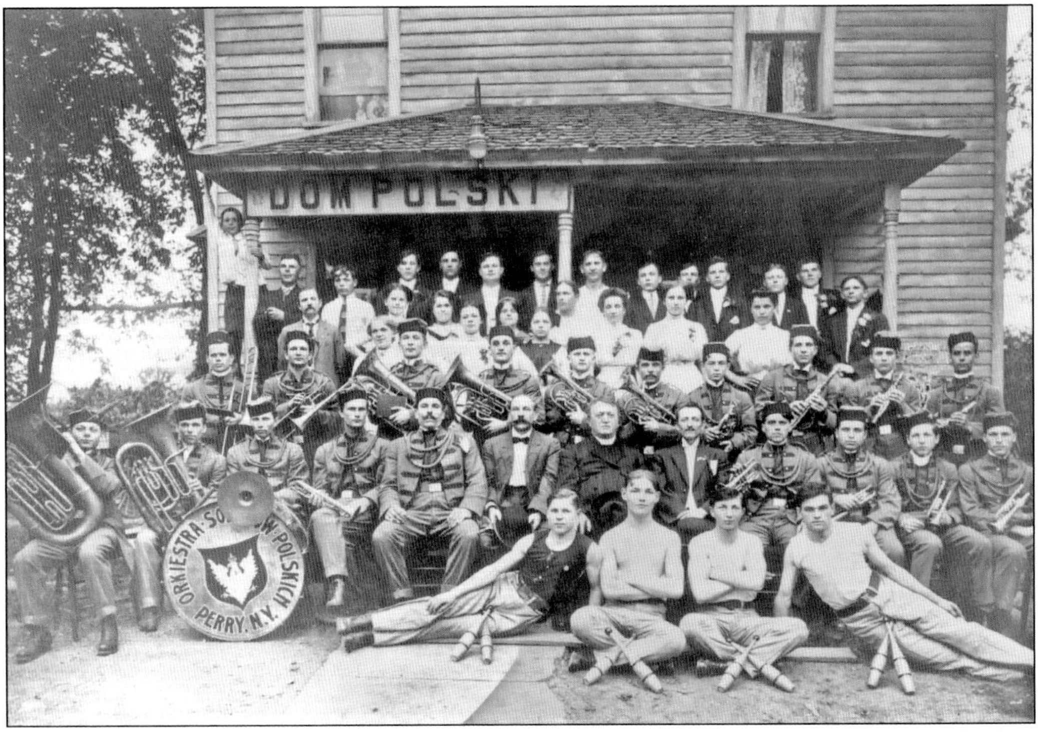

Polish immigrants came to Perry to work in the mills and settled on Water Street. This is the first Dom Polski social club, which burned in 1913. The Polish Falcon band is pictured, along with a singing group. A priest is in the center, and an athletic group is in front with clubs. The present Dom Polski hall was built in 1929.

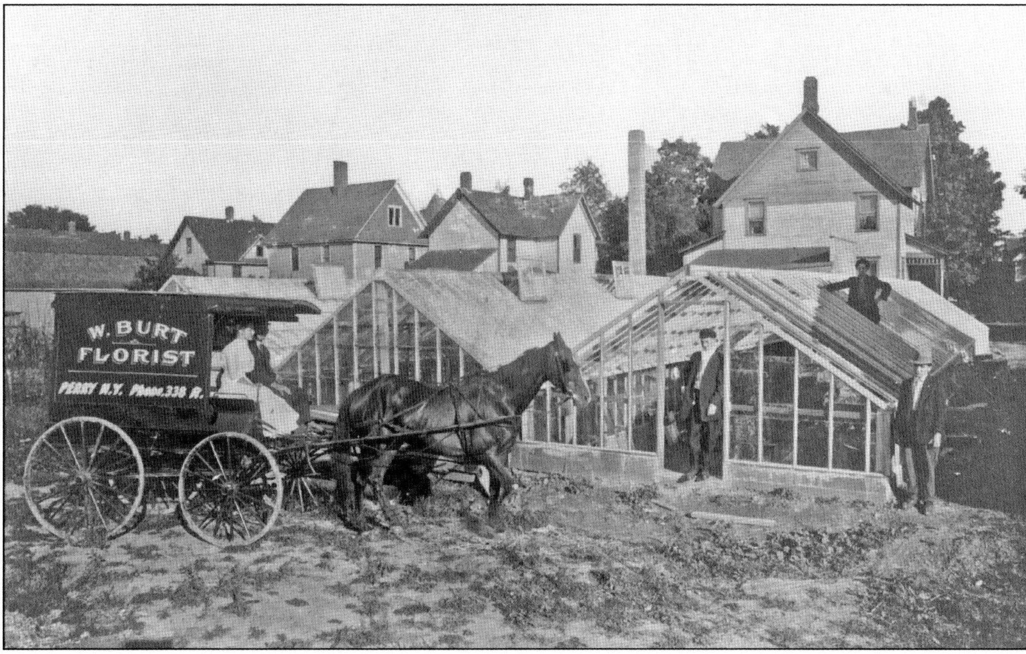

The greenhouses for the W. Burt Florist business were behind his home on the west side of North Main Street, almost across from Genesee Street. A flower shop was downtown. Burt's Lumber was founded by his son in 1953, with the first building on the west side of South Federal Street near Washington Boulevard. In 1973, a new building was constructed across Federal Street, still serving customers today.

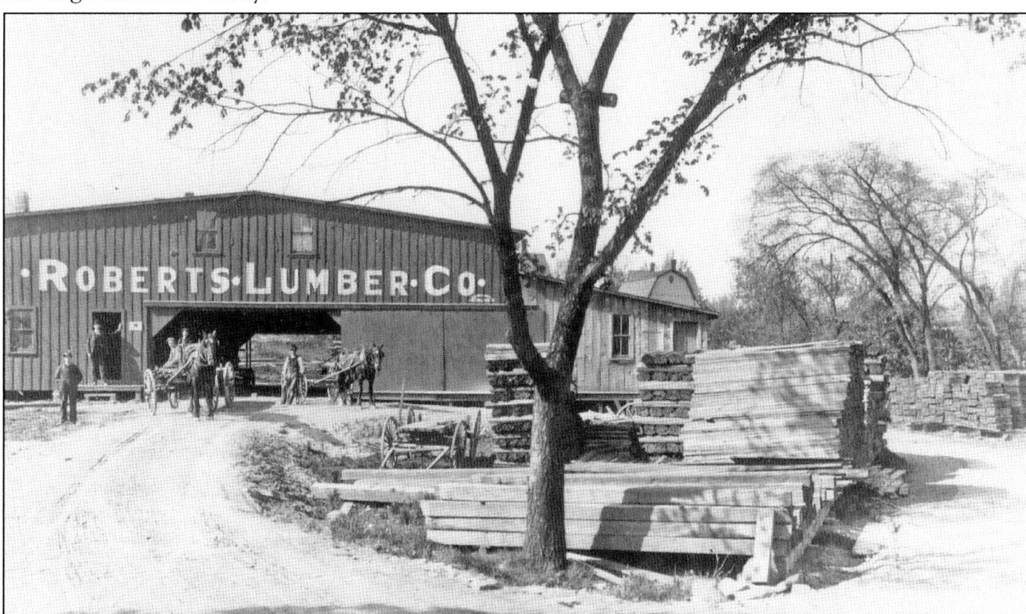

Roberts Lumber Company was formed in 1908 by W. J. Roberts. The lumberyard was constructed on the south side of Gardeau Street back along the east bank of the Silver Lake Outlet. All the machinery in these buildings was operated with electricity. Today this is a storage facility, which can be seen from the back of the present post office.

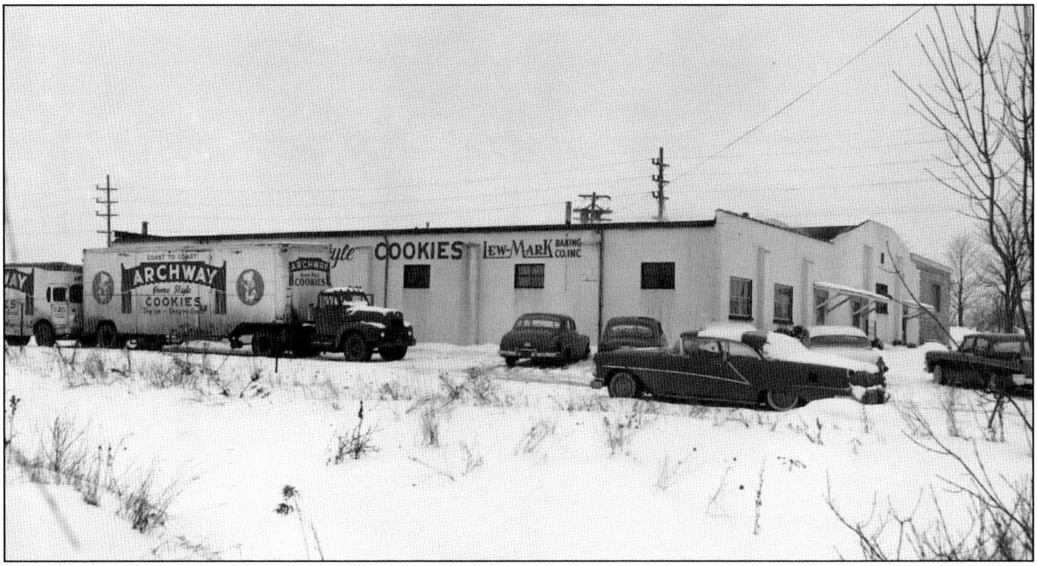

This building on Washington Boulevard and South Federal Street was constructed in 1953 as the first home of Lew-Mark Baking Company, the makers of Archway home-style cookies. After several additions, a new facility was built in 1967 on Lincoln Avenue, across South Main Street from Needham Street. Today Creative Food Ingredients continues to make cookies.

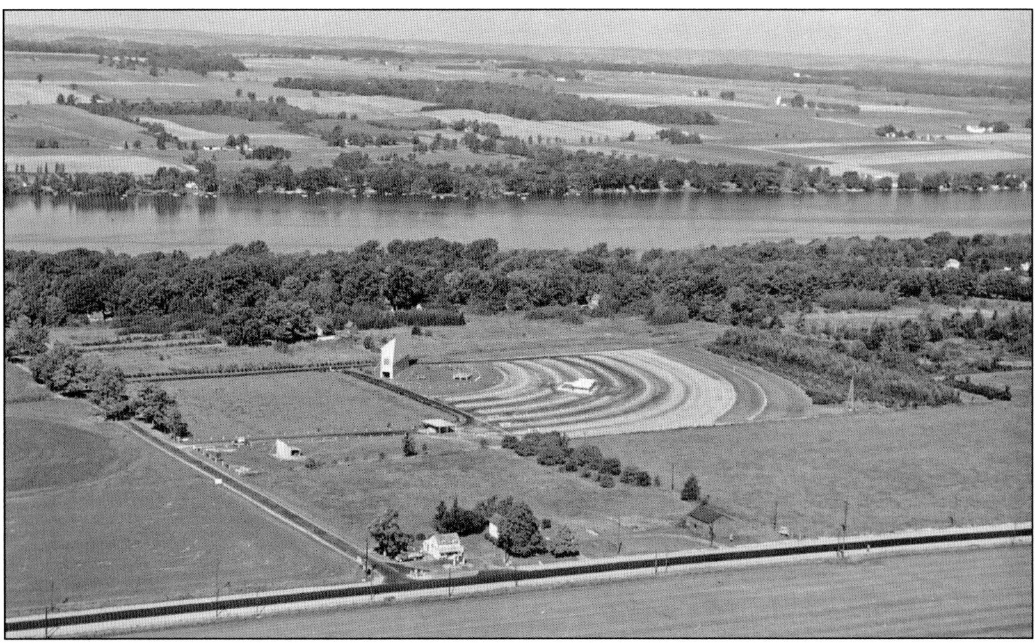

This aerial shot shows Harry Martin's drive-in theater in the early 1950s. It is south of the village of Perry in the town of Castile, at the intersection of Route 39 and Camp Road. Silver Lake is in the background. Today it is the Charcoal Corral with a restaurant and pizza parlor, a miniature golf course, and a two-screen drive-in theater.

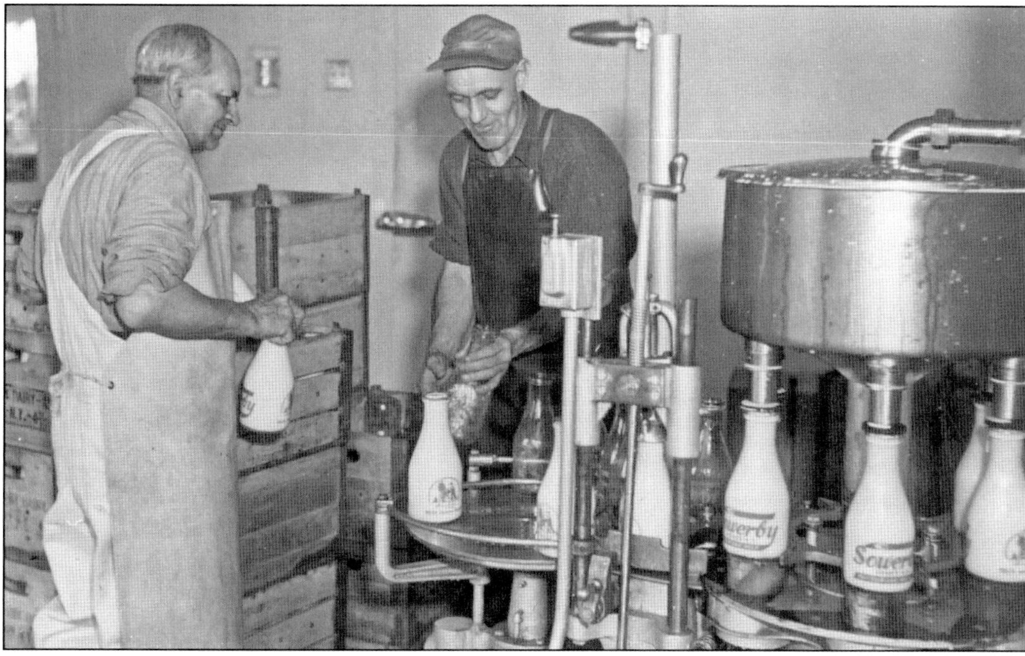

This is at the milk processing plant of Sowerby Dairy on the west side of North Center Street. Milk, ice cream, and other dairy products were sold in the front of the building. A drive-through was also available. This was next to the Perry Service Center, which is today McClurg's Chrysler dealership. Today the Sowerby building is John and Sarah's restaurant.

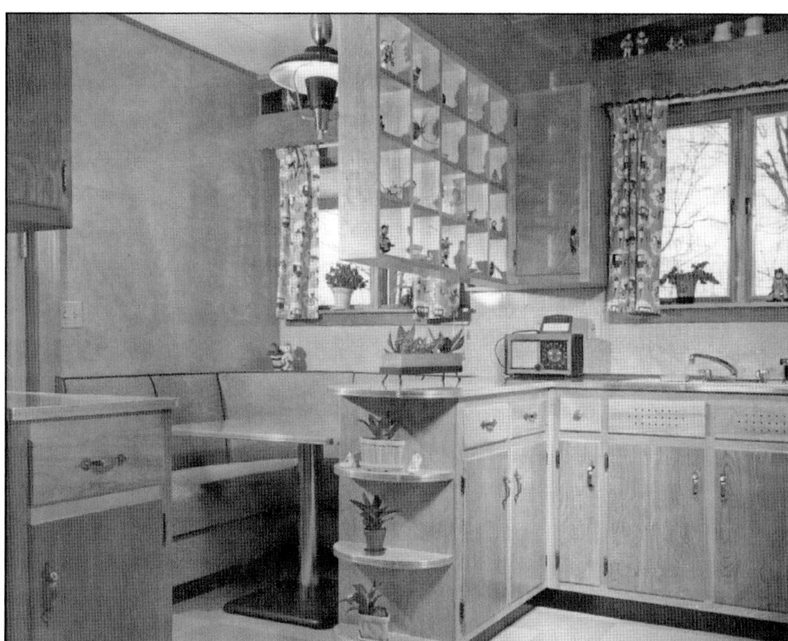

The building north of the Sowerby Dairy site was constructed in 1947 as the Towers cabinet shop. This picture is a sample of their work. They also did work for Robeson, who later acquired the structure for their Shur-Wood plant. Today J. N. White Design is in the building after buying it in 1977.

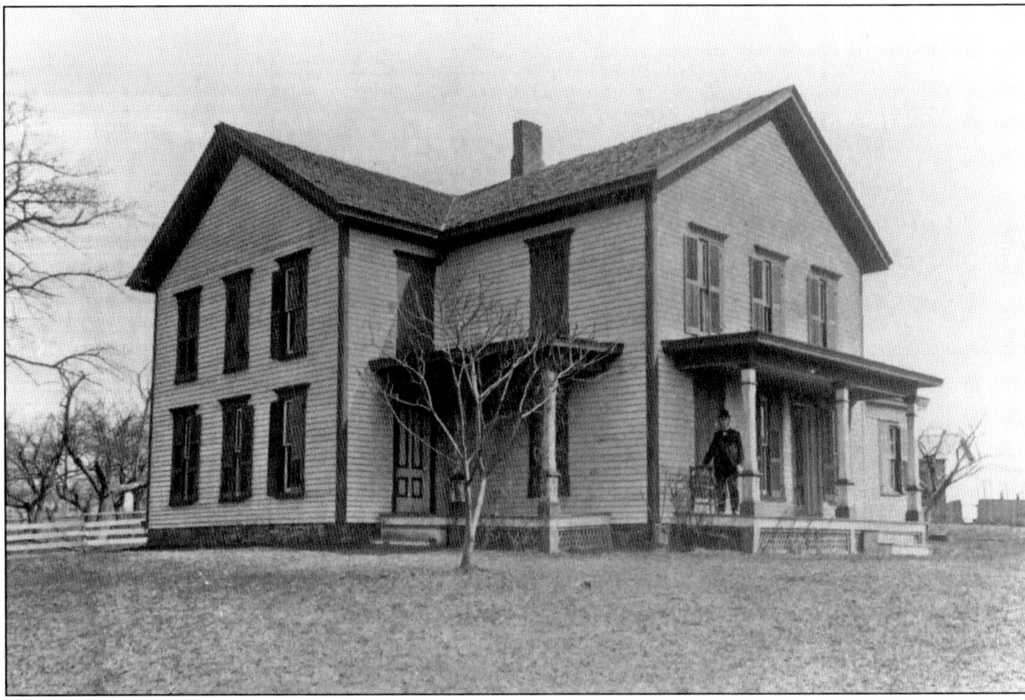

This is the Carl Parker homestead on the east side of North Center Street, or Route 246, in 1897. This farm was demolished and today is the site of the present Parker Lane with many new businesses. University Eye Specialists is on the corner. At the roundabout are McClurg's Chevy, the Pioneer Credit building, and Wyoming County Power Sports.

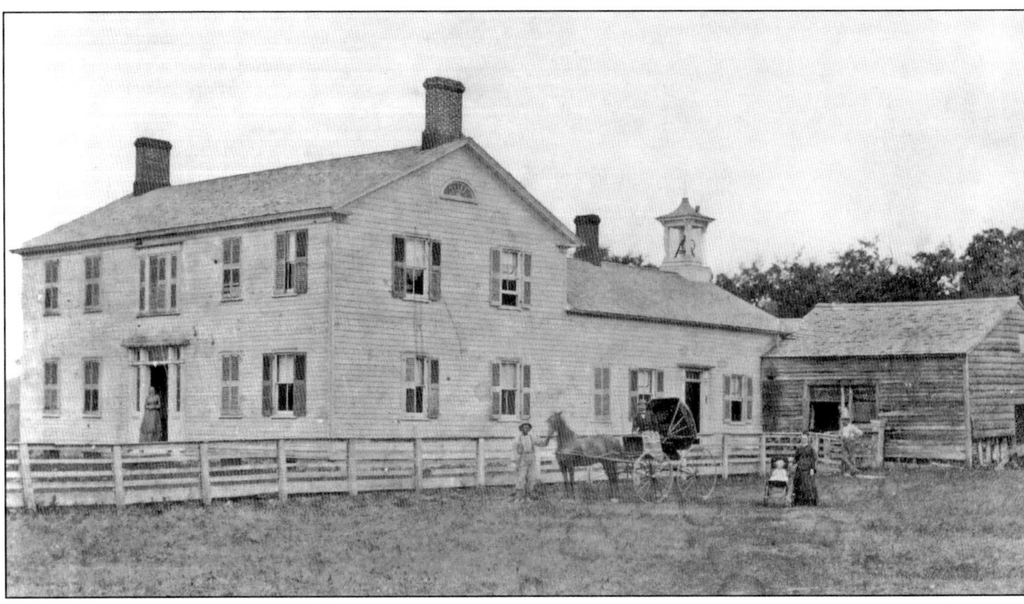

Dr. Jacob Nevins was the second physician to settle in the town of Perry, arriving in 1816. Dr. Jabez Ward had been the first, settling in Perry Center in 1813. This is Dr. Nevins home on the west side of the Perry Center Road, or Route 246, between the village of Perry and Perry Center. Today it is the main house on the True Farms dairy operation.

Seven

COMMUNITY

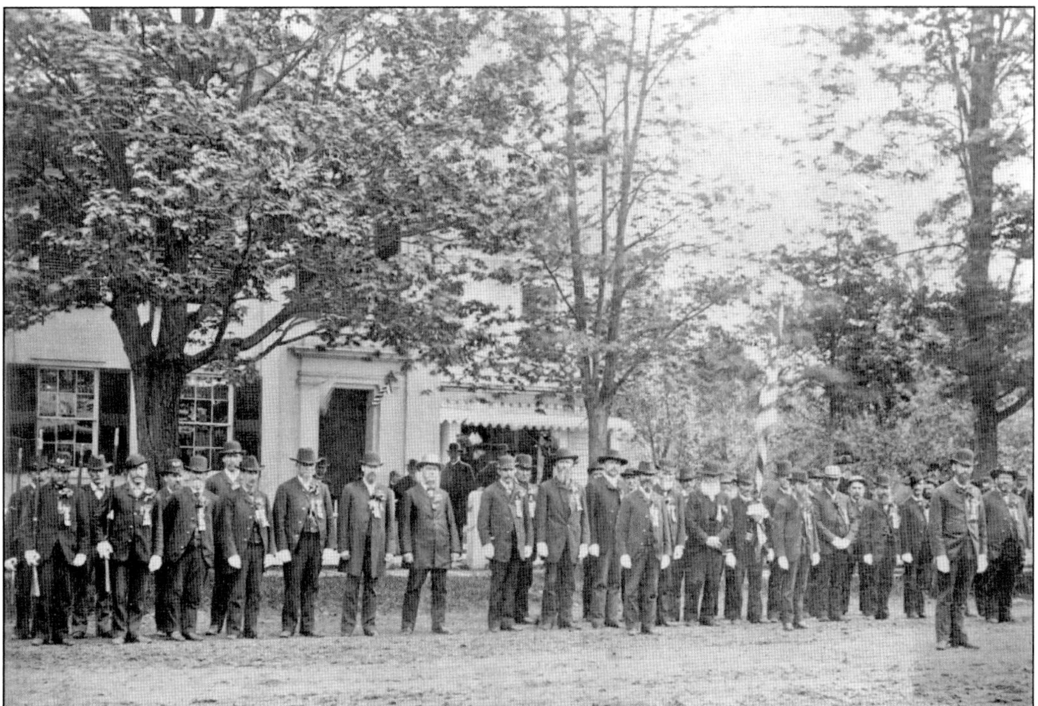

The Civil War veterans are gathered in front of Dr. Goodwin's home on the east side of South Main Street. The war had been hard on the men of Perry. Of the 80 men enlisted in the 24th New York Battery, only 22 had returned, and all but two had died in the Andersonville Prison. Others served in the 9th New York Cavalry and the 1st New York Dragoons.

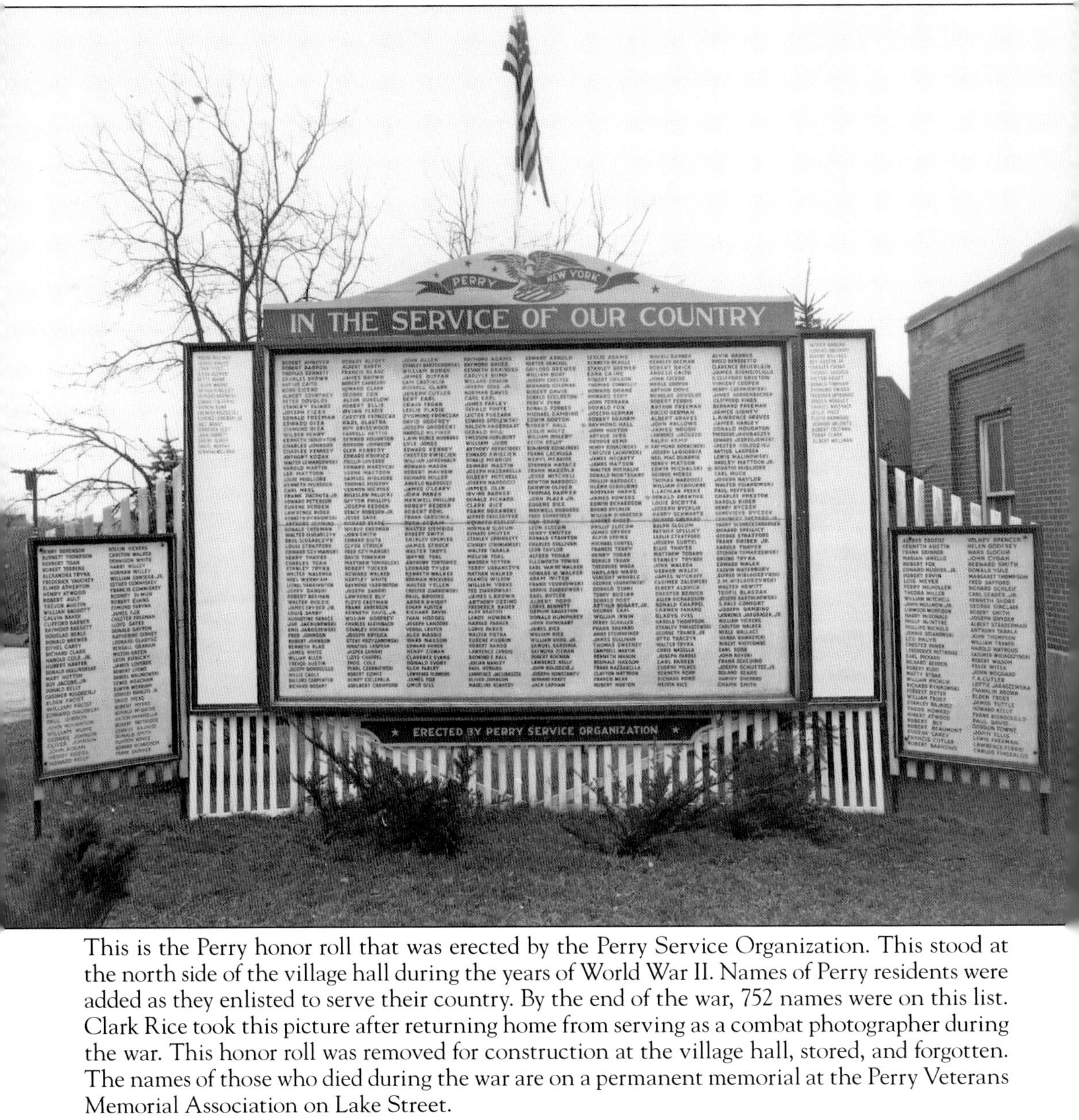

This is the Perry honor roll that was erected by the Perry Service Organization. This stood at the north side of the village hall during the years of World War II. Names of Perry residents were added as they enlisted to serve their country. By the end of the war, 752 names were on this list. Clark Rice took this picture after returning home from serving as a combat photographer during the war. This honor roll was removed for construction at the village hall, stored, and forgotten. The names of those who died during the war are on a permanent memorial at the Perry Veterans Memorial Association on Lake Street.

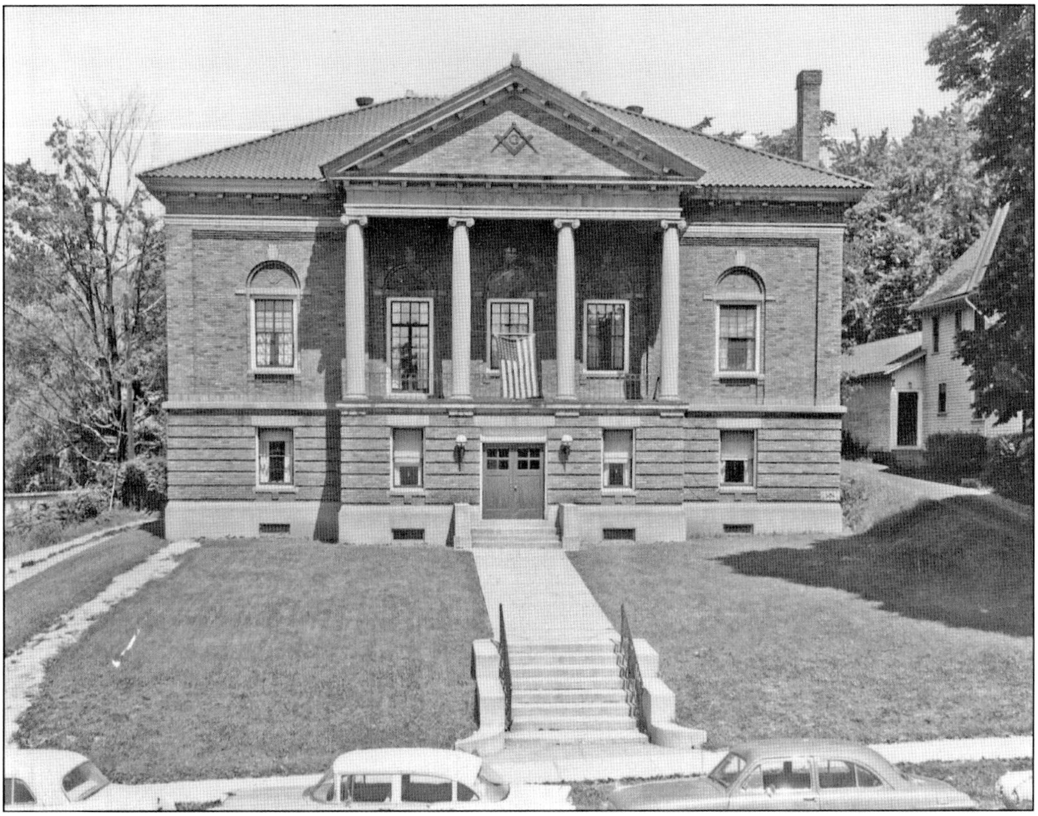

These two pictures were both taken in the late 1950s. The top picture is the Masonic temple on the west side of North Main Street, north of the business district. The cornerstone was laid in 1914 with the first meeting held in September 1915. The Masons and the Order of the Eastern Star meet here, as well as other community organizations. The Perry Rotary Club, a service organization founded in 1923, meets here weekly. The bottom picture is the house to the north, which at this time was the Moose Club, before it moved to a new location farther north on Main Street. This had been a Page family residence before. Today it is again a residence.

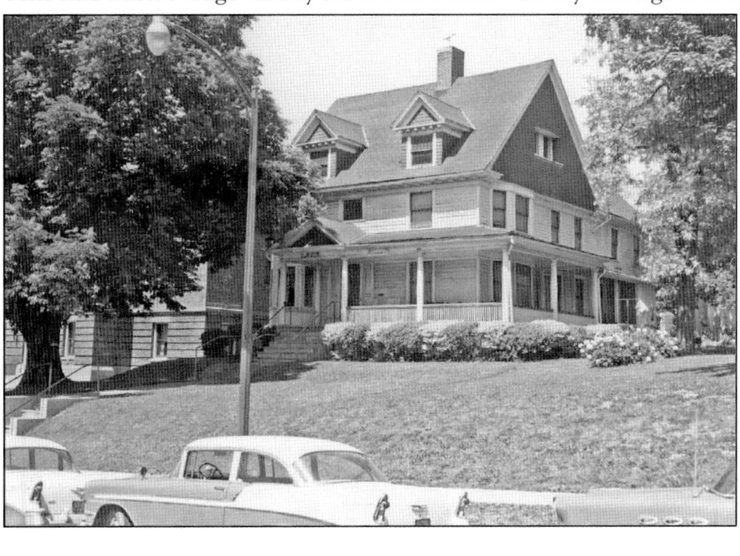

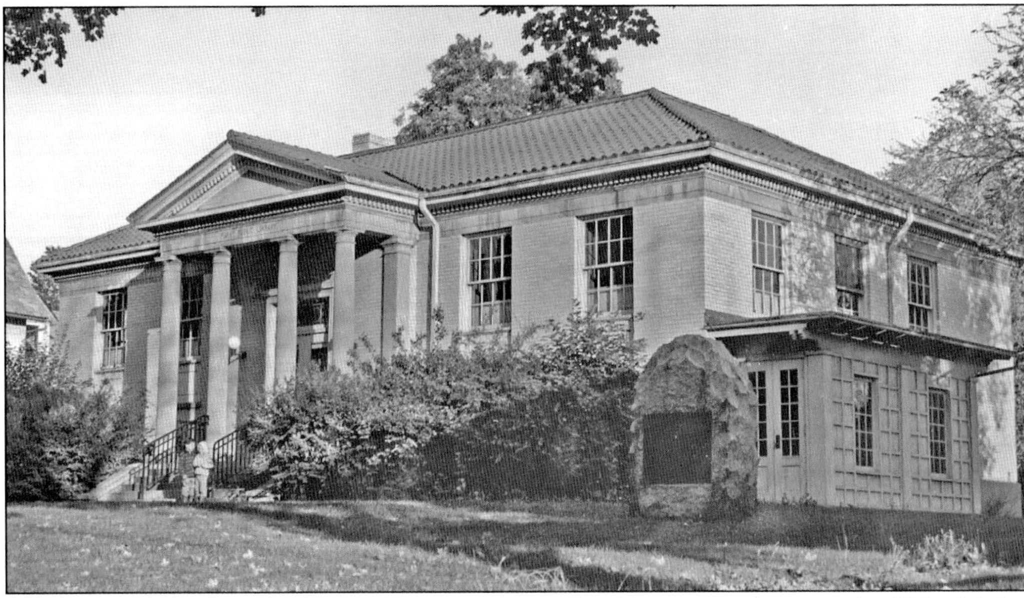

The Perry Public Library, in the top picture, was completed in 1914 on the east side of North Main Street, on the site of the old pioneer cemetery. It had been funded by the Carnegie Corporation, with the site and annual maintenance provided by the Town of Perry. To the right, in front of the building, is a memorial stone placed in memory of the World War I veterans. This was moved to Hope Cemetery in 1970. The bottom picture of the interior of the library was taken in June 1935, when the gallery addition opened. The main desk is in the center, and a skylight brightens the interior. Today the skylight is covered, the desk moved to the north side, and computers are in use.

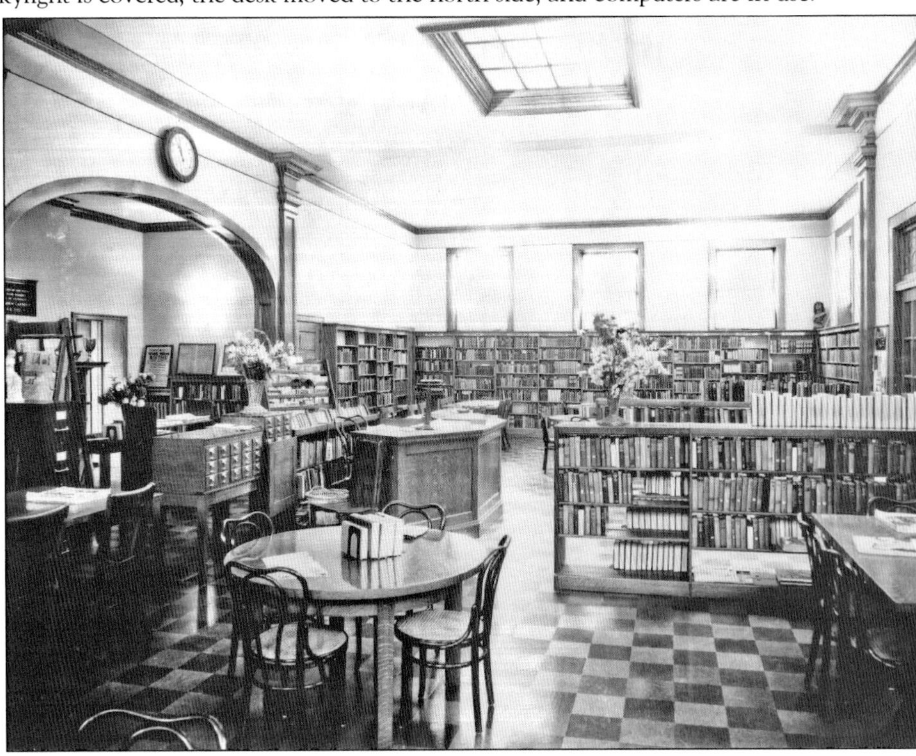

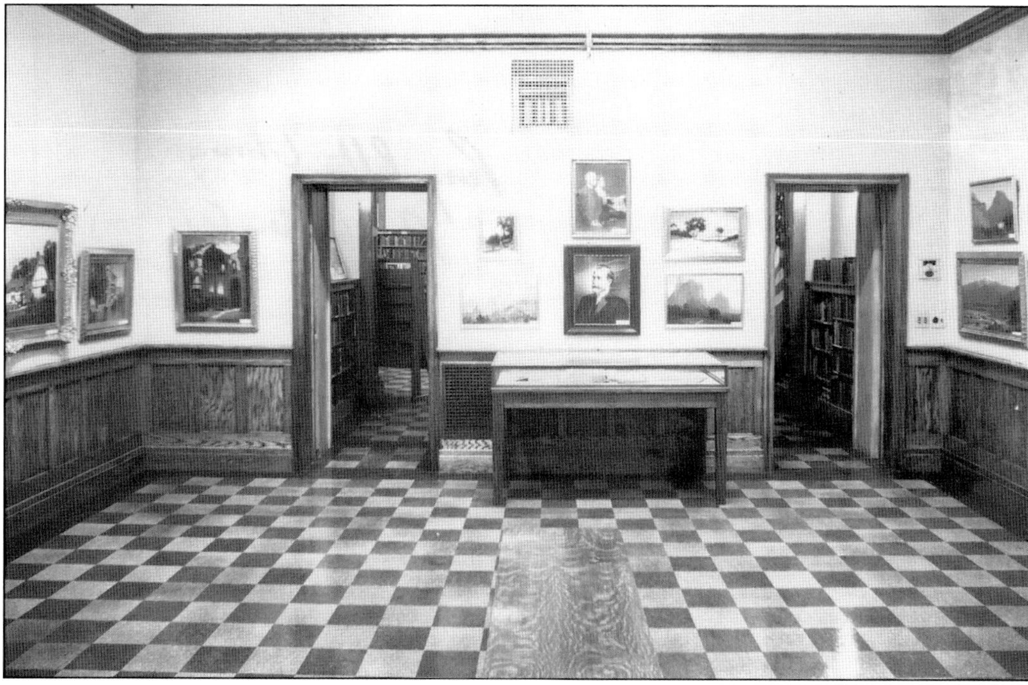

This is inside the Stowell-Wiles Art Gallery at the Perry Public Library. This 1935 addition and the paintings were a gift from Dr. Charles Stowell (bottom center portrait), the nephew of artist Lemuel M. Wiles (top portrait with wife). The artist grew up in West Perry and later with his son conducted a summer art school on the west side of Silver Lake.

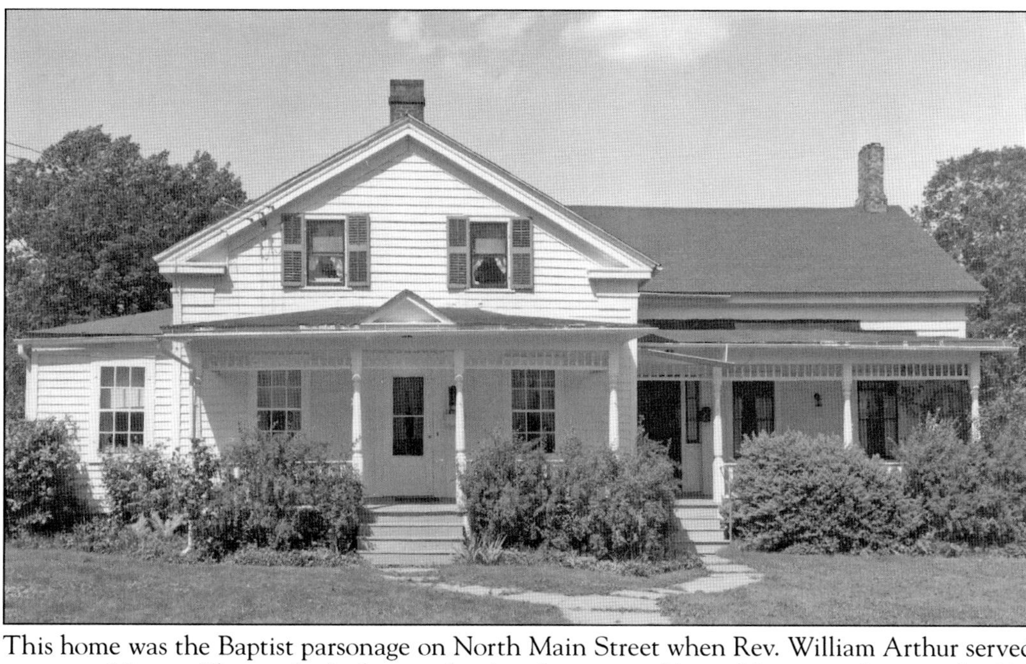

This home was the Baptist parsonage on North Main Street when Rev. William Arthur served as pastor. His son Chester A. Arthur, at the time four years old, would go on to become the 21st president of the United States. The family stayed only four years in Perry, leaving in 1837. This home was moved to Elm Street, where it is today, to make room for the house of W. T. Olin.

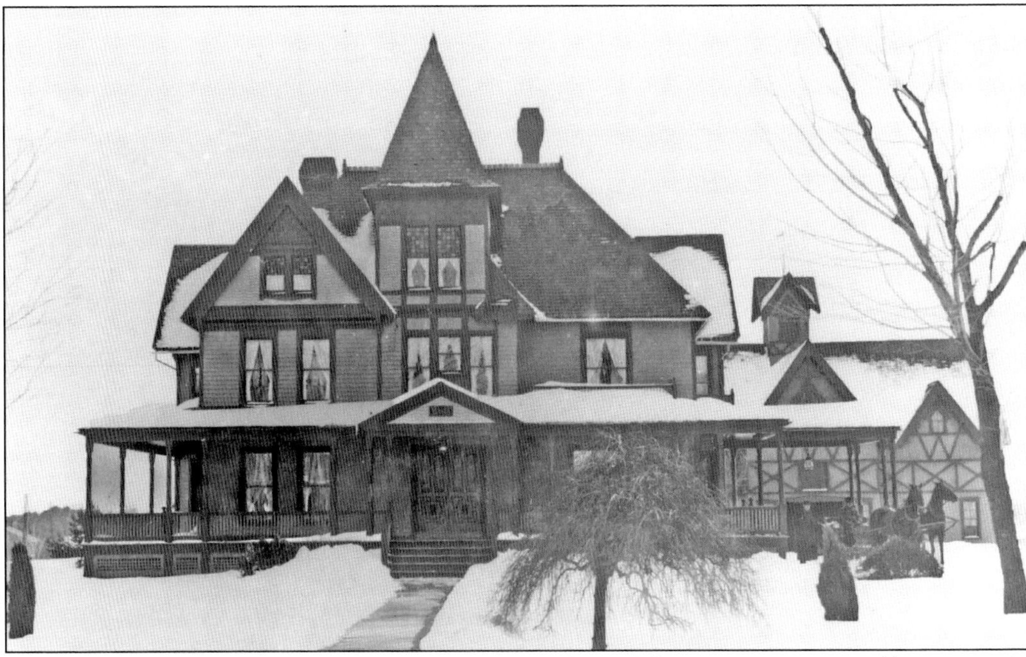

The home and carriage barns of Milo H. Olin, president of the Perry Knitting Mill, were on the east side of Main Street opposite Benedict Street. This later became a Wyckoff residence, and then the Hettig Highway House. It was destroyed by fire in 1963, when it was the Marco Inn. The Moose Club was located on this site, until the Eaton Watson Funeral Home was built here.

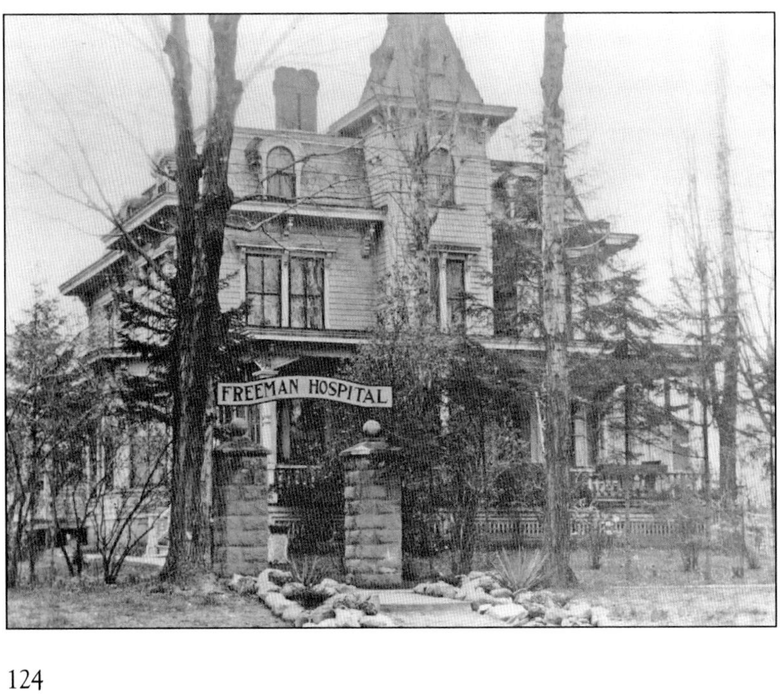

In 1927, the Freeman Hospital opened in the former home of T. H. Bussey on North Center Street across from Watkins Avenue. This later became the Perry Home for Adults and today is an Arc group home. A water trough from Main Street was in the side garden until 1989 when it was removed to a Main Street park.

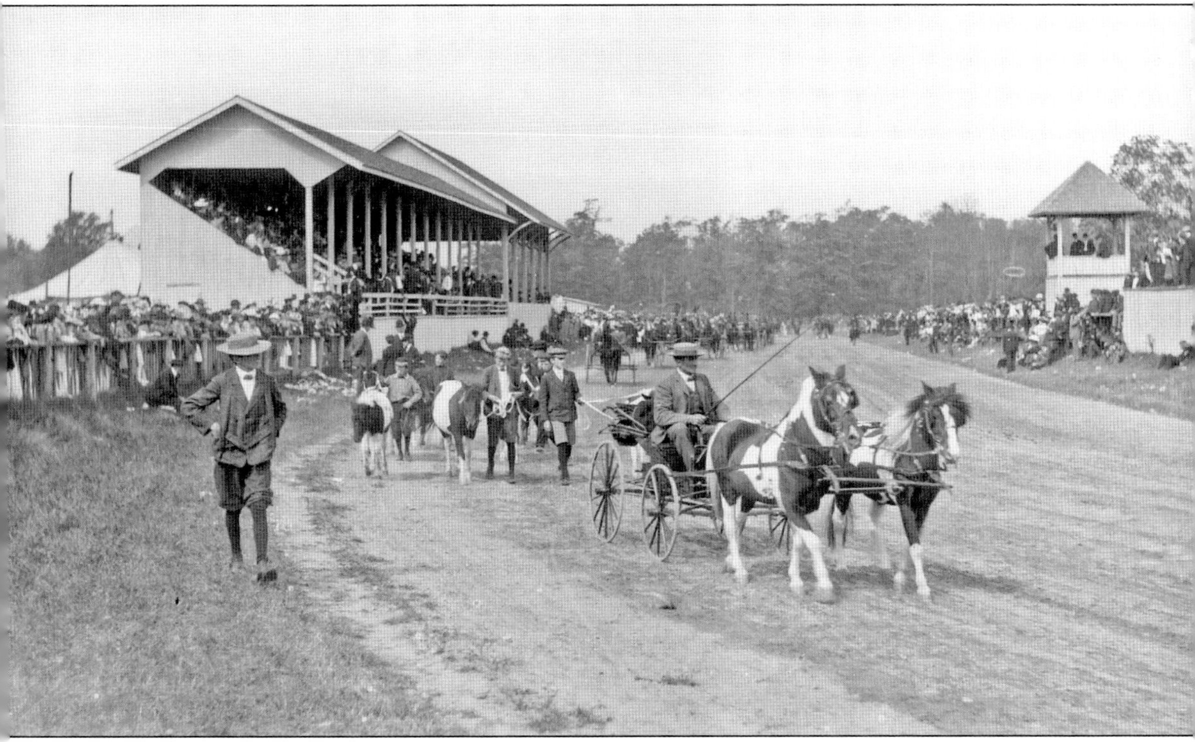

The Perry Fair was conducted from 1880 to 1933 on the grounds that now hold the Perry Village Park. This was run by the Silver Lake Agricultural and Mechanical Association, and the first year, 6,000 people attended to look at more than 900 exhibits. In this picture, Charles Bow of Perry Center Road and his Shetland ponies lead a parade around the track. The grandstand at the left was near the present tennis courts, and the judges stand for the horse races is on the right. Due to the Depression, the fair was forced to close in 1933, and the village acquired the property. The track in the village park is all that is left of the Perry fairgrounds.

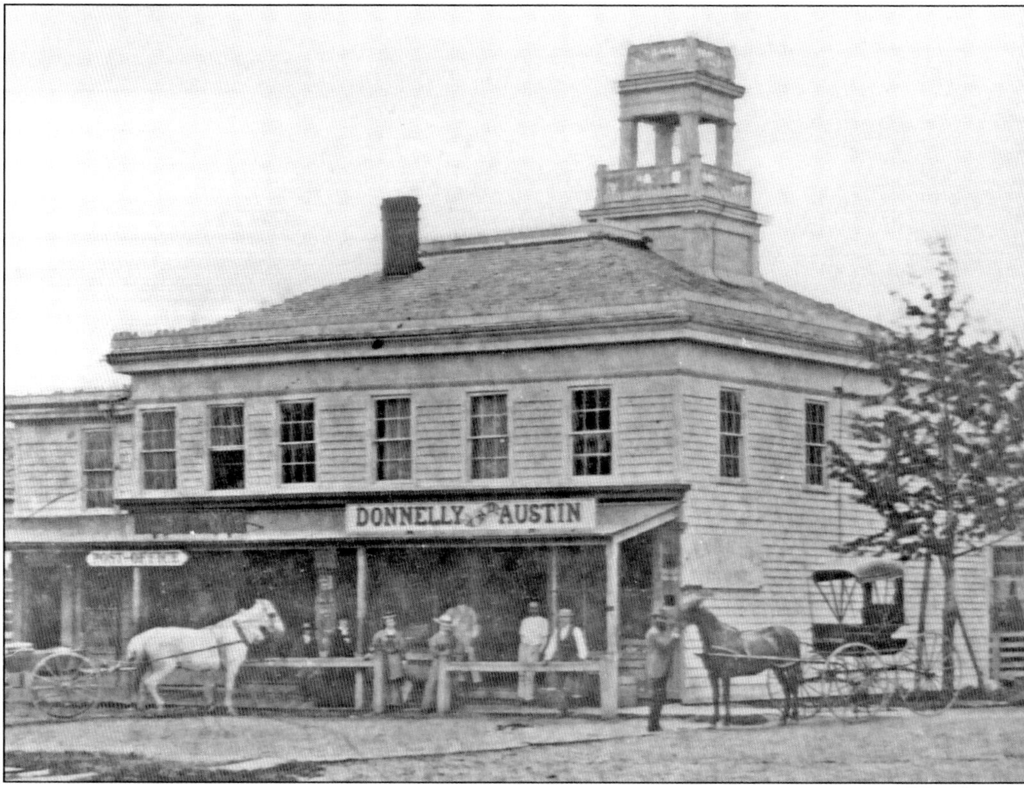

Donnelly and Austin was a general store in Perry Center at the southeast corner of the intersection of Routes 20A and 246. This building was constructed in 1839 on the northeast corner of the intersection and served as the Perry Center Institute into the 1840s. It was moved across the street to become a shoe store, then the general store and post office, and today is Kelly's Motors.

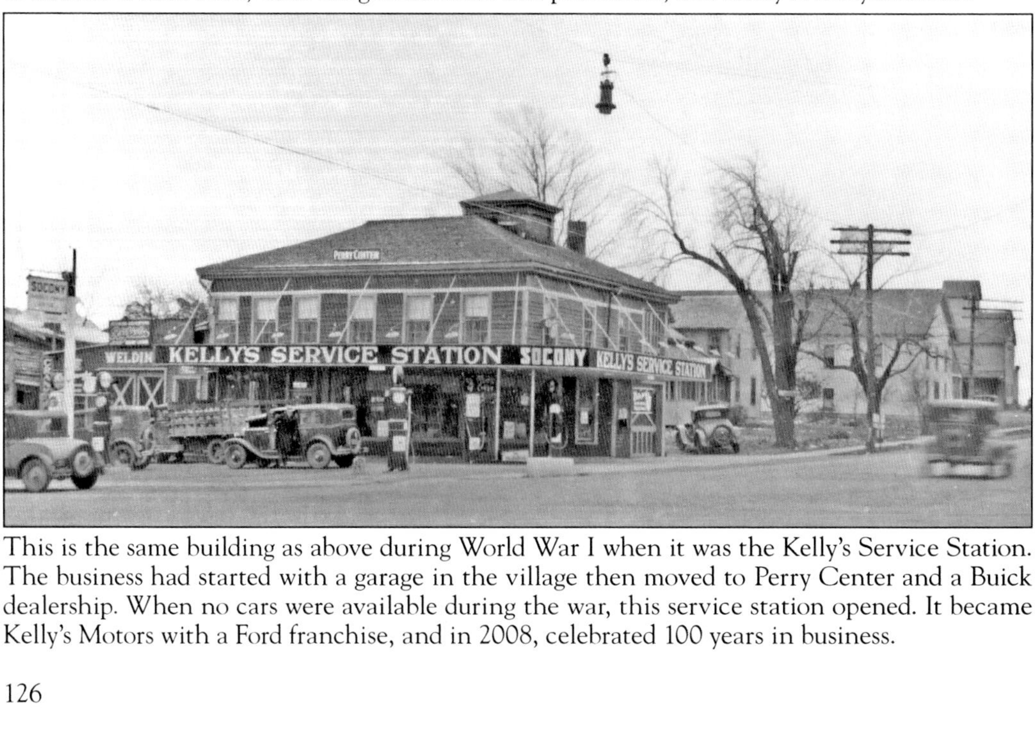

This is the same building as above during World War I when it was the Kelly's Service Station. The business had started with a garage in the village then moved to Perry Center and a Buick dealership. When no cars were available during the war, this service station opened. It became Kelly's Motors with a Ford franchise, and in 2008, celebrated 100 years in business.

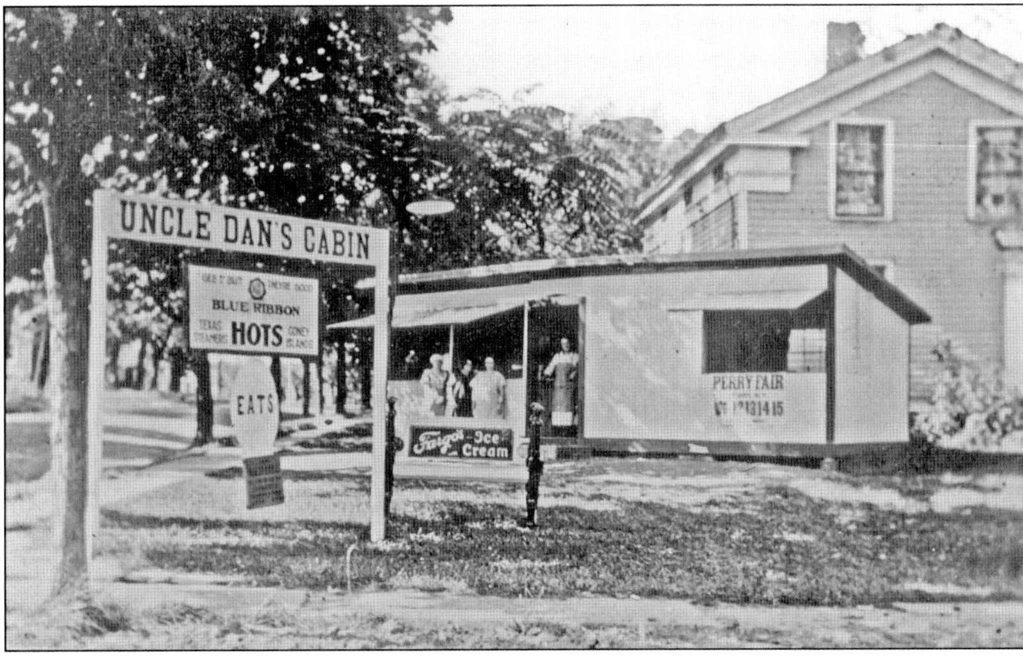

This is in Perry Center looking north at the northeast corner of Routes 20A and 246. Uncle Dan's Cabin, with a Perry Fair advertisement on the front, was a hot dog stand located in front of Daniel Ball's residence. When the home became a Kelly residence, this corner became the site of the Perry Center Diner. In 1967, the street was widened and curbed, and the diner was forced to close.

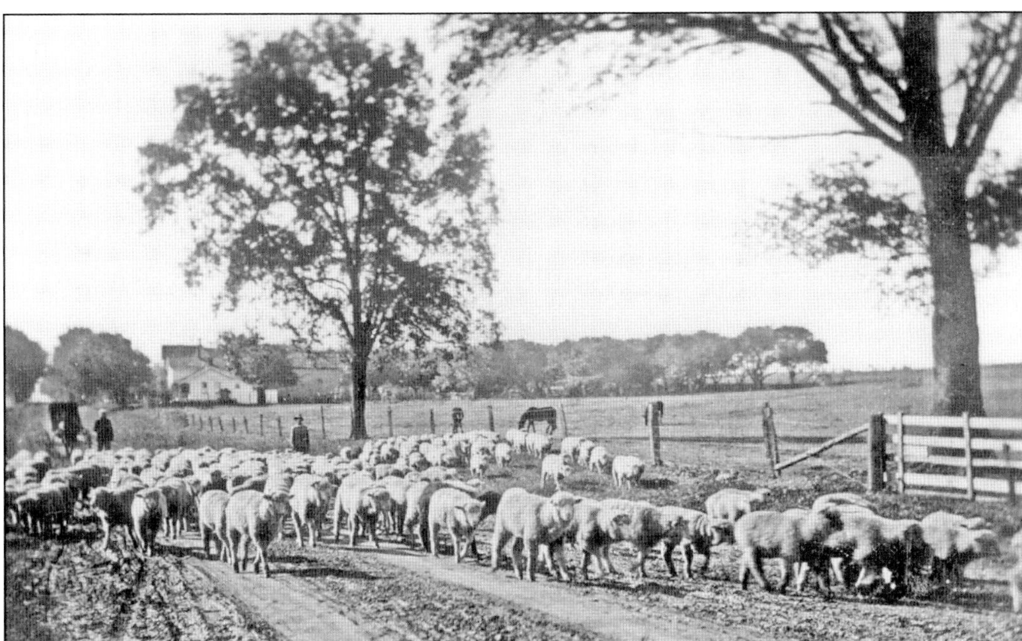

This is one of the joys of living in a rural community. This picture was taken in 1925 on Route 246, looking south towards Perry Center. The sheep, indeed, have the right of way.

Consistent with our mission to preserve history on a local level, this book was printed in South Carolina on American-made paper and manufactured entirely in the United States. Products carrying the accredited Forest Stewardship Council (FSC) label are printed on 100 percent FSC-certified paper.

MADE IN THE USA